D1528462

LUKE, JUDAISM, AND THE SCHOLARS

LUKE, JUDAISM, AND THE SCHOLARS

Critical Approaches to Luke-Acts

JOSEPH B. TYSON

UNIVERSITY OF SOUTH CAROLINA PRESS

Published in Columbia, South Carolina, by the
University of South Carolina Press

Manufactured in the United States of America

03 02 01 00 99   5 4 3 2 1

Library of Congress Cataloging-in-Publication Data

Tyson, Joseph B.
   Luke, Judaism, and the scholars : critical approaches to
Luke-Acts / Joseph B. Tyson.
      p. cm.
   Includes bibliographical references and index.

   ISBN 1-57003-334-X (alk. paper)
   1. Jews in the New Testament. 2. Bible. N.T.—Luke—Criticism,
interpretation, etc.—History—19th century. 3. Bible. N.T.
Acts—Criticism, interpretation, etc.—History—19th century.
4. Bible. N.T. Luke—Criticism, interpretation, etc.—History—20th
century. 5. Bible. N.T. Acts—Criticism, interpretation, etc.—
History—20th century. I. Title.
BS2589 .T97 1999
226.4'083058924—dc21   99-6596

For Peggy

CONTENTS

PREFACE

Studies in the sociology of knowledge have shown how scholarship has been profoundly influenced by the culture in which it develops. The critical study of the New Testament is no exception, and an examination of the scholarly portraits of Judaism in the days of Jesus serves as a striking illustration. Nineteenth-century scholars tended to portray first-century Judaism as moribund and casuistic and to see the God of the Jews as distant and unapproachable. But at the end of the twentieth century, scholars of the New Testament tend to portray Judaism at this early period in far more positive ways. Even the terms have changed. Judaism at the time of Jesus was almost uniformly referred to as "late Judaism," a term that signified both its inferiority to the religion of the Hebrew Bible and its approaching death. New Testament scholars today prefer to use the term, "early Judaism," by which they mean to signify a vital phenomenon that has a continuing history.

It is becoming increasingly clear that the Holocaust of 1933–45 was a major turning point in the history of New Testament scholarship. Reflection on the events of these years has brought about a reconsideration of Christian teaching about Jews and the effect of this teaching on Christian-Jewish relations. Although it is inappropriate to equate these Christian teachings with Nazi antisemitism, it is necessary to question the relationships. Did Christian attitudes support Nazi goals, or at least prepare people not to object to them? Is there something basically anti-Jewish in fundamental Christian concepts, and if so, how far back in Christian history is this motif to be found? Is it even possible that the foundational Christian documents, implicitly or explicitly, grant permission to believers to give vent to anti-Jewish expressions?

As a result, a number of post-Shoah scholars have engaged in an examination of elements in the New Testament and in the interpretation of the New Testament that may have contributed to or supported anti-Jewish attitudes. The present book is intended to survey the history of critical scholarship on two New Testament texts, the Gospel of Luke and the Acts of the Apostles, with particular attention to the ways in which scholars have interpreted Luke's treatment of Jews and Judaism in these texts. The book does not attempt to give a definitive answer to the question of anti-Judaism in Luke-Acts, but it asks about the ways in which certain scholars have dealt with this issue.

Luke-Acts is an appropriate object of our study, because these books, written by the same author, contain a mass of material about Jesus and his first followers, most of it reporting events that occurred among Jewish people. In these texts some Jewish people are supportive of the new messianic movement, but others are shown to be in vigorous opposition. Some materials in Luke-Acts leave the reader with a highly positive impression of Jewish people, while others are deeply negative. As a result it is not obvious whether these texts lead readers to be positive or negative about Jews and early Judaism, and this leaves a great deal of room for scholarly interpretation. Thus, our purpose is to trace the history of scholarship on Luke-Acts in regard to the treatment of Judaism in these texts. How have particular critical scholars weighed this issue in their analyses of these New Testament texts?

Chapter 1, a history of anti-Judaism in critical New Testament scholarship, forms a background for our study. There I attempt to explain what is meant by anti-Judaism and to show how it became dominant in scholarly interpretations of the nineteenth century. Chapters 2–7 deal with selected scholars who have made major contributions to the understanding of Luke-Acts. No attempt is made to be exhaustive, so not every book and article on the subject is considered, but the major scholars who have treated our issues are featured. Some of these scholars have produced important studies of other texts as well as Luke-Acts, but the focus here is on those publications that have made a major impact on Lukan studies. Chapter 2 deals with Ferdinand Christian Baur, whose understanding of competing Christian parties in the early church had important implications for the study of Luke-Acts. Chapter 3 examines the work of Adolf von Harnack, who is generally acknowledged as one of the greatest nineteenth-century interpreters of Luke and Acts. In chapter 4, an important representative of German conservatism, Adolf Schlatter, a contemporary of Harnack, is treated. In chapter 5, two of the most important twentieth-century Lukan scholars are featured: Ernst Haenchen and Hans Conzelmann. Jacob Jervell, who issued a significant challenge to the Conzelmann-Haenchen consensus in Lukan studies, is the subject of chapter 6. Chapter 7 examines the work of three contemporary American scholars: Jack T. Sanders, Robert L. Brawley, and Robert C. Tannehill. The final chapter attempts to isolate the major issues that remain to be resolved in the interpretation of Luke's view of the Jews. Other scholars, whose work on Luke-Acts has been important but who have not focused attention in an extensive way on the issue of Jews and Judaism, are acknowledged at appropriate points in order to provide context.

In the case of books and articles originally published in German or French, I have made use of published English translations when available. When such editions were not available, the quotations included here are my own translations. Unless otherwise noted, scripture quotations are from the New Revised Standard Version Bible. Transliteration of Greek, abbreviations of the names of biblical books, and abbreviations of commonly used periodicals, reference works, and serials follow the guidelines of the Society of Biblical Literature (see *JBL* 117 [1998]: 555–79).

Much of the research and writing on this book was done during academic leaves awarded me by Southern Methodist University, most recently in the fall semester, 1997. I am grateful for this and for the bibliographical, secretarial, and technical assistance that even after my retirement from teaching continues to be available to me. I am also grateful to my colleagues in the study of Luke-Acts, from whom I have learned a great deal and among whom I have always enjoyed support and critical encouragement. Some of these scholars are featured in this book. They are in no way responsible for anything presented here and may well disagree with much of it. I hope, however, that they will find that their work has been carefully considered and fairly presented.

CHAPTER 1

ANTI-JUDAISM AND NEW TESTAMENT SCHOLARSHIP

Perhaps the most striking illustration of the relationship between historical events and critical scholarship has taken place in our own twentieth century. Now, at the end of this century, it is becoming increasingly clear that the Holocaust of 1933–45 was a watershed event in human history and especially in relations between Christians and Jews. Remarkably, it also seems to have marked a turning point in the history of New Testament scholarship. Awareness of the horrors of these times has not only had a sobering effect on philosophical and theological approaches that assume a kind of progress in the human condition, but it has also had an energizing effect on historical studies and, in particular, on the study of early Christian and early Jewish relationships. New questions, new issues, and new approaches have emerged to enable scholars to gain a clearer picture of the early relationships and their potential to affect the dismal conditions that made the Nazi Holocaust possible. Is there something basically anti-Jewish in fundamental Christian concepts, and if so, how far back in Christian history is this motif to be found? Is it even possible that the foundational Christian documents, implicitly or explicitly, grant permission to believers to give vent to anti-Jewish expressions?

Scholars who wrote prior to the rise of National Socialism in Germany were certainly aware of anti-Jewish motifs in the Christian writings, but their approach to the understanding of these motifs was characteristically different from that of many postwar scholars. In some cases the anti-Jewish motifs were more or less taken for granted, as if no explanations were needed. In other cases they were explained as justified by some supposedly well-known Jewish practice, belief, or character trait. In still other cases the NT documents were called upon to provide justification for modern expressions of anti-Judaism and anti-Semitism. But rarely were anti-Jewish charges in the NT documents questioned for historical accuracy or condemned as misleading or damaging.

In post-Holocaust times and especially in the last quarter of the twentieth century, however, the discussion of anti-Judaism in the NT has been vigorously debated among scholars, among whom, however, there is no consensus. While some scholars have maintained that the history of Christian anti-

Judaism may be traced back to the NT, others have been anxious to exonerate the NT from any such charges. A fascinating feature of these discussions has been a focusing of attention on Luke-Acts. Among the NT texts, Luke-Acts seems to be the most perplexing in terms of the ambivalent attitudes toward Judaism that appear to be included. Here is a pair of documents by the same author, in which viewpoints and attitudes are not altogether clear and perhaps not even consistent.

The present book is intended to serve as a history of critical scholarship on Luke-Acts with particular attention to the ways in which scholars have understood the ancient author's views about Jews and Judaism. In the process we shall examine the work of some of the leading writers on Luke-Acts in the nineteenth and twentieth centuries, including a number of recent authors. Before approaching the individual critics, however, it is essential to grasp the significance of a strong tradition in NT scholarship generally. This tradition, which dominated scholarship in the nineteenth and early twentieth centuries, draws an exceedingly dark picture of first-century Judaism, emphasizing negative qualities and depreciating the importance of more positive aspects. It is a tradition of anti-Judaism in NT scholarship, which exercised a profound influence on many of the earlier scholars we shall examine. More recent scholars have had the benefit of a newly developing tradition that expresses a much greater appreciation for Judaism at the time of Jesus.

In his excellent study of the treatment of Judaism in Christian scholarship, Karl Hoheisel claims that the year 1947 marked a significant change in the ways in which Christian scholars looked at Judaism in the time of Jesus.[1] By 1947 we knew the horrors of the Holocaust and were beginning to become more sensitive to the implications of Christian anti-Judaism. Also in 1947, the Dead Sea Scrolls were discovered, and we gradually became aware of the multiplicity of Jewish groups and the diversity of religious viewpoints and practices among Jews at the time of Jesus. The term by which we began to designate this first-century phenomenon changed. We ceased to call it late Judaism, which implied something that had come out of the Hebrew Bible, had become moribund at the time of Jesus, and had no genuine future. We began to call it early Judaism, by which term we meant to signify a phenomenon that had a new beginning, coming out of the history of ancient Israel and making use of the writings of the Hebrew Bible, of course, but with a vital future, pointing toward the developments that led to the Mishnah, the Talmuds, and modern Judaism.

These developments sometimes brought with them fundamental changes in the ways in which early Judaism was portrayed. In some cases, rabbinic writings began to be perceived more positively. The change may be illustrated by reference to two editions of Emil Schürer's *History of the Jewish People in the Time of Jesus Christ*. The English edition of 1897, in a short chapter titled "Life under the Law," refers to several early Jewish writers, including Antigonus of Socho. The reference to Antigonus says, "The saying of Antigonus of Socho: 'Be not like servants who serve their master for the sake of reward, but be like those who do service without respect to reward,' is by no means a correct expression of the keynote of Pharisaic Judaism, which was in fact like the servants who serve for the sake of recompense."[2] In the 1979 edition, revised by Geza Vermes and others, the chapter is retitled "Life and the Law," and at the comparable place we have the following: "The saying of Antigonus of Sokho, 'Be not like servants who serve their master for the sake of reward, but be like those who do service without consideration of reward,' foreshadows many similar counsels preserved in rabbinic literature."[3] In 1897, Schürer, implicitly applauding the saying of Antigonus, confidently labeled it an exception to the rule. In 1979, Vermes maintained that it is not untypical of rabbinic teaching.

Despite positive movements in some quarters, Hoheisel is not optimistic about Christian scholarship. He contrasts general studies of Jewish religious history and studies that concentrate on the connection between early Judaism and early Christianity. Among the former, "there is a long line of relevant representations of Jewish religious history at the beginning of the Christian era. The understanding of the Torah is given proper assessment in them."[4] In the latter, however, which I take to include studies by NT scholars, "the historically incorrect view of 'the late Jewish religion of law' has persisted. . . ."[5]

Hoheisel is correct in his judgment that the older view has persisted, but it is nevertheless important not to overlook the more positive aspects of contemporary NT scholarship. The examination of scholarship on Luke-Acts in the following chapters will suggest that some change is perceptible but that it began to occur some decades after 1947. In any event it is necessary first to describe the tradition of anti-Judaism in Christian scholarship by calling attention to the major participants and the most important issues in the history of nineteenth- and twentieth-century critical scholarship on the NT.

There are a number of excellent essays on the treatment of Judaism in Christian NT scholarship. The book by Karl Hoheisel has already been mentioned. George Foot Moore's 1921 article is still important,[6] especially in its contrast of scholarship in the nineteenth century with that in previous times. Although the focus is on Pauline studies rather than on the gospels, a section of E. P. Sanders's *Paul and Palestinian Judaism* cannot be overlooked.[7] In a section titled "The persistence of the view of Rabbinic religion as one of legalistic works-righteousness," Sanders clearly shows how this anti-Jewish tradition developed. Geza Vermes has also provided important insights on some of the most significant scholarship.[8] In a recent article, Susannah Heschel shows how the work of Abraham Geiger, a leader of Reform Judaism in the middle of the nineteenth century, had the potential of providing an alternative view of Jesus in his relationship to the Pharisees.[9] Heschel maintains that Christian scholars knew but intentionally ignored Geiger's work.

Drawing on the studies cited above I will survey the work of those scholars who made important contributions to the development of anti-Judaism in critical biblical scholarship. Professor Heschel has pointed out that many of the concepts that we will find expressed by these scholars were not really new. They had become familiar and popular through centuries of Christian teaching. She writes, "One wonders how much difference there really was between the attitudes toward Judaism of a village pastor in nineteenth-century Germany and those of Schürer or Harnack, other than the idiom in which they were expressed. . . . These historians apparently did not try to free themselves from traditional Christian biases toward Judaism, even when alternative historical models and interpretive modes had been developed by Jewish historians such as Geiger."[10]

Curiously, one of the earliest of the nineteenth-century scholars had become familiar with early Jewish literature, and he came away with relatively positive views of Judaism. George Foot Moore claims that August Friedrich Gförer (1803–61) represents the beginning of the modern period in Christian studies of Judaism. Moore found a major change in Christian scholarship beginning in the mid-eighteenth century: "The seventeenth century was the great age of Hebrew learning among Christian scholars; it lasted on till toward the middle of the eighteenth and then abruptly ended."[11] Nineteenth-century scholars claimed to be writing history but "for this purpose they employed chiefly the material that came down from their predecessors, without giving sufficient consideration to the fact that it had been gathered for every conceivable motive except to serve as material for the historian."[12] Moore adds, "a delectus of quotations made for a polemic purpose is the last kind of a source to which a historian would go to get a just notion of what a religion really was to its adherents."[13] Indeed, the opening sentence of Moore's article claimed that "Christian interest in Jewish literature has always been apologetic or polemic rather than historical."[14] And Moore has adequately shown this statement to be true.

But Gförer appears to be an exception. His "was the first time that the attempt had been made to portray Judaism as it was, from its own literature, without apologetic, polemic, or dogmatic prepossessions or intentions."[15] And Moore claims that "it is to this day [1921] the most adequate presentation of the subject from the hand of a Christian scholar. . . ."[16] Heschel notes that Gförer made the then popular association between Jesus on the one hand and Essenic and Philonic ideas on the other. Even so, "Gförer's conclusions are particularly significant because of the weight of research behind them."[17] Heschel adds, "His presentation of Jewish thought draws extensively on the collections of rabbinic, midrashic, and kabbalistic texts prepared by earlier Christian scholars, from Raymund Martini (thirteenth century) onward, as well as on his own readings of Talmudic texts. . . ."[18]

Heschel laments that, for the most part, Christian scholars ignored the work of Gförer. Of far greater influence was Ferdinand Weber (1836–79). Although some scholars find the origin of anti-Judaism in Christian scholarship with earlier writers, Moore and Sanders agree that it began with Weber.

Moore says he was the chief resource of Christian writers for forty years. He served the needs of Christian writers by providing a system of theology for Judaism at the time of Jesus, but it was a modern German system that he used, not an ancient Jewish one. For him, legalism was the sum and substance of Jewish religion. Actually, Moore questions Weber's originality: "Most of his quotations come out of the common stock which had been accumulated by the labors of many generations, not all of them even verified. Confiding successors have appropriated these errors, and not always given Weber the credit of them."[19] Although he notes Weber's characterization of Judaism as legalism, he says that what Weber calls "transcendentism," is on his part a fundamental misunderstanding: "Weber's original contribution to the misunderstanding of Judaism was what he calls 'transcendentism,' the inaccessibility of God, wherein he finds the characteristic difference of the Jewish idea of God, and its immense inferiority to the Christian idea."[20]

Sanders has a fairly full summary of Weber's most important concepts, beginning with the story of the universal fall of humankind, which resulted in human estrangement from God. Weber believed that, in Jewish thought, a divine account is kept of sins and fulfillments, and that we have two ways to overcome our estrangement: repentance, understood as a work, and obedience to the law. In regard to Israel, Weber believed that the Mosaic covenant restored Israel to a pre-Adamic position but this was short-lived: "Because of the incident of the golden calf, Israel loses its restored status: as Adam's fall resulted in the separation of mankind from God, 'es ist Israels Sündenfall' (p. 274). Thereafter it becomes the goal of the individual Israelite to regain what had been lost through the fall of Israel."[21] The individual Israelite does this though meticulous obedience to Torah, through the sacrificial system, through good works, and through the treasury of merit. According to Weber, "Judaism is a religion in which one must *earn* salvation by compiling more good works ('merits'), whether on his own or from the excess of someone else, than he has transgressions."[22]

Hoheisel also recognizes Weber's importance. He notes that today we know there is nothing that may be called the Talmudic system. But he writes that "Weber found not just the 'tenor' or the 'central complex of ideas' in these writings, but he also thoroughly systematized them, not by using representatively selected material, but by means of the system of Lutheran theology."[23] Hoheisel claims that Weber invented the theory of legalism as a pejorative description of Jewish religion, and Moore also implicitly confirms this assertion. Near the end of his essay, in commenting on Christian scholarship before Weber, Moore says that legalism "is not a topic of the older polemic; indeed, I do not recall a place where it is even mentioned. Concretely, Jewish observances are censured or ridiculed, but 'legalism' as a system of religion, not to say as the essence of Judaism, no one seems to have discovered."[24]

Although his major interest was not in NT studies, Julius Wellhausen (1844–1918) is clearly a contributor to the tradition of anti-Judaism in critical scholarship. Commenting on his source criticism of the Pentateuch, Hoheisel says that Wellhausen was romantically attracted to origins and primitive times. He tended to look upon Israel's pre-exilic period as a time of freedom and spontaneity, without Mosaic law. The post-exilic period, by contrast, was one of degeneration, in which the priestly cult became a substitute for what Wellhausen regarded as genuine religion. Hoheisel points out that "with the religious liberalism of his time, Wellhausen was filled with a deep mistrust of law and statutes."[25] Geza Vermes also shows how Wellhausen's religious leanings influenced his scholarship: "Liberal Protestantism—represented, say, by Wellhausen—promoted a sort of academic anti-Judaism which, in an oversimplified way, may be summed up thus. Authentic Judaism—i.e., all that a nineteenth century enlightened Christian found acceptable in the Old Testament—was propounded by the prophets before the Babylonian exile. After the return of the Jews to Palestine, came the Law which completely suffocated the free impulses of a living religion."[26]

The relationship between Wellhausen and Weber may be shown by reference to the fact that the latter adopted the former's historical construction. Weber wrote in his introduction, "Something new arose with Ezra's return to the Jewish community. Through him the law of Moses became the exclusive means of religious thought and the life of all the people's piety. The influence of the prophetic words retreated behind the law; indeed, the law became the sole religious principle."[27]

Wellhausen also wrote on the Sadducees and Pharisees, explicitly intending to counter the claims of Abraham Geiger. He pictured the Pharisees as "characterized by their 'religious materialism . . . the Pharisees killed nature through the commandments. 613 written commandments and 1000 other laws and they leave no room for conscience. One forgot God and the way to him in the Torah.'"[28] Thus, in Wellhausen's view, Jesus could not have been a Pharisee, as Geiger had claimed.

In a recent appraisal of the work of E. P. Sanders, Martin Hengel and Roland Deines write about Paul Billerbeck (1853–1952), "who was himself—as was his teacher H. L Strack—a decided opponent of anti-Semitism, and who in our opinion did more to spread the knowledge of rabbinic texts in academic theology than any other Christian theologian, including Sanders."[29] Sanders's judgment about Billerbeck is, however, decidedly negative: "Billerbeck, who carefully compiled countless 'parallels' to New Testament passages from Rabbinic literature, more than any other passed on Weber's soteriological scheme to the present generation."[30] Sanders notes that many NT scholars do not perceive a theory at work in the selection of passages in the *Kommentar,* but he insists that Billerbeck nevertheless distorted the clear meaning of some texts and by his selections prejudiced the questions addressed to them. In his own statement of soteriology, Billerbeck talks about Torah as providing an occasion for individuals to earn merit and reward, of God as bookkeeper, and of the merits of the fathers: "Billerbeck summarizes: 'the old Jewish religion is thus a religion of the most complete self-redemption (*Selbsterlösung*); it has no room for a redeemer-saviour who dies for the sins of the world' (p. 6). The last clause indicates what is *really* wrong with Judaism."[31] Later in the same volume, Sanders's comments on Billerbeck's *Kommentar* are even more devastating: "Billerbeck may retain some usefulness as a collection of passages on individual points, with several provisions: that the user be able to look up the passages and read them in context, that he disregard as much as possible Billerbeck's own summaries and syntheses, and that he be able to imagine how to find passages on the topic not cited by Billerbeck."[32] In other words, "Billerbeck's *Kommentar* should not be used by those it was designed to serve: New Testament scholars who have no ready independent access to Rabbinic material."[33] Hoheisel would agree, and he says that Billerbeck "developed the Pharisaic teaching on righteousness as the pure negation of the magnificent evangelical teaching of justification, which Jesus is supposed to have brought into the world."[34] He adds that Billerbeck's portrayal is so totally dark that no one can make use of it to claim that Judaism was a preliminary stage of the gospel.[35]

Moore reserves some of his most negatively critical comments for Wilhelm Bousset (1865–1920). He claims that Bousset's knowledge about Judaism was only negligible. He was only twenty-seven years old when he wrote his *Religion des Judentums:* "What Bousset lacked in knowledge, he made up, however, in the positiveness and confidence of his opinions and for the failure to present evidence, by an effective use of what psychologists call suggestion—unsupported assertion coming by force of sheer reiteration to appear to the reader self-evident or something he had always known."[36] Jewish scholars have censured Bousset for his exclusive use of Apocrypha and Pseudepigrapha, especially apocalypses, and his secondary use of "the writings which represent the acknowledged and authoritative teachings of the school and the more popular instruction of the synagogue."[37] Bousset would defend himself by saying that he used works that appeared before the first century, not afterward. But Moore writes: "The relative age of the writings is of much less importance than their relation to the main line of development which can be followed from the canonical Scriptures through many of the postcanonic writings, including the Synoptic Gospels and the liturgy of the synagogue, to the Midrash and Halakah of the second century."[38]

Hoheisel also notes the criticism about Bousset's limited use of sources, but he argues that the sources were pre-Christian and that, while rabbinic literature might show us the religion of the scribes, the literature Bousset used was that of popular piety. Nevertheless, Hoheisel claims that a "detailed source analysis confirms that Bousset did not write a history, but painted a dark background for the proclamation of Jesus."[39]

One of Bousset's basic emphases is the contrast between the Jewish idea of God and that of Jesus. He conceives of the Jewish God as distant and estranged. Moore explains that Bousset's concept comes from his preoccupation with apocalyptic literature, which characteristically pictures God as remote and approachable only through intermediaries. Sanders, however, traces Bousset's concept of Jewish theology to Weber, and he judges that for this reason the idea of the remoteness and inaccessibility of God dominated Bousset's work.[40]

Heschel notes that Bousset was heavily dependent on Geiger in his characterization of the relationship between Sadducees and Pharisees, but that he presented the Pharisees in a way very different from that of Geiger. She writes that, according to Bousset, "although the Pharisees were originally the representatives of progress in Judaism, 'piety in their hands soon became stiff and lifeless,' and the Pharisees, once they attained power, 'very quickly developed into the conservatives, the representatives of a hard and rigid piety, a new aristocracy which forcibly displaced the old.' Ultimately, he concludes, Judaism is a religion of external observance lacking sincerity."[41]

Bousset stressed the legalistic aspects of what he called late Judaism: Jewish piety means a divine demand of righteousness and countless requirements for good works. Life is thus an account book or a balance sheet.[42] He wrote, "If we should ask about the foundation of the late Jewish religious community, there can be no doubt that only one answer can be given: that foundation is the law."[43] He calls attention to the fact that a number of tractates in the Mishnah are concerned, in the smallest detail, with sacrifice, observances, and the Temple cult. The civil law, he says, covers almost everything—marriage, rights of elders and children, relations of masters and slaves, trials and punishments. Moral law also covers every conceivable detail, but it is limited. Obligations of Jews to fellow Jews is of a different order from their obligations to Samaritans and the Am-Ha-Aretz. So "Judaism knows nothing of the interest and unconditional good will of persons to other persons."[44] Nevertheless, the rigid demands of the law called on the people to bear astounding and almost impossible burdens.[45] And, as Sanders points out, Bousset rejected the concept of the treasury of merit, found in Weber's theology, and this had a profound effect on his description: "Thus, in Bousset's view, the one hope of Jews—the transfer of the merits of the fathers—was doomed to frustration, and Judaism was consequently judged to be an inadequate and non-functional religion."[46] There is also the character of casuistry. Next to each other are ritual, cult, civil law, important and unimportant matters, large and small details.[47] Bousset's judgment is similar to that of Harnack, as we shall see: "Judaism knows so many higher and more excellent demands of ethical culture, but it knows so much more besides."[48] Over against all this stands Jesus' Sermon on the Mount, which is a great polemic against the legalistic character of Jewish religion. It is intended to replace the many individual commands with a way of thinking.[49]

Hoheisel claims that Emil Schürer (1844–1910) wrote his history in the spirit of Wellhausen. It has a great deal of important data on the 300-year period that is covered, but only two chapters specifically on religion: "His choice of the topics, 'Messianic Hope,' and 'Life under the Law,' shows his apologetic Christian interest."[50] Schürer added his own authority to the equation that he did not discover, namely, "Judaism=Legalism," which "plays a dominating role in theological teaching and research up to the present day."[51] Heschel claims that Schürer's purpose in painting such a negative picture of Judaism is to provide a contrast with Christianity. She also points out that, although he had argued against the use of rabbinic literature "for reconstructing political developments within Second Temple Judaism, he nonetheless uses rabbinic texts for his reconstruction of the alleged legalism and religious sterility of first-century Jewish life."[52]

Schürer's brief treatment of "Life under the Law" is a prime example of the negative portrayal of Judaism in Christian scholarship. The law, he says, was intended to govern all of life, and Jews were enthusiastic about it because they had total belief in divine retribution, "a retribution in the strictest juristic sense."[53] In the law all commands, large and small, are on the same level: "Not the doing of the good as such, but merely formal accuracy in fulfilling the letter of the law is the aim."[54] "All law is necessarily casuistic, for it lays down a multiplicity of individual statutes. All casuistry is by its nature endless."[55] And so Schürer concludes, "Life was a continual torment to the earnest man, who felt at every moment that he was in danger of transgressing the law; and where so much depended on the external form, he was often left in uncertainty whether he had really fulfilled its requirements."[56]

Sanders claims that Rudolf Bultmann (1884–1976) continued the practice of picturing Judaism negatively and lent enormous prestige to the tradition of Weber, Billerbeck, Bousset, and Schürer. Sanders is convinced that Bultmann had no independent access to the rabbinic literature but depended on Schürer, whom he commended for his work on both history and religion. But, writes Sanders, "It is a testimony to Bultmann's mental prowess and theological sophistication that his presentation of Judaism, though derivative, is often more acute and better nuanced than the works of those from whom he derived his information."[57] Bultmann believed that second-Temple Judaism no longer regarded God as an important factor. God had acted in the past but does not in the present. Ritual observances were elaborated in Judaism "to the point of absurdity." Bultmann thus emphasized legalism in Judaism, referred to the laws as complex and often unintelligible, and he believed that, in Jewish thought, one could do an excess of good works, which could balance transgressions. This legalism could lead either to "an unhealthy anxiety" or to "smug self-righteousness."[58] Even repentance and faith are counted as good works. Sanders shows that alternative views were available to Bultmann in the works of George Foot Moore and Erik Sjöberg but that Bultmann chose to ignore them in favor of the view of Weber, which "is simply repeated."[59] Hoheisel underscores this judgment and alludes to the reason for Bultmann's acceptance of the negative picture. He writes, "With Bultmann as well as with the research on late Judaism that preceded him, questions about work, reward and retribution are so exclusively oriented toward the Protestant understanding of justification that the significance of the law for collective salvation . . . is generally not perceived."[60]

In Bultmann's *Primitive Christianity,* the first section in the chapter on "Synagogue and Law" is titled "Jewish Legalism."[61] There is little difference here between Bultmann and Weber. The Bible, Bultmann affirms, "was no longer primarily a historical record of God's dealings with his people, but a book of divine Law."[62] Bultmann acknowledges that "life under the Law was still worship and service of God."[63] But the Pharisees imposed harsh and restrictive laws on the people: "These regulations went into detail to the point of absurdity."[64] The emphases on honesty and marital fidelity were still upheld, and in these matters Judaism was exemplary. But, "most important of all, no distinction was drawn between the moral and ritual law in respect of their divine authority."[65] A failing of this religion is that it is something other than "radical obedience," which is what Jesus taught: "What was required was specific actions, or specific abstentions from action. Once these had been got through, a man was free to do what he liked."[66] "Where the motive of obedience is simply that a certain course of action is prescribed, there is no personal assent to the requirements of the Law. Radical obedience is possible only where the Law is understood and answered by personal assent."[67]

A review of the critical scholarship treated here shows that there is no exaggeration in speaking of a dominant anti-Jewish tradition in Christian biblical scholarship. From Weber to Bultmann, critical scholarship has created a foil against which the teachings of Jesus and Paul may be seen as clearly superior. The Judaism of the time of Jesus, which does not go back to the earliest strata of the Hebrew Bible but only to the time of Ezra, is a legalism that emphasizes the individual's efforts at self-salvation, concepts of merit, reward, and punishment. Almost as a caricature, God is pictured as an accountant, making entries in each individual's balance sheet. But God is not directly accessible, as God had been accessible in early Israelite times. The Judaism of Jesus' time nevertheless emphasizes a special relationship of Jews to God, and this particularism and nationalism add to the shortcomings of this religion. To be sure, some of our scholars recognized that there were brilliant insights and commendable ethical teachings among the rabbis, but, they said, there was so much trivia that the brilliance was hidden. Although individual scholars provided different emphases of this portrait and wrote with different nuances, the above description emerges as a consensus of scholarship. There were demurrals, mostly from Jewish scholars, and it is clear that these did not go unnoticed. But they were largely ignored in the effort to paint the dark portrait of first-century Judaism that we have observed.

In the chapters that follow we shall analyze the work of some of the leading critical scholars on Luke and Acts and ask about their understanding of Luke's views about Jews and Judaism. In asking this question, it will be useful, when possible, also to examine the scholars' own views about Judaism and to consider the relation of their views to their critical analysis of the ancient

NT texts. We begin with works associated with the Tübingen school of NT studies, since contentions of Ferdinand Christian Baur about the history of early Christianity set the agenda for studies, especially of Acts, for a number of decades and affected the ways in which scholars thought of the narratives recorded in Acts. After an examination of relevant works from the Tübingen school, this book will proceed chronologically to survey a selection of the works of major scholars who have devoted attention to issues relating to the treatment of Jews and Judaism in Luke-Acts.

CHAPTER 2

FERDINAND CHRISTIAN BAUR
(1792–1860)

When Jacob Jervell announced what he claimed were revisions in Lukan scholarship, he explicitly did so against the background of a forcefully maintained consensus interpretation.[1] This interpretation was, according to Jervell, primarily associated with the names of Hans Conzelmann and Ernst Haenchen. But Jervell was aware that the roots of this consensus interpretation go back to Ferdinand Christian Baur and the Tübingen school of New Testament scholarship.

The point of view that Jervell associates with Conzelmann and Haenchen is one that sees Luke-Acts as the story of an early Christian mission that began with Jews and, following Jewish rejection, focused attention upon Gentiles. He describes Haenchen's view as follows: "According to Luke, the leaders of the primitive Christian mission were Jews who were faithful to the law and who did not originally intend to undertake any Gentile mission. They were, however, driven irresistibly to it by God himself."[2] In a later chapter we shall devote significant attention to the work of Conzelmann and Haenchen, as well as Jervell. In the present chapter it will be useful to explore the roots of this consensus interpretation by considering the formative work of Ferdinand Christian Baur. In fundamental ways Baur established a pattern for the investigation of early Christian literature, especially Luke and Acts, and called attention to many of the issues that we propose now to investigate.

Baur was not the first to use a critical approach in the study of Luke-Acts, but he probably was the earliest scholar to engage in a systematic effort to place these documents in their historical contexts and to interpret the various narratives, not as in some way recording historical events, whether accurately or not, but as expressions of particular tendencies or theological biases. In an essentially negative assessment of Baur's major contentions, Horton Harris nevertheless acknowledges his significance and that of the school he founded: "No single event ever changed the course of Biblical scholarship as much as the appearance of the Tübingen School. All New Testament criticism and, derivatively, much Old Testament criticism from the mid-nineteenth century onwards finds its origin, consciously or unconsciously, in this School."[3] In this judgment Harris is certainly correct; it is a judgment that makes the work of Baur the appropriate place to begin our own study.

Ferdinand Christian Baur was born in 1792, the son of an Evangelical cleric in Württemberg. He studied philosophy and theology at the University of Tübingen from 1809 to 1814, following which he was appointed to a professorship at Blaubeuren. In 1826, after much controversy, he became professor of NT exegesis at Tübingen, where he remained until his death in 1860. His tenure was marked by frequent controversy with persons both within and outside the university. Much of the controversy was precipitated by the publication in 1835 of *The Life of Jesus* by Baur's student, David Friedrich Strauss.[4] Baur himself at first remained silent about the book but finally could not avoid being associated with the views of its author. Baur himself wrote, "Seldom has a work of literature produced such a great sensation so quickly and so universally, and summoned the forces of war with great excitement to a battleground on which the most varied parties opposed each other and raised the ardour of the conflict to the most intense passion."[5] Though often engaged in controversy, Baur's strongly positive influence over his contemporaries cannot be doubted. Among his immediate students one may number not only Strauss, but Eduard Zeller, who married Baur's eldest daughter in 1847, and Matthias Schneckenburger, whose work on Acts inspired some of Baur's own most significant work.

Baur was born just after the French Revolution, which at least in France led to the emancipation of Jews, and the first half of the nineteenth century was a time of significant progress for many Jews in Germany as well. Enlightenment values informed the Jewish *Haskalah,* and Jewish philosophers enthusiastically read the works of Goethe, Hegel, and Kant. Abraham Geiger and other leaders of Reform Judaism envisioned an accommodation between traditional Jewish values and those of the modern world. Jewish life in Germany persisted and often flourished despite the legal and social restrictions that prevented Jews from entering many professions and despite the strength of continuing hatred of Jews.

Baur's views about Jews and Judaism adhere closely to the tradition of anti-Judaism in Christian critical scholarship. In his study of early Christian history, however, he expressed a genuine appreciation for one aspect of Judaism: "The special superiority which distinguished the Hebrew religion from all the religions of the heathen world was the pure and refined monotheistic idea of God, which from the earliest times had been the essential foundation of the Old Testament faith."[6] But Baur was quick to qualify this judgment:

> But on the other hand the Old Testament conceived God as the God, not of the human race, but of a particular nation. And the particularism, the limitation of the blessings and hopes of religion to the Jewish race, which was partly the cause and partly the effect of this conception of God, stood in the strongest contrast to the spirit of Christianity. If the Old Testament notion of God was ever to

be a sufficient form for the consciousness of God which belonged to the universal and absolute nature of Christianity, it was necessary that it should first be
freed from this national one-sidedness and defectiveness. It was necessary that
it should discard all that belonged only to the narrow range of vision of the Jewish theocracy, and that it should no longer, in accordance with the conceptions
of antiquity, ascribe to God a human form and human passions.[7]

Baur thus makes no secret of his assessment of Judaism as, except for its
monotheism, narrow, particularistic, racial, and anthropomorphic.

By contrast, Baur maintained that Jesus' message was intended to focus
religious devotion in a quite different direction. He states that the heart of
Jesus' message was in Matthew's beatitudes, which he summarizes as saying
that only human disposition counts for morality. In Jesus' teaching "the inner
is opposed to the outer, the disposition to the act, the spirit to the letter. This is
the essential root-principle of Christianity; and, in insisting that the absolute
moral value of a man depends simply and solely on his disposition, Christianity was essentially original."[8] The lines along which Judaism and Christianity
are to be contrasted are clear. Judaism has a kernel of truth surrounded by a
husk of narrowness and particularism. Christianity, at least in the teachings of
Jesus, breaks through all of this to focus attention on the inner human life.

Baur's approach to an understanding of early Christian history is well
known. He characterized early Christianity as a kind of battle between competing sides. On one side were the Jewish Christians, led by Peter, who saw in
Jesus the hope for the fulfillment of Jewish expectations but in other respects
held strictly to Torah. In early Jewish-Christian theology, Gentiles would be
able to join with the Jewish Christians, just as Gentiles have always been able
to do and under the same conditions. Torah was to hold its position as the dominant and defining force for both Christian and non-Christian Jews. On the
other side were the Gentile Christians, led by Paul. In this group, faith in Jesus
was the only condition for entry, and Torah was denounced as ineffective in
addressing the problem of human guilt. Given this supposed historical situation, the Acts of the Apostles is seen to play a crucial role.

It has been customary to understand Baur's approach as an expression of
a Hegelian view of history, in which a thesis and its antithesis finally come to
a resolution in a synthesis. Clearly Hegelian philosophy exercised an influence
on Baur's thought at some point. Alan Richardson is typical of those scholars
who find themselves unsympathetic with Baur and the Tübingen school: "The
celebrated Tübingen School in the eighteen-forties made the first consistent
attempt to explain the origins of Christian doctrine by the principles of historical criticism. Its weakness, like that of so much German biblical criticism,
was that it took over an *a priori* scheme from the then fashionable philosophy
(Hegel's) and forced the evidence into it: the dialectic of the Petrine and
Pauline elements within the Church resulted in the synthesis of second-century
Catholicism."[9]

But questions have recently been raised about the influence of Hegelian thought on Baur. In two major works, Peter Hodgson has maintained that this influence is, to say the least, overstated.[10] Hodgson maintains that, "although he [Baur] believed that history as it appears in events and in their interpretation is the outward patterning of an inward idea, the idea of reconciliation, the self-mirroring of God in free human acts, he also insisted that independent critical or positive historical research alone determines the shape of our understanding of the way these events are connected and the direction in which they move."[11] Hodgson also pointed out that Baur had come to his major concepts about early Christianity before he came in contact with Hegelianism. In 1833 Baur himself had criticized the use of Hegelian dialectic in the writing of church history.[12] Hodgson also showed that it was 1835 before Hegel received significant attention from Baur, and he wrote, "In other words, by the time Baur first came under the influence of Hegel, he was in his early forties, and already a mature scholar in his own right."[13]

The discussion of Hegelian influence on Baur continues, but for the purposes of assessing his work on Luke-Acts it is not necessary to settle the question. Baur would be among the first to insist that we should judge his work on the NT as we judge all others, by the quality of the exegetical studies rather than by the philosophical associations.

Baur and the Acts of the Apostles

Baur's fundamental views about the course of early Christian history are closely connected to his studies of the book of Acts, and so it is useful to begin our examination with his work on Acts and turn later in this chapter to his treatment of the Gospel of Luke.[14] A. J. Mattill, Jr., has shown how Baur was influenced by the work of Matthias Schneckenburger on Acts.[15] Baur considered the work of Schneckenburger, who had been his student, as a watershed in the history of NT scholarship. In his review, Baur observed, however, that scholarship cannot be left where Schneckenburger had left it. He wrote, "We must either go backward from the aim stated by the author or go forward beyond that aim to further investigations of the historical character of Acts."[16] Baur beckoned the way forward.

Following suggestions of Baur himself, Schneckenburger produced a detailed study of the extensive parallels in Acts between Peter and Paul. The two characters perform similar miracles, experience life-changing visions, deliver apologetic and evangelistic speeches, and undergo imprisonments followed by remarkable releases. In content, some of the speeches of Peter sound like Paul. In his speech to the household of Cornelius, Peter states: "I truly understand that God shows no partiality, but in every nation (ἐν παντὶ ἔθνει) anyone who fears him and does what is right is acceptable to him" (Acts 10:34–35). After Peter has reported to the other apostles in Jerusalem about his vision and experience with Cornelius, they all are led to say, "Then God has given even to the Gentiles the repentance that leads to life" (Acts 11:18). And in the meeting of the apostles, with Paul present, Peter affirms that "we believe that we will be saved through the grace of the Lord Jesus, just as they will" (Acts 15:11).

Contrariwise, the speeches of Paul, with one exception, do not sound like the Paul of the letters. The one exception is in Paul's speech at Pisidian Antioch, where he announces that forgiveness of sins is available through Jesus Christ and that "everyone who believes is set free from all those sins from which you could not be freed by the law of Moses" (Acts 13:39). Here Paul sounds like the author of Romans and Galatians. Elsewhere in Acts, however, the themes of the Lukan Paul are fundamentally Jewish, more specifically Pharisaic. Paul stresses monotheism, creation, and resurrection. Most important, there is a great deal of stress on his acknowledgment of Torah for himself and for fellow Jews. In his apologetic speeches in Acts 21–26, he repeatedly denies that he has done anything contrary to the laws of Moses or the traditions of his people. Nor has he taught any contrary practices. Precisely to avoid suspicion that he has taught contrary practices, Paul is counseled by James to pay the expenses of four men who have taken on Nazirite vows (Acts 21:17–26). Paul is totally willing to do this, and in his defensive speeches that follow his arrest he stresses his connection with the Jews and identifies himself with the party of the Pharisees (Acts 23:6; 26:5). It is made clear in the hearing before the Sanhedrin that belief in resurrection is distinctively Pharisaic, and consequently fundamentally Jewish (Acts 23:8).

The parallels mean that Peter is made to sound like Paul, and Paul like Peter. Schneckenburger explained these and other phenomena by reference to the apologetic purpose of the text of Acts, to justify Paul to the Jewish Christians. Mattill observes, "A mere historical purpose cannot explain why Luke, who [according to Schneckenburger] was in Rome, devotes only one verse (28:15) to Paul's visit with the church there, and yet stresses Paul's meeting with Jews. Moreover, Luke does not end his narrative in Rome simply because he desired to describe the geographic spread of Christianity from the centre of Judaism to the centre of heathenism, but because he now wants to represent Paul . . . as permanently rejected by the Jews themselves and predominantly sent to the Gentiles, thus fulfilling Jesus' own command (1:8)."[17] For Schneckenburger Paul was a problem to Jewish Christians, and he needed to be explained.

Baur was impressed that Schneckenburger had contested the historical purpose of the author of Acts, and he saw this as a signal of release from concern with historicity. To a certain extent he also approved of Schneckenburger's designation of Acts as an apology. The writing of an apology means that some group needs to explain itself to another, and thus the Baurian concept that there were two groups in the church is implicitly affirmed in Schneckenburger's work. But for Baur this is not a fully adequate explanation of the character of Acts. For what we may observe is a modification on both sides. In other Christian apologies there is no attempt to describe the opponents in terms that would be acceptable to Christians. But Acts explicitly deals with both parties and attempts to show that there is no genuine disagreement, that Peter is really Pauline and Paul is really Petrine.[18] Baur described Acts as "the apologetic attempt of a Paulinist to introduce and thus to produce the mutual approach and uniting of the two opposing parties, so that Paul appears as Petrine as possible and Peter as Pauline as possible."[19] Although he could use the term "apology" to describe Acts, Baur preferred to think of this text as a proposed reconciliation between the two opposing parties. And as such it would require concessions on both sides. So, acknowledging his debt to Schneckenburger, Baur concluded that "its [Acts'] chief tendency is to represent the difference between Peter and Paul as unessential and trifling."[20]

Baur was struck with the absence from Acts of any mention of conflict between Peter and Paul, such as Paul described in Gal 2:11–14. He insisted that we must accept Paul's report as basically factual. According to Baur, there was an actual controversy between Peter and Paul, and the issue appears to be related to dietary regulations. In his report in Galatians, Paul portrays Peter as wavering, at first eating with Gentiles and apparently compromising the food restrictions, but later as withdrawing under pressure from the people associated with James. Even if Paul presented a biased report of the incident, Gal 2:11–14 is evidence that there was conflict in the earliest days of the church between the two great apostles over issues relating to Torah and Jewish practices. So Baur regards Galatians 2 as the best illustration of this early church conflict, and he is impressed that "throughout all the Epistles of Paul we do not find the slightest indication that the apostles ever drew nearer to each other in after years."[21] Remarkably, Baur failed to mention Gal 2:9, where James, Cephas, and John extend to Paul and Barnabas "the right hand of fellowship." Although it is not clear what Paul means by this statement, it should not be overlooked. Minimally, it suggests that, despite the controversy, some accommodation was found between the disputing parties. But Baur would emphasize the statement in Gal 2:7, in which a more or less permanent split is accepted: Paul goes to the uncircumcised; Peter to the circumcised. Presumably Baur would also emphasize the sequence of events narrated in Galatians 2. The extension of fellowship and the agreement to divide the Christian mission (Gal 2:7–9) come before Paul accuses Peter to his face (Gal 2:11). Thus the Galatians passage calls attention quite explicitly to the two parties, associates the names of Peter and Paul with them, and then goes on to point out that one of the continuing issues between the parties was that of table fellowship.

Here for Baur is the key to understanding early Christianity as a continuing controversy between two powerful parties. But there are other confirming indications that such a view is correct. In 1 Cor 1:12, Paul refers to factions and gives four names to them: Apollos, Christ, Peter, and Paul. Baur is convinced, however, that the significant opposition alluded to here is between the parties of Peter and Paul. He thinks that the parties of Apollos and Paul were allied against those of Peter and Christ. The attachment of the Christ party to the party of Peter means that these groups refused to grant Paul the title of apostle, a point that Paul addresses in both 1 and 2 Corinthians.[22]

Baur points out that, even in Acts, where every effort is made to minimize the conflict, there is nevertheless an important indication that Jewish Christians in Jerusalem "were by no means so unconcerned in the outbreaks of hatred to which the apostle fell a victim, as is generally supposed."[23] He has in mind the suspicion of Torah-observant believers that Paul had led diaspora Jews to withhold circumcision from their sons and to forsake Mosaic Torah. Notable also is the lack of support from this quarter when Paul fell under attack from Jews and was arrested by the Roman *chiliarch* (Acts 21:27–36). One wonders what happened to the myriads of believers among the Jews (Acts 21:20), none of whom came to Paul's defense on any of the occasions of his hearings and trials. Baur also notes the opposition to Paul in the Pseudo-Clementines, where he is identified with the Simon Magus of Acts 8:9.

If it is correct to assume that there was a continuing conflict between Jewish (Petrine) Christians and Gentile (Pauline) Christians, where then does the Acts of the Apostles most reasonably fit in this historical context? The clue for Baur is to be found precisely in Schneckenburger's study, which showed that Luke made every attempt to minimize the differences between Peter and Paul, to portray Paul as Petrine and Peter as Pauline. Why would a writer do this? Baur answered that a writer such as Luke would produce this kind of history as the first step toward reconciliation between the opposing parties. If there is to be any form of agreement between the two groups, argues Baur, that agreement could be regarded as well established if it "could be regarded as one which the two apostles had themselves contemplated, and could be traced to their mutual agreement. This is the point where the Acts of the Apostles not only finds its place as a literary product, but also plays its part as an independent factor of the history in the development of these relations."[24] And Baur asserts, "The Acts is thus the attempt at conciliation, the overture of peace, of a member of the Pauline party, who desired to purchase the recognition of Gentile Christianity on the part of the Jewish Christians by concessions made to Judaism by his side, and sought to influence both parties in this direction."[25]

From Baur's point of view it is not difficult to discern some of Luke's strategies. His method was to recommend concessions on both sides by showing the large areas of agreement between the two leaders. So for this reason, it is Peter, not Paul, who baptizes the first Gentile, Cornelius (Acts 10:44–48). Baur noted that Luke portrayed Paul's conversion and Peter's openness to Gentiles as results of visionary experiences, and he commented that we know from the Clementines that Jewish Christians suspected the apostolic calling of Paul and generally suspected the reliability of visions. They also insisted on the primacy of Peter. Baur writes, "[Acts] seems to ask from the Jewish-Christians the concession that there might exist another mode of being called to the apostolic mission, namely, through apparitions and visions, especially as the Apostle Peter himself had, by special divine appointment, and in furtherance of the important aim of the conversion of the Gentiles, been the recipient of similar visions."[26]

In dealing with the so-called apostolic conference of Acts 15, Baur first notes that it is impossible to harmonize this account with that in Galatians 2, a fundamentally trustworthy account: "But the most important point is, that the Acts of the Apostles represents the elder Apostles as agreeing with the Apostle Paul with regard to his views and principles in such a manner as we can see from the Epistle to the Galatians could never have been the case."[27] For, according to Galatians, the result of the meeting was a division: "in one the Mosaic law had force, in the other it had none, and these two systems simply co-existed without being in any way harmonised."[28]

Baur's approach has significant implications for the issue of Judaism in Acts. It is clear that, for Baur, Acts played a major role in reconciling the two parties, which opposed one another on issues relating to Torah and the Jewish people. But our concern at this point is in determining how Luke's alleged strategy of reconciliation affected the ways in which, in Baur's judgment, he portrayed Judaism. Baur is by no means silent on this matter, and at a number of points he reveals his biases.

For the most part, Baur's treatment of specific narratives in Acts reveals his interest in questions of historicity. For example, in the story of Ananias and Sapphira (Acts 5:1–11), the only thing that might constitute a historical kernel is the statement that the believers laid their possessions at the feet of the apostles.[29] But as for the story itself, the author of Acts created it out of the general statement. Baur says, "So little do we here stand on firm historical ground, that even the fact that persecutions did arise against the Apostles and the early Church could scarcely be deemed to be proved beyond all question, if it rested on no other evidence than what this narrative supplies."[30]

But Baur continues with a surprising approval of the basic historicity of the story of Stephen: "What follows this ideal scene, however, the martyrdom of Stephen and the persecutions of the Christians which was connected with it, wears the indubitable stamp of historical reality."[31] Although he thinks Stephen's speech is the composition of the author of Acts, Baur nevertheless is convinced that "it cannot be doubted that the attack of Stephen on the Jewish national worship was the cause of the outbreak of indignation to which he fell a victim."[32] The reason the reader can have such confidence in this claim is never explicitly stated. But Baur's analysis of Stephen's speech strongly suggests that its historical value is related to its anti-Judaism. That is, from Baur's point of view, the speech of Stephen is a trustworthy section of Acts because in it the Christian hero attacks in Judaism what should be attacked. Here is Baur's interpretation of Acts 7:46–47, a section of Stephen's speech that treats the age of David and Solomon: "But now the godless and carnal temper of the people manifested itself more openly, for they changed the general aspect of their religion with the change of the place where they worshipped. Now they possessed a permanent Temple, their religion took the form of a Levitical worship attached to the Temple, and became a formalism composed of outward rites and ceremonies."[33]

Despite appearances, Stephen did in the speech answer the charges against him, for in it he attacked "the outward ceremonial service to which at that time the true essence of the Jewish religion had been perverted. . . ."[34] Stephen's attack was, in fact, motivated by the same concerns as those of the Hebrew prophets: "But in dwelling upon this he is also exhibiting the grossness of the people's perversity; ingratitude and disobedience, with that overwhelming bias toward materialism, which the people had always manifested, must really have been their truest and most characteristic nature, because from the beginning—from the first moment in which they began to be a nation— they showed no other inclination."[35] The reader of Baur thus learns that the Judaism of Stephen's day was altogether characterized by negative factors, which Luke fully recognized.

The anti-Jewish character of the Baurian Acts is confirmed in his analysis of Paul's arrest in Jerusalem. He comments that the catastrophe that occurred when Paul went for the last time to Jerusalem was predictable. It was "brought about by the hatred which the Jews had all along cherished against the Apostle as an apostate and enemy of the national religion."[36] Throughout the narrative of Paul's ministry, "the Jews appear as the Apostle's bitterest enemies, who not only resist with all their might his preaching of the Gospel, but also attempt in every way to wreak their hatred on his person."[37]

The ending of Acts simply confirms the course of the narrative that precedes it, and here we have the Baurian statement of what came to be the consensus view that Jacob Jervell described: "The step which the Apostle was about to take in preaching the Gospel to the Gentiles was to be justified by the opposition of the Jews which had preceded it."[38] Baur also points out the incongruity in the narrative of Acts 28:23–28, which reports that some of Paul's Jewish hearers accepted what he said but others refused to believe. Yet, as Baur notes, the condemnation in Acts 28:25–28 allows for no distinctions, and thus, despite the lack of logic, Jewish opposition is "a mere pretext to give some colour of justice to a step which seemed to be unjustifiable without it."[39] The step to which Baur refers is, of course, announced in Acts 28:28, the determination to go to the Gentiles.

Baur insists that the authorial purpose of Acts is an irenic one, to attempt a reconciliation between the Jewish-Christian and Gentile-Christian parties. But Baur also maintains that a major aspect of Luke's strategy is to refocus the hatred that the two Christian groups have against one another and direct it toward unbelieving Jews. According to Baur, Luke's hope was that the mutual hostility between Jewish Christians and Gentile Christians would be forgotten "in the common hatred of both toward the unbelieving Jews," who had opposed Paul at every turn.[40] From this perspective, hatred of Judaism is seen as part of the rhetorical strategy at work in Acts, and, hence, anti-Judaism is part of the very structure of this document, which is ironically characterized as irenic.

Baur and the Gospel of Luke

Baur devotes a few pages to the Gospel of Luke in the first volume of his church history of the first three centuries.[41] But a more detailed analysis of this gospel had appeared a few years earlier in a study of all four gospels.[42] After a discussion of the history of gospel criticism, Baur devotes a chapter each to the gospels of John, Luke, Mark, and Matthew, in that order. His treatment of the issue of Judaism in the Gospel of Luke can be understood only in the context of his analysis of the complex history of this document.

Baur begins his discussion of the third gospel by questioning its relation to Marcion. He explicitly rejects the patristic belief that Marcion used canonical Luke and altered it so that it supported his own beliefs about the separation of law and gospel. Using the remarks of Tertullian and Epiphanius, he examines the probable text of Marcion's gospel and finds little evidence to support the theory of a mutilated text of Luke. Baur depends on Albrecht Ritschl in his analysis of a number of passages in Luke that are not found in Marcion's gospel and claims that some of the omissions might tend to support Marcion's theological position and that others are simply irrelevant to it.[43] In some cases, the narrative of canonical Luke reads better without the so-called Marcionite omissions, and in others the Marcionite order appears to be closer to the original. For example, in canonical Luke, the story of Jesus' first appearance in Nazareth (Luke 4:16–30) is followed by the first visit to Capernaum (Luke 4:31–37). But within the former narrative there is a reference to a prior visit to Capernaum (Luke 4:23), a reference that makes no sense in Luke in its present form. But in the Marcionite gospel, says Baur, the order is reversed, and the reference to the prior visit to Capernaum in Luke 4:23 points back to a visit that is actually described in the text. The author of canonical Luke changed the Marcionite order, which made perfect sense, because he wanted to emphasize the significance of the Nazareth pericope as the initial proclamation of Jesus about his mission. The perplexing joining of two apparently conflicting verses in Luke 16:16–17 is probably due to a modification of the gospel used by Marcion. According to both Tertullian and Epiphanius, Marcion had Luke 16:16, which proclaims the end of the law with John the Baptist. But in the next verse Marcion had, "it is easier for heaven and earth to pass away than for one stroke of my [Jesus'] words to fall." This version not only removes the contradiction with the previous verse but also conforms with the style and plan of the original gospel of Luke. This analysis leads to Baur's basic theory of the history of the composition of the Gospel of Luke.

Baur accepts the then dominant view of synoptic relations, namely that Matthew was the earliest gospel. In Baur's theory, "the original Gospel of Luke," as he designates it, was a revision of Matthew, written by a Paulinist who felt that the gospel should be purged of the Jewish-Christian tendencies to be found in Matthew's gospel. Original Luke was not a Marcionite gospel, but its strong Pauline character made it easily adaptable for Marcionite use. Some time after Marcion, a second author revised the original gospel of Luke in the interest of reconciling the Jewish-Christian and Gentile-Christian wings of the church, and this second author reintroduced some of the seemingly pro-Jewish parts of Matthew.[44] Baur then gives attention to these two editions of Luke.

If Marcion used the original gospel of Luke, then it is clear, says Baur, that there were significant sections missing from this gospel. The following longer sections were missing in the Marcionite gospel and hence probably not included in the original gospel of Luke: (1) the narratives of Jesus' birth and infancy, his baptism, and temptation (Luke 1:1–4:15); (2) three significant parables: Pilate's killing of the Galileans and the fig tree (13:1–9); the prodigal son (15:11–32); and the rebellious vineyard workers (20:9–18); (3) the narrative of Jesus' entry into Jerusalem (19:29–46). In addition, since the original gospel of Luke was a revision of Matthew, "the particular character of the original gospel of Luke may be shown above all in negative ways by its distinctions from Matthew."[45] So Baur observes that the original gospel had no affirmation of the validity of Torah. Jesus is not said to be born of a woman or born under Torah. There is in original Luke an emphasis on Jesus' Samaritan ministry, in which Samaria is taken to be Gentile territory.

The distinctions between Matthew and original Luke seem especially marked in Baur's discussion of Jesus' disciples. In both Matthew and original Luke Jesus sends out his twelve disciples (or apostles) on a mission (Matt 10:1–16; Luke 9:1–6, 10). But Luke alone has a parallel mission of the seventy (Luke 10:1–20). For Baur, the twelve, for obvious reasons, represent the Jewish Christians, and he takes the number seventy to represent the number of Gentile nations, a figure apparently based on the table of nations in Gen 10:2–31.[46] The author of original Luke apparently could not omit the former narrative but decreased its significance by the addition of a mission authorized by Jesus that anticipates the mission to the Gentiles in Acts. Although Jesus' instructions to the two groups are similar, his responses to their return are strikingly different. In 9:10, Luke simply reports the return of the twelve and goes immediately to the next narrative of the feeding of the crowd. But upon the return of the seventy (Luke 10:17–20), Luke says there was great joy, and he includes Jesus' declaration that he has witnessed the fall of Satan and his statement about granting authority to the seventy over snakes, scorpions, and the power of the enemy. Baur also notes that original Luke transferred the words of Jesus, "whoever welcomes you welcomes me," from Matt 10:40, where they are addressed to the twelve, to Luke 10:16, where they are attached to the seventy.[47]

Original Luke omitted from Matthew Jesus' declaration that Peter is the rock on which the church will be built and is destined to hold the keys of the kingdom (Matt 16:17–19). Neither does original Luke have the statement in which Jesus gives to the disciples the power to forgive or not forgive sins (Matt 18:18). In a number of other places original Luke included negative comments about the disciples. In the story of the transfiguration, it is said that Peter did not know what he said (Luke 9:33). Immediately after this a man brings a demoniac whom the disciples were unable to heal (Luke 9:37–43). Luke 9:44–45, in contrast to the parallel in Matt 17:22–23, shows that the disciples were uncomprehending about the deepest meaning of Jesus' fate. In the story of Jesus' mother and brothers (Matt 12:46–50; Luke 8:19–21), Jesus designates the disciples as his family in Matthew but not in Luke.

The distinctions between Matthew and original Luke may also be seen in the ways in which the latter has transformed the Sermon on the Mount. In Matthew the sermon has the character of a messianic inaugural address, but not in Luke. By transposing the scene of the sermon from a mountain to a valley, Luke diminishes its importance. He reduces the eight blessings in Matthew to four and adds corresponding woes, which sharpen the distinction between this world and the world to come. Here too the disciples hold a much less elevated position than in Matthew. Baur notes that in Matt 5:2, the sermon is addressed to αὐτούς, an indefinite article signifying both the crowd and the disciples, who are said to be with Jesus in Matt 5:1. But in Luke, although the presence of the crowd is noted in 6:19, the words of Jesus that follow are explicitly addressed to the disciples: Καὶ αὐτὸς ἐπάρας τοὺς ὀφθαλμοὺς αὐτοῦ εἰς τοὺς μαθητὰς αὐτοῦ ἔλεγευ (Luke 6:20). Baur takes this to mean that both the blessings and the woes in Luke 6:20–26 are addressed specifically to the disciples. Although they are given promises for the world to come (kingdom of God, fullness, joy, reward in heaven), they are also presented with threats. The fact that both blessings and woes are given in the second person in Luke, in contrast to the third in Matthew, also tends to support Baur's view that they are meant quite specifically for the immediate listeners, Jesus' disciples.

The bias of original Luke against Jewish Christianity carries with it an anti-Jewish bias. This is shown particularly well in the parable of the great dinner in Luke 14:16–24. Baur understands that the first ones invited are the Jews, who proceed to make excuses. But the blind and lame are brought in, as are those from the roads and lanes (Luke 14:23). These would be Gentiles, to whom the Christian message is presented later, and thus the word of rejection in Luke 14:24 comes to the Jews, who reject the invitation: "none of those who were invited will taste my dinner." Likewise, the story of the rich man and Lazarus in Luke 16:19–31 points up the obstinate refusal of Jews to accept the Christian message. Although they have Moses and the prophets, they have not heeded them, and they will not even listen to one who appears from beyond the grave (Luke 16:31). They will therefore refuse to repent of their sins and will be separated from the comforts of the bosom of Abraham. The story of Mary and Martha in Luke 10:38–42 tells of two women, one of whom listened to Jesus and the other who "was distracted by her many tasks" (Luke 10:40). Baur is convinced that Luke means to suggest that Martha is distracted by the many tasks imposed on her by the obligations of Torah.

Original Luke is thus a revision of Matthew by one who totally sympathizes with Paul and rejects all traces of Jewish Christianity. Baur describes this unknown author as follows: "So the author of the gospel lives totally in the consciousness of a Pauline universalism, which has overcome and abandoned all Jewish particularism and envisioned the finest development of the Christian idea, its highest triumph, not in Judaism but only among Gentiles, among all the people of the Gentile world."[48]

Canonical Luke was the work of a second author, writing some time after the Marcionite challenge. According to Baur, this edition of Luke was produced by a Paulinist who (a) rejected Marcion and (b) wanted to make peace with the Jewish Christians. These two purposes coalesce, since the reintroduction of passages favorable to Jewish Christianity would also tend toward the rejection of Marcionism. Canonical Luke is, therefore, a "neutralizing collection of Pauline and Judaistic discourses and narratives, a work of collecting, in which the Pauline elements appear as the basis of the gospel and the Judaistic as the interpolations and additions."[49] The result is an irenic gospel.

Although the second author of Luke displays no Judaistic tendencies, he includes in the gospel some sections that do. For example, the birth and infancy narratives of Luke 1–2, which must have originated in Jewish-Christian circles, present Jesus as the expected Jewish Messiah. Baur comments on these narratives: "The entry of the Messiah into the world is accompanied by everything which the Jewish fantasy [*jüdische Phantasie*] could muster. . . ."[50] But the universalizing interest of this Paulinist is not lost. Although the birth narratives have Jewish settings, elevated Gentiles, such as Augustus and Quirinius are also mentioned prominently. The genealogy of Jesus, in contrast to that in Matthew, which begins with Abraham, is expanded to include Adam and shows that Gentiles are also sons of God.

The complex history of the writing of Luke, together with the competing interests of the two authors, produces a complex gospel. Baur recognizes five different kinds of passages in canonical Luke: (1) those with an anti-Marcionite tendency; (2) those with a pro-Pauline tendency; (3) those with a Judaistic tendency; (4) those with a relationship to later party conditions; and (5) those which merely complete the picture of gospel history.[51] Some examples of each will be helpful.

(1) Although the original gospel of Luke was not Marcionite, it contained some anti-Jewish passages that were compatible with Marcion's views. The second author would need to change these passages. For example, in the original gospel of Luke, 16:16 ("the law and the prophets until John") might be used to support the Marcionite separation of law and gospel, especially with its reference to the durability of Jesus' words in 16:17 ("it is easier for heaven

and earth to pass away than for one stroke of my words to fall"). The second author, drawing on Matthew, changed the latter saying to read, "But it is easier for heaven and earth to pass away, than for one stroke of a letter in the law to be dropped" (Luke 16:17). Thus canonical Luke contains an anti-Marcionite reference to the permanence of Torah.

(2) Some passages in canonical Luke exhibit Pauline tendencies with particular clarity. Perhaps the best example of this is Luke 17:7–10, especially verse 10: "So you also, when you have done all that you were ordered to do, say, 'We are worthless slaves; we have done only what we ought to have done!'" The parable of the barren fig tree in Luke 13:6–9 also exhibits Pauline tendencies. Baur comments, "The fig tree, finally cut down after such a long time of unfruitfulness, is a picture of the Jewish people and their guilt, which the apostle Paul always remembers, when he compares Jews and Gentiles in relation to the Kingdom of God."[52]

(3) Probably the most significant section added by the second author to give a nod toward Jewish Christianity is Luke 1–2, the birth and infancy narratives, which we noted above. In addition, the entry of Jesus into Jerusalem (Luke 19:28–44) is presented as the entry of the Jewish Messiah.

(4) By passages that exhibit a relationship to later party struggles, Baur means to signify those that relate in some way to the conflicts between Pauline and Jewish Christianity and to the author's hope for reconciliation. Perhaps the best illustration in this category is the parable of the prodigal son in Luke 15:11–32. In its present form, the parable appears to echo the conditions set in Rom 11:11–14, where the jealousy of the unbelieving Jews is contrasted with the joy of the Gentile Christians. Clearly, says Baur, the elder brother in Luke 15 is the Jewish Christian, who has never left home, and the younger brother is the Gentile, who has repented his former life in order to come to the father. The author of canonical Luke knows that Jewish Christians have a sense of priority in the faith and are suspicious of the more recent converts from among the Gentiles. But the motif of conciliation is also present, when the father assures the older brother of his position in the family and encourages him to accept the younger: "Son, you are always with me, and all that is mine is yours. But we had to celebrate and rejoice, because this brother of yours was dead and has come to life; he was lost and has been found" (Luke 15:31–32).

(5) The last category consists of incidental verses and pericopes that are needed in order to present a more complete account. These interpolations agree more or less with Matthew and probably come from this source.

More readily than many scholars before or after his time, Baur has recognized the complexities in canonical Luke. In its present form, Luke appears to be unusually ambivalent in the treatment of Judaism and the Jewish people. Whatever may be the deficits of his approach, Baur has clearly seen this phenomenon and provided a way to make sense of it. For the most part, passages in Luke's gospel that seem to be anti-Jewish belong to the original gospel, while those that seem pro-Jewish were interpolated by the second author.

There is no doubt that Baur expresses deep appreciation for the work of the second author and his attempt at reconciliation. But there is also a sense in which his reconstructed original Luke not only has a chronological priority to canonical Luke but also carries more theological weight. Despite its irenic purpose, canonical Luke is not, in Baur's judgment, an improvement on original Luke. Its interpolations and its alterations, as well as its reintroduction of material explicitly omitted by the first author, result in a gospel with an unclear focus and diminished impact. Since the author of original Luke had no need to try to satisfy disparate groups but only intended to present a Pauline point of view in narrative form, his gospel is less complex and more sharply focused than is canonical Luke. Its anti-Judaism is a product of its Paulinism and its opposition to the kind of Jewish Christianity represented in Matthew, whereas the pro-Jewish passages of the second author seem to be merely nods in the direction of the opponents and are dictated by the need to compromise. Baur's own summary statement in his discussion of Luke in the *Church History* confirms his basic view: "by repeated declarations, the great truth is clearly set forth, that Judaism is not the true or appropriate field for the accomplishment of the work of Jesus."[53]

Although Baur is careful to point out the complexities in Luke, his overall approach to the treatment of Judaism in both the gospel and Acts is uncomplicated, and it conforms well with his own conception of Judaism in NT times. Thus, in Baur's reading, Judaism in Luke-Acts is, fundamentally, a religion that emphasizes formalism, materialism, particularism, and legalism. The ritual of the Temple is a matter of outward rites and ceremonies, empty of spiritual meaning. The Jewish people are disobedient, unbelieving, and obdurate. Their rejection of Paul and the Christian message is virtually total. They misperceive their scriptures not only by failing to recognize the truth of the Christian message but by their preoccupation with Torah. Jewish messianic expectation is described as fantasy or illusion. The fundamental strategy of the author of Acts, and presumably of canonical Luke as well, is to refocus the hatred that Christian groups had against each other and direct this hatred toward unbelieving Jews. The only relief from these startlingly negative images of Judaism is provided by interpolations required by the need for intramural reconciliation but not supplied by philo-semitic sentiments.

Finally, I want to return to the question of the influence of Hegelian thought on Baur's study of early Christianity. Peter Hodgson is probably correct in his observations, which question the significance of Baur's contact with Hegel. In the work examined here on Luke-Acts, Hodgson's judgment also seems to be confirmed: the character that Baur sees in early Christianity is not solely the product of his alleged adherence to Hegelian philosophy. It depends in the first instance on his interpretation of the NT texts. In these exegetical studies, there is no explicit attention given to Hegelian or any other philosophy of history. To be sure, a lack of explicit mention does not mean a lack of influence in the exegetical studies, but it does mean that, as Hodgson observed, Baur intends to let his case rest on the critical interpretation of NT texts, an interpretation that can and should be defended or attacked without recourse to philosophies of history. Our studies confirm Hodgson's view that it is no longer permissible to dismiss Baur's work as nothing more than the imposition of Hegelian philosophy on the history of early Christianity.

At the same time, however, one cannot overlook the relationship between Baur's exegetical work and his historical reconstructions. In some cases the historical reconstruction is dependent on the interpretation of texts. Galatians 2, for example, is probably the bedrock of Baur's theory of the opposition of Pauline and Petrine Christianity. In other cases the historical reconstruction affects the exegesis. The relation of Luke to Marcion, the reconstruction of the original text of Luke, its relation to Matthew, and the history of the composition of canonical Luke—all rest on speculative judgments that shape the ways in which Baur reads this gospel.

Baur was not the first to use hypothetical historical reconstructions in the interpretation of Luke-Acts. And we shall see that he is by no means the last. The value of his interpretation will become clearer by comparison with subsequent writers.

The Tübingen School and Its Challengers

Ferdinand Christian Baur was a giant among NT scholars. His viewpoints became dominant within a school of interpretation, the Tübingen School, named for his university. His critical methods and interpretation opened new vistas for some and provided difficult challenges for others. His work inevitably had a profound influence on the study of Luke-Acts.

The most extensive commentary on Acts produced by a member of the Tübingen school was written by Baur's son-in-law, Eduard Zeller.[54] Zeller's views on Acts are, in most respects, similar to Baur's, and it may not be far from the truth to say that Zeller's commentary on Acts is the one that Baur would have written, had he written one. Zeller is keenly interested in the historical accuracy of Acts, and, for the most part, he is skeptical. In particular, he questions the historicity of the character of Paul as portrayed in Acts. On Acts 23:6, where Paul announces to members of the Sanhedrin that he is a Pharisee, Zeller asks, "How could Paul say this of himself with even a semblance of truth? He certainly had been a Pharisee; but was he *at that time still* a Pharisee,—he who unremittingly waged war against the observance of the Law, the groundwork of this Jewish orthodoxy?"[55] And later he writes, "We hear but the maxims of Jewish Christianity from the lips of the Apostle of the Gentiles."[56]

Zeller insists that Acts is not simply an apology for Paul. A better apology would have consisted of a clear picture of Paul's character, principles, and work. Rather, Acts is, as Baur had said, a conciliatory document, "an attempt at mediation between Judaists and Paulinists."[57] More particularly, "it is the project of a treaty of peace submitted to the Judaists by the Paulinist side."[58]

The most vigorous objection to the contention that Acts is a proposal for reconciliation came from Franz Overbeck, who in many respects found himself in agreement with Baur.[59] Overbeck agreed with Baur and Zeller that Acts cannot be understood without reference to the antagonisms between parties within early Christianity, but he was more sensitive than they about the anti-Jewish character of Acts and was unable to accept their views about its conciliatory character. Overbeck writes,

> But to regard the Acts as a conciliatory work aggravates the difficulty of the assumption that the book was designed for Judaists—at least if by the latter we understand Christians who were of Jewish parentage. Against this view we have the *national Anti-Judaism* of the Acts, its antagonism to the Jews as a nation. This book, which unequivocally attributes the development of the Christian community to the stubborn unbelief of the Jews, which from the outset pointedly emphasizes their past culpability, and which as a matter of fact charges upon the Jews every additional advance made in the preaching of the Christian Messiah . . . such a book cannot have been intended to exercise a conciliatory influence upon the Jewish Christians.[60]

Overbeck returns to the view that Acts is an apology written to Gentiles, and, among other reasons, it was written "to avert political suspicions from Christianity."[61]

Although a number of objections to the Tübingen school were raised by conservative scholars, Albrecht Ritschl, at one time a student of Baur, is usually given the credit for destroying general confidence in the school.[62] Ritschl begins his own study of early Christianity with Jesus. Drawing initially from the Gospel of Mark, which he believes to be the original gospel, he maintains that Jesus demonstrated the nonbinding character of the commandments about Sabbath rest and ritual purity, as well as the Mosaic permission of divorce. For Jesus, the highest goal for human beings is the love of God and the love of the neighbor. Whatever from Torah supports this goal is valid, and whatever does not is invalid. Ritschl maintained that Jesus intended to substitute his own words for those of Torah. He acknowledged that Jesus did not actually abrogate circumcision, the concept of God's choice of Israel, or the sacrificial system, but he maintained that these changes would naturally follow from Jesus' teachings. Ritschl saw no reason to suggest a wide gap between the teachings of Jesus and the theology of his earliest followers. So the earliest Jewish Christians, although they maintained circumcision, did not adhere to Torah in an inflexible way and so did not find themselves in deep opposition to Pauline Christianity. Moreover, Ritschl showed that Christianity was far more diverse in the first two centuries than Baur had imagined. There were controversies, and there were extreme Jewish Christians, but the controversies were more complex than Baur had thought, and the extreme Jewish Christians had less influence than Baur's reconstruction would allow. Although he, like Baur, saw a conflict in early Christianity with Jewish traditions, he traced the conflict to the time of Jesus rather than to that of Peter and Paul.

Although Ritschl is usually given credit for providing an answer to the Baurian challenge, we shall see that some scholars even in the late twentieth century are still struggling with problems that Baur first posed. His creative exegesis of NT texts, especially Luke and Acts, remains a signal contribution to the history of the interpretation of early Christianity, and his approach to the treatment of Judaism in Luke and Acts is still worthy of serious consideration.

CHAPTER 3

ADOLF VON HARNACK
(1851–1930)

In a recent study Susannah Heschel has shown that Albrecht Ritschl's attack on the Tübingen school carried with it the potential for a more vigorous anti-Judaism in Christian scholarship than had been the case with Baur.[1] Baur had concentrated on the conflicts in the early church between Jewish Christians and Pauline Christians and had clearly shown that such conflicts involved issues of Torah observance. He characterized early Jewish Christianity as legalistic and nationalistic and Pauline Christianity as free and universalistic. He saw Pauline Christianity as hostile to those matters that could be characterized as Jewish. But Heschel notes that Ritschl traced this hostility to Judaism back to Jesus himself. She writes, "Whereas Baur was anxious to keep Jesus within the environment of his day, for Ritschl, Jesus presented not an extension but a renunciation of Judaism and its law that became a sharp dividing line between his teachings and those of the Jews. That break, according to Ritschl, occurred at the beginning and was decisive; there was no gradual evolution out of Judaism."[2] In addition, Ritschl restricted the differences between Pauline Christianity and the religion of the earliest apostles, and this change also affected the ways in which Christian anti-Judaism was perceived. According to Heschel, "Whereas Baur had made Jewish Christianity the basis for the oldest, original form of religious expression, that of the surviving eleven apostles, in contrast to Pauline Christianity, Ritschl demolished that schema by arguing for a far greater affinity between Paul and the other apostles. . . . This meant that Ritschl created a picture of an early Jesus movement united in a goal of eliminating Jewish elements; . . . Jewish Christianity remained a marginal sect, closed in on itself, which eventually withered to death; Catholicism, he claimed, was the product of Pauline Christianity, not Jewish Christianity, as the Tübingen school had asserted."[3] Ritschl exercised a profound influence on a number of subsequent scholars, most notably Adolf Harnack. Harnack met Ritschl in 1877, and he later wrote, "The future of Protestantism as a religion and a spiritual power lies in the direction which Ritschl has indicated."[4]

Harnack was born on May 7, 1851, at Dorpat, in a region then known as East Prussia, now Estonia. Martin Rumscheidt notes that the "Harnacks were

Lutheran and belonged by education, social position and, by a strong degree too of consciousness-reinforcement, to the ruling minority of Prussians who maintained the language and customs of Germany in this far outpost of German ecclesial and commercial missionary work."[5] The father, Theodosius Harnack, taught church history at the University of Dorpat until 1853, when he accepted a position at Erlangen. When Adolf was in his mid-teens, the father, now widowed with five children, moved back to Dorpat, and at eighteen Adolf began his studies at the university there. In 1872 he left Dorpat to study at Leipzig, where he quickly produced a doctoral dissertation and a habilitation-dissertation. He began teaching at Leipzig in 1875, then moved to Giessen in 1878 and Marburg in 1886. From 1888 on, he was professor of church history at the University of Berlin. The appointment was controversial from the beginning. Church officials objected to Harnack's views on the authorship of a number of NT documents as well as to his views on miracles. But Kaiser Wilhelm II supported him and signed the call for his appointment. Even so, the controversy surrounding Harnack continued and led to the appointment in 1893 of a counter-professor, Adolf Schlatter, whose contribution will be examined in the chapter that follows. For the next three decades Harnack had a personal relationship with the Kaiser, with whom he met privately on several occasions. To prepare the German people for war in 1914, Kaiser Wilhelm asked Harnack to write his speech, and Harnack accepted. Through the emperor he also met Houston Stewart Chamberlain, whose theories of race and antagonism between Teutons and Jews were very influential in Germany.[6]

Harnack's *History of Dogma* appeared in three volumes between 1885 and 1889, and the appearance of each volume was surrounded by controversy. Many church officials regarded the work as heretical, while Harnack's academic colleagues regarded it as tame. On the part of the church leaders, "the chief critique was that Harnack made use of the New Testament and Christianity as *sources,* rather than as *norms,* for the formation of personal faith."[7] A similar controversy surrounded the publication of Harnack's most famous work, *Das Wesen des Christentums,* in 1900. The first of his studies on Luke-Acts, which will be of greatest interest to us here, appeared in 1906.

By the time that Adolf von Harnack began his studies of Luke-Acts, the influence of the Tübingen school had greatly diminished. The interim between the death of Baur in 1860 and Harnack's first major publications on Luke-Acts in 1906 was a significant period for NT studies in several respects. Attention to two major developments in this period will help us to understand the significance of Harnack's work on Luke and Acts.

In the first place, extensive studies of the synoptic problem had drastically altered the paradigm with which most scholars carried on their studies of the gospels. Although Baur worked confidently with the concept that Matthew was the earliest gospel, Ritschl was able to assume Markan priority even before Baur died. But Heinrich J. Holtzmann, who noted that there was no consensus on the solution to the documentary relationships among the synoptic gospels, is to be given the credit for establishing the two-document hypothesis as a convincing solution for scholars and theologians in the late nineteenth century.[8] Werner G. Kümmel characterizes Holtzmann's work as "a study that summed up all previous research in magnificent fashion."[9] William R. Farmer, who is critical of the process by which the two-document hypothesis became established, wrote that "at the beginning of the twentieth century nearly all Gospel criticism was being carried on within the limits of Holtzmann's synthesis, and the Marcan or two-document hypothesis was regarded by most as one of the assured results of nineteenth century criticism."[10]

A second development between the time of Baur and that of Harnack that affected NT scholarship was the greater attention that was given to early Judaism (although it was still called "late Judaism") and its relationship to early Christianity. Baur had identified Judaism fundamentally with the Hebrew Bible, and he acknowledged no Jewish development beyond NT times. But in the latter part of the nineteenth century, rabbinic literature came to be seen as a significant source of information about early Judaism. Studies by Jewish scholars, such as Abraham Geiger, who demonstrated the usefulness of rabbinic literature in historical studies of both Judaism and Christianity, were widely used in the late nineteenth century.[11] Geiger maintained that Jesus taught nothing different from the Pharisees and that his teaching may be most closely compared with that of Hillel.[12] In an appraisal of Geiger's work and its influence on Christian scholarship, Heschel writes that his *Urschrift und Übersetzungen* "is not only Geiger's best-known book; it is the single book by a Jewish author which attracted the greatest amount of attention in the Christian scholarly world in Europe during the nineteenth century."[13]

Mindful of the research on the synoptic problem and the improved information about first-century Judaism that came to light in the late nineteenth century, we may now approach the work of Adolf Harnack, to explore, first, his understanding of first-century Judaism; second, his treatment of Luke-Acts; and, third, his assessment of Judaism in Luke-Acts.

Harnack on First-Century Judaism

Harnack exhibits an awareness of Geiger's work, but his own views about Judaism in the time of Jesus are almost totally unaffected by Jewish scholarship. In a discussion of the distinctiveness of the teaching of Jesus in the third lecture of his *Das Wesen des Christentums,* Harnack raises the question of the relationship of this teaching to Judaism and makes an oblique reference to Jewish scholarship, perhaps Geiger's.

"What do you want with your Christ," we are asked, principally by Jewish scholars; "he introduced nothing new." I answer with Wellhausen: It is quite true that what Jesus proclaimed, what John the Baptist expressed before him in his exhortations to repentance, was also to be found in the prophets, and even in the Jewish tradition of their time. The Pharisees themselves were in possession of it; but unfortunately they were in possession of much else besides. With them it was weighted, darkened, distorted, rendered ineffective and deprived of its force, by a thousand things which they also held to be religious and every whit as important as mercy and judgment. They reduced everything to one dead level [*Fläche*], wove everything into one fabric; the good and holy was only one woof in a broad earthly warp.[14]

Even if the German *Fläche* does not carry quite the same negative quality as the English "dead level," there is no doubt about the force of Harnack's statement.[15] Harnack continues with similar imagery to speak of the purity and strength of the gospel, and he uses the metaphor of the spring to signify the holiness of truth: "As regards purity, the spring of holiness had, indeed, long been opened; but it was choked with sand and dirt, and its water was polluted."[16] With Jesus this truth burst forth in pure clarity, without the pollution of priests and Rabbis.

Harnack's judgment about Judaism is evidently not based on extensive study of Jewish literature. It is rather a product of his conviction about the distinctiveness of Jesus. This distinctiveness could not be allowed, however, to play itself out in absolute terms, for Harnack fully recognized the weight of Jewish objections. It was possible to cite parallels in the Hebrew Bible and later Jewish literature to many of the sayings of Jesus. So the distinctiveness must be established in a different way, by emphasizing the purity of the teaching of Jesus, and this required Harnack to characterize the Jewish tradition as a kernel of truth hidden within a husk that threatened to obscure whatever truth it contained.[17]

Harnack was, however, less than explicit when it came to describing the character of first-century Judaism. The reader is left to fill in the negative characterization with whatever content might seem appropriate, and Harnack only hints at what the appropriate content might be. The essential distinction appears to be between matters such as justice and mercy, which may be characterized as inward dispositions, and ritual and worship, which are characterized as external acts. Later in *What Is Christianity?* Harnack includes what appears to be a carefully nuanced statement about Pharisees: "To judge the moral ideas of the Pharisees solely by their childish and casuistical aspects is not fair. By being bound up with religious worship and petrified in ritual observance, the morality of holiness had, indeed, been transformed into something that was the clean opposite of it. But all was not yet hard and dead; there was some life left in the deeper parts of the system."[18] In this light, Harnack points out that Jesus' contribution was a breaking of the connection between ethics and ritual: "He [Jesus] would have absolutely nothing to do with the purposeful and self-seeking pursuit of 'good works' in combination with the ritual of worship."[19]

In *The Expansion of Christianity,* Harnack allows that there was a kind of

preparatio evangelium in Jewish proselytism. He notes that the Jewish missionaries found it necessary to de-emphasize ritualistic elements in order to
call attention to the significance of monotheism.[20] But this alteration in Jewish
concepts appears to be motivated only by political and rhetorical considerations and is not a matter of principle. Besides, says Harnack, there was a vital
omission in Jewish proselytism, namely that "no Gentile, in the first generation at least, could become a real son of Abraham. His rank before God
remained inferior. Thus it also remained very doubtful how far any proselyte—to say nothing of the 'God-fearing'—had a share in the glorious
promises of the future. The religion which will repair this omission will drive
Judaism from the field."[21]

Although Harnack displays a modicum of appreciation for the contribution of Jewish missionary preaching as a preparation for Christian preaching
to Gentiles, he makes it clear that there is no fundamental connection between
Jewish and Christian theology. His *History of Dogma* begins without a treatment of the Jewish ideology that might have formed a context for Jesus and
the early church. Indeed, Harnack is convinced that Christianity is new,
despite its relation to Jewish history, concepts, and practices. As a fundamental presupposition to his history of dogma, Harnack maintains that "the Gospel
presents itself as an Apocalyptic message on the soil of the Old Testament, and
as the fulfilment of the law and the prophets, and yet is a new thing, the creation of a universal religion on the basis of that of the Old Testament."[22] This
principle would appear to cause trouble for a consideration of Jesus, whom
Harnack is careful to associate, though loosely, with Judaism and not at all
with Hellenism. But his approach is problematic. He admits that Jesus "did not
withdraw from the religious and political communion of his people, nor did he
induce his disciples to leave that communion. On the contrary, he described
the Kingdom of God as the fulfilment of the promises given to the nation, and
himself as the Messiah whom that nation expected."[23] But this connection to
Judaism appears to be a political strategy on Jesus' part, to secure "for his new
message, and with it his own person, a place in the system of religious ideas
and hopes, which by means of the Old Testament were then, in diverse forms,
current in the Jewish nation."[24] The Hebrew Bible, transformed by the message
of Jesus, provided the believer a sense of comfort and strength, and it supplied
a firm footing that preserved the gospel "from dissolving in the glow of enthusiasm, or melting away in the ensnaring dream of antiquity. . . ."[25] Even so, the
result of Jesus' preaching "was not only the illumination of the Old Testament
by the Gospel and the confirmation of the Gospel by the Old Testament, but
not less, though indirectly, the detachment of believers from the religious community of the Jews from the Jewish Church."[26] The movement of Christian
believers away from Judaism and toward Hellenism is not surprising, for the
latter exercised a powerful attraction: "Israel, no doubt, had a sacred treasure
which was of greater value than all the treasures of the Greeks,—the living
God; but in what miserable vessels was this treasure preserved, and how much

inferior was all else possessed by this nation in comparison with the riches, the power, the delicacy and freedom of the Greek spirit and its intellectual possessions."[27]

Negative appraisal of Judaism in the *History of Dogma* becomes radical rejection in Harnack's study of Marcion.[28] Harnack's emphasis on the newness of Christianity is a reflection of his fascination with Marcion, and his explanation of Marcion's motivation appears to be in harmony with his own. For example, Harnack states that Marcion's point of departure is *"provided in the Pauline contrast of law and gospel, on the one side malicious, petty and cruel punitive correctness, and on the other side merciful love."*[29] Harnack finds no basis for disagreeing with Marcion in this characterization. For him Marcion's theology is an extension of Paulinism, and this recognition led Harnack to sympathize with Marcion's attitude toward the Hebrew Bible. "If one carefully thinks through with Paul and Marcion the contrast between 'the righteousness that is by faith' and 'the righteousness that is by works' and is persuaded also of the inadequacy of the means by which Paul thought that he could maintain the *canonical* recognition of the Old Testament, consistent thinking will not be able to tolerate the validity of the Old Testament as canonical documents in the Christian church."[30]

Later in the same chapter, Harnack states the following thesis, for which he argues: *"The rejection of the Old Testament in the second century was a mistake which the great church rightly avoided; to maintain it in the sixteenth century was a fate from which the Reformation was not yet able to escape; but still to preserve it in Protestantism as a canonical document since the nineteenth century is the consequence of a religious and ecclesiastical crippling."*[31] Harnack recommends that the Protestant churches make it clear that the Hebrew Bible is useful for reading but is not canonical, that it is not to be put on the same level as the NT, and that it has no compelling authority for Christians.

In summary, Harnack's view of first-century Judaism may be characterized as radically negative. Judaism plays only a minor role in the history of early Christianity and contributes nothing of significance to the theology. Although there are similarities between Jewish teachings and the teaching of Jesus, there are no grounds for any meaningful comparisons. One would need to dig through mountains of valueless Jewish teachings in order to find what presents itself in purity and simplicity in the teaching of Jesus. Judaism emphasizes the external duties of correct worship and ritual. It teaches the doctrine of righteousness by works, the very opposite of the Pauline doctrine of righteousness by faith. Thus, Christianity is new, and its relation to Judaism and to the Hebrew Bible is not essential. Even if NT documents speak of Jesus as the fulfillment of law and prophets, this fulfillment is to be understood as a severance from Judaism, a separation that should result in the Christian rejection of law and prophets as canonical.

In the first volume of his study of the history of Christianity, Harnack has a revealing statement about the relationship of Christianity to Judaism. He raises the question of justice in consideration of the appropriation of the Hebrew Bible by the Gentile-Christian church, on the one hand, and the rejection of Judaism, on the other: "The Gentile church stripped it [Judaism] of everything; she took away its sacred book; herself but a transformation of Judaism, she cut off all connection with the parent religion. The daughter first robbed her mother, and then repudiated her! But, one may ask, is this view really correct? Undoubtedly it is, to some extent, and it is perhaps impossible to force anyone to give it up. But *viewed from a higher standpoint,* the facts acquire a different complexion. By their rejection of Jesus, the Jewish people disowned their calling and dealt the death-blow to their own existence. . . ."[32] One may reasonably ask what the "higher standpoint" is from which Harnack is making his judgment, and if this standpoint is appropriate for the kind of historical investigation he intends. The answer is obvious. The "higher standpoint" is nothing other than the Christian conviction about Jesus, a faith standpoint that motivated Harnack's historical work throughout his life.

Harnack on Luke-Acts

Harnack produced no commentary on either Luke or Acts. Instead he devoted three volumes of the series, New Testament Studies, to introductory studies of these documents.[33] In addition, volume two in this same series dealt with the so-called Q material in Matthew and Luke.[34] Taken together, these volumes give us a clear analysis of most of the major problems of an introductory nature in Luke and Acts.

Not only in *Luke the Physician* but also in *The Date of the Acts* and to a lesser extent in *The Acts of the Apostles,* Harnack deals with the problem of the authorship of our documents, and he consistently maintains that the author was the traveling companion of Paul, known as Luke the physician. In *Luke the Physician,* Harnack begins by noting that Lukan authorship of both the third gospel and Acts has been universally accepted since the middle of the second century. He assumes that the name of the author must have originally appeared in the title, and he asserts that it is more likely that the name contained there was the same as the one recognized by all commentators than that it was some other person: "If St. Luke was not the author, then the real author's name must have been purposely suppressed either when the book was combined with the three other gospels or at some previous time."[35] Of these alternatives, the most likely is that Luke was the author and his name appeared originally in the title. In addition, the work itself provides us with some information about the author. For one thing, "St. Luke is never mentioned in the Acts, which is just what we should expect if he himself was the author of the book."[36] Luke and Acts also show that they were composed by one who was Greek by birth, who was a physician and a member of "the middle or higher plane of contemporary culture."[37] In addition, the author of Acts was a companion and fellow-worker with Paul, and a native of Antioch.

The pieces of information provided about the author by the text are not of equal weight. Some pieces are, in fact, curious. It is true that Luke is not mentioned by name in Acts, where he might have played a minor role in some episodes, but of course an indefinite number of other people are also not mentioned. And, as we shall see, according to Harnack, the author frequently refers to himself in the "we" sections, although not by name. The argument that Harnack states here has validity only if, on other grounds, we have reason to believe that Luke is the author of Acts. Similarly, the composition of Luke and Acts by a person who was Greek by birth, if shown conclusively, would not definitively point to authorship by Luke.

Much more weight should be given to the evidence that the author is a physician and a fellow-worker with Paul. On the identification of the author as a physician, Harnack leans heavily on the work of William K. Hobart,[38] who had compared the language of Luke-Acts with that of known Greek physicians of the time. Harnack complained that Hobart had gone too far in his citation of evidence, but he found the argument on the whole convincing. In support, Harnack included an appendix to *Luke the Physician,* in which he cited the pertinent evidence: the character of the gospel narrative as dominated by the author's emphasis on Jesus as healer, the preference in the gospel for stories of healing, and the medical coloring of the language.[39]

The key to Harnack's approach to the authorship of Luke and Acts is, however, the contention that the author was a companion of Paul. To support this contention Harnack does two things. First, he demonstrates that the "we" sections of Acts were written by the same person who wrote the rest of the book, and second, he answers the objection that the author of Acts has either misunderstood or misrepresented Paul. It is necessary to devote some attention to these two arguments.

In the English edition of Harnack's *Luke the Physician,* almost one hundred pages are devoted to a discussion of the "we" sections of Acts, and Harnack returns to a summary of the discussion in *The Date of the Acts.* In *Luke the Physician,* he provides a detailed analysis of Acts 16:10–17 to show that almost everything in it is either characteristic of the language of Luke-Acts or at least not unusual. The study leads him to reject the assumption that this passage is drawn from a source: "After this demonstration those who declare that this passage (xvi.10–17) was derived from a source, and so was not composed by the author of the whole work, take up a most difficult position. What may we suppose the author to have left unaltered in the source? Only the 'we'? For, in fact, nothing else remains! As such a procedure is absolutely unimaginable, we are simply left to infer that the author is here himself speaking."[40] Harnack then analyzes Acts 28:1–16, with the same results, and provides vocabulary statistics of all the "we" sections to show that the vocabulary of these sections has more in common with other parts of Luke and Acts than with the other gospels. He concludes that the author of the "we" sections is the author of the entire work, Luke-Acts.

The other main support for Harnack's contention about the authorship of
Luke-Acts consists of an attempt to address objections to it. The chief objection that was raised against the theory that Acts was written by a companion
of Paul is that the picture of Paul in Acts is very different from the picture of
Paul that emerges from a study of the letters. As we have seen, Baur and Zeller
used this observation in major ways, and, as we shall see, the problem has not
gone away. But Harnack argues vigorously that, although Luke is no more
immune than any other writer from making historical errors, we have no right
to substitute our impressions, drawn from the letters, for his. "If he [Luke] has
here assigned less honour to St. Paul than from his epistles seems to be due to
him, and if in chaps. xxi. ss. he makes him appear more Jewish in his behaviour than we, judging from the same epistles, should imagine possible, it is at
least permissible to ask which is right—our imagination or the representation
given in the Acts."[41] Harnack also observes that Paul must have been a perplexing person, that "he must more than once have appeared very incomprehensible to his Gentile Christian as well as to his Jewish Christian
companions."[42] Since Luke had not come to grips with the problem of Torah
in the way that Paul had, he cannot be called a Paulinist in the strict sense of
that term, and it is natural that he would not have been able to portray Paul
with full understanding. Besides, Luke was certainly not the only companion
of Paul who was not a Paulinist. "If all of them, or even only the majority of
them, were Paulinists in the strict sense of the word, how was it that the Gentile Church in Asia, in Greece, and in Rome, became so un-Pauline?"[43]

Harnack returns to a discussion of this issue in *The Date of the Acts.*[44] He
notes that the argument is usually made that Paul's attitude toward Judaism is
contained in Galatians and that he never departed from the judgments
expressed there. But Harnack calls attention to some things that suggest that
Paul's attitude was more complex than it has been represented to be. Even in
Gal 5:11, Paul is accused of still preaching circumcision, and there must be
some ground for this accusation. In 1 Cor 7:18–20, Paul implies "that the converted Jew should remain faithful to the customs and ordinances of the
fathers."[45] Romans 9–11 constitutes a serious qualification to Paul's judgments
in Galatians, since here he holds out a future hope for historical Israel. Strict
logic would have required Paul to abandon this hope, but "the Jew in him was
still too strong and his reverence for the content of the Old Testament still too
devoted!"[46] The observation that historical Israel will follow the Gentiles into
salvation sheds light on Paul's command that God's ordinances should continue to be observed, "for if the nation no longer observes its Law, then it is no
longer the Jewish nation; and thus there is now no nation for which the special
promise belonging to the Jewish nation can be fulfilled."[47] Also in 1 Cor 9:20,
Paul says, "To the Jews I became as a Jew, in order to win Jews." Harnack
maintains that this was not simply a pragmatic consideration: *"His limitation
lay in this, that he had not thought this conception out to the end, and accord-
ingly held fast to an indefinite compromise with Jewish convictions; and that,*

instead of carrying on the fight along the whole line, he on important points yielded to the Jew in the Jewish Christian—not from cowardice or insincerity, but because the Jew in himself was still too strong."[48]

Harnack concludes that there were more pro-Jewish tendencies in Paul than most critical commentators have heretofore recognized and that Acts brings out these tendencies in ways that the letters, because of their occasional contexts, only leave implicit. Thus, the author of Acts, although not free from historical errors, was not unfaithful in his portrait of Paul: "Our conclusion, therefore, is that the author of the Acts, in his description of St. Paul's relations with Judaism, is in essential agreement with St. Paul's own epistles."[49] Harnack blames the *Tendenzkritik,* associated with Baur, for a failure to recognize this essential agreement.

Harnack's argument is convincing to the degree to which the traces of Paul's alleged pro-Judaism in the letters might be compared with the portrayal in Acts. There is something persuasive about the contention that Paul was, among his own contemporaries, perplexing if not incomprehensible. It must be admitted that Harnack has presented a more balanced picture of Paul than has Baur, and his calling attention to the possible implication of remarks such as that in Gal 5:11 is helpful. Still, there seems to be a vast difference between these passages and statements such as Acts 23:6, where Paul claims to be a Pharisee. In addition, Harnack has not discussed the evidence that would tend to support a position such as Baur's or Zeller's. What might he say, for example, about Phil 3:8, if it is right to understand Paul's deprecating comment as directed toward circumcision, Torah, and Pharisaism? Furthermore, there seems to be some confusion about the relationship of 1 Cor 7:18–20 and Romans 9–11. Harnack says that there must be a recognizable Torah-observant Israel to be saved after the salvation of the Gentiles and that Paul's command in 1 Corinthians is directed toward the end of preserving this Jewish nation. But the words of 1 Cor 7:18–20 are directed toward Christians, not to the unbelieving Jews contemplated in Romans 9–11.

In my judgment, Harnack's most impressive argument asserts the common authorship of the "we" sections of Acts and the rest of Luke-Acts. To my knowledge, this argument has not yet been answered, even by those who hold that the "we" sections come from a source used by the author. Harnack has won the day on this issue, and it only remains to determine whether his argument compels acceptance of the contention that the author of Acts was a companion of Paul. The argument is frequently made that the "we" sections were composed by the author and included for their value as verisimilitude. Under this supposition, the author used the "we" sections to increase the reader's confidence. The point is that Harnack's linguistic argument, as impressive as it is, is not sufficient to prove that the author of Acts was Luke the physician and companion of Paul.

Harnack's argument about the "we" sections does not mean that the author of Luke-Acts worked without sources. In the case of the gospel, Harnack accepts the two-document hypothesis, which, as we have seen, had by his time become dominant, and so he thinks of Luke as working with Mark and Q. In the first part of Acts, Harnack claims that the author used a source that was probably derived from Philip or his daughters and in which we can have great confidence as to its historicity. But it is intermingled, said Harnack, with other sources, some of which (notably source B, represented in Acts 2:1–47; 5:17–42) are historically worthless. "Where it [source B] is trustworthy in its record the order of events is confused, it combines things that have no real connection with one another, it omits what is important, it is devoid of all sense of historical development."[50] After Acts 15:35, however, the author is, according to Harnack, no longer dependent on sources; he is writing from personal memory.

These considerations lead Harnack to believe that certain parts of Acts, which was written before the death of Paul, deserve our confidence as regards historicity.

Harnack on Judaism in Luke-Acts

Harnack's high regard for the historical competence of the author of Luke-Acts and for the general accuracy of his work affects also his consideration of this author's treatment of Judaism and the Jewish people. He characterizes the author as unbiased. Luke not only accepts the divine rejection of the Jewish people, he also includes favorable notes about Jews whenever he can. Harnack remarks that "this impartiality of the narrative, in a point where there was such an extraordinary temptation to partiality, is a valuable proof of the careful sense of justice of the historian St. Luke."[51] But Luke is not consistently unbiased. In his reporting of the missionary work of Paul, he pictures Jews as forever stirring up Roman authorities against him. But, says Harnack, "*this bias is in accordance with actual fact.*"[52] Harnack's confidence in Luke's historical competence and the eye-witness character of his report serve to underline the anti-Jewish emphases in his narrative.

But Harnack is not so consistent as Baur in his assessment of Luke's portrayal of Judaism. Baur was able to address the issue of ambivalence on this matter by positing multiple stages in the composition of the gospel and by assuming Luke's need in writing Acts to please both Pauline and Jewish Christians. Harnack, however, cannot follow this route. He notes that Luke is sometimes more pro-Jewish than Paul but in other places, the reverse is the case. In his answer to those who think that the author of Acts misrepresented Paul, Harnack admits, as we have seen, that Paul was a complex figure. He also notes Luke's pro-Jewish stance, vis-à-vis Paul: "And we must also remember that St. Luke as a 'theologian,' like all Gentile Christians, was more a man of the Old Testament than St. Paul, because he had never come to a real grip with the problem it presented."[53] But in a note in the preface to *The Acts of the Apostles,* Harnack seems to suggest that Luke is more anti-Jewish than Paul. Here Harnack addresses the question of anti-Judaism in early Christianity generally and ranks various writers in an order ranging from no anti-Judaism to extreme anti-Judaism. The order is: Paul, Luke, John, the apologists, the Epistle of Barnabas, and Marcion. About Luke, Harnack writes: "St. Luke himself has adopted from St. Paul the theory of the hardening of Israel without Rom. xi. 25ff; yet he regards the religion and piety of the Old Testament with the deepest reverence; he still joys over every Jew who is converted, and does not in the least place the individual under the ban of his general theory."[54] Although the order in the list implies that Luke is more anti-Jewish than Paul, the explanation suggests that the order might be reversed. The explanation says that whatever anti-Jewish concepts Luke had he got from Paul and that these were moderated to a significant extent by his own admiration for the Hebrew Bible. The problem may be more with Paul than with Luke, however, for Harnack's substantive statements about Luke stress the ambivalence. Perhaps Harnack thought that Paul could have no anti-Jewish sentiments because he was a Jew, a rather curious assumption. In any event, there is some confusion about Harnack's view at this point.

For Luke, the Jewish rejection of the Christian message was not, according to Harnack, the problem that it might become for later generations. Jewish rejection was not a sign of the weakness of the gospel, since it was the result of divine predestination that had been foretold in the prophets. Jewish rejection of the gospel has not only led to divine rejection of the Jewish people but has also assured the legitimacy of Gentile Christianity: "This negative theme, which runs like a scarlet thread through the whole book, is summarised once again with impressive emphasis in the antepenultimate verse of the Acts: 'Be it known therefore unto you that this salvation of God is sent unto the Gentiles; they will also hear.'"[55] This means that, for the most part, Jews are treated unfavorably in the text of Luke-Acts, but Harnack is careful to note a major difference between Luke and John at this point: "The Jew is in a sense the villain in this dramatic history, yet not—as in the Gospel of St. John and the Apocalypse—the Jew in the abstract who has almost become an incarnation of the evil principle, but the real Jew without generalisation and exaggeration in his manifold gradations of Pharisee, Sadducee, aristocrat, Jew of Palestine or of the Dispersion."[56]

For the most part, Harnack stresses a balance in Luke-Acts between anti-Judaism and admiration for the Hebrew Bible: "In hostility to the Jews—so far as that people had rejected the gospel—he certainly cannot be surpassed; but just as certainly (see also the gospel, especially chaps. i and ii) he had a theoretical reverence for Old Testament ordinances and Old Testament piety. . . ."[57] In addition, Harnack denies that Luke thought of Christianity as the new people of God, replacing the Jews: "According to St Luke there is no new 'People' which takes the place of the old; the Jewish nation still remains the People, to the believing section of which the Gentiles are added."[58] As we shall see, Jacob Jervell recaptures this theme and makes it fundamental to his entire approach.

As a liberal theologian, who sympathized with Marcion, and a conservative biblical critic, who was convinced that a companion of Paul wrote Luke-Acts, Harnack is a fascinating study. Despite his own bias against the Hebrew Bible, he was not blind to Luke's reverence for it. What he called Luke's lack of bias counted for him as a confirmation of the historical character of Luke-Acts.

Harnack does not take a back seat to Baur in recognizing ambivalence in the attitude toward Jews and Judaism to be found in the text of Luke-Acts. Clearly he does not reconstruct the history of tradition that Baur used to explain the ambivalence, and thus he is less vulnerable to criticism on this point. But precisely here Harnack is less satisfying than Baur. He is able to observe that Luke-Acts contains both pro- and anti-Jewish tendencies, but his explanation for these contrary tendencies is thin. In fact, I could find only one sentence that attempts to provide an explanation. The sentence, quoted above, suggests a comparison between Luke and Paul on the issue of the Hebrew Bible: "And we must also remember that St. Luke as a 'theologian,' like all Gentile Christians, was more a man of the Old Testament than St. Paul, because he had never come to a real grip with the problem it presented."[59] The evidence cited for this contention presumably is to be found in Luke 16:17, to which Harnack calls attention in a footnote.[60] Apparently we are to conclude that Luke is a representative of those Gentile Christians who, because they were not Jewish and had not had the experience of Paul, held a higher view than he of Jewish religion. This suggestion, built on a number of unsubstantiated assumptions, seems remarkably inadequate as an explanation for the deep ambivalence to be found in Luke-Acts on the issue of Israel. And when we recall Harnack's almost total neglect of any description of first-century Judaism in his other historical studies, we gain the impression that the whole issue had little importance for this great scholar. Perhaps Baur's historical and literary reconstructions are fanciful. But Harnack's reduction of the problem of anti-Judaism to the psychological experience of the alleged author of Luke-Acts tends to trivialize it in an equally unconvincing way.

CHAPTER 4

ADOLF SCHLATTER
(1852–1938)

Adolf Schlatter and Adolf Harnack (1851–1930) were contemporaries, and, in fact, both were on the theological faculty of the University of Berlin from 1893 until 1898. But much of Schlatter's exegetical study was published late in his life. Although his commentary on Acts appeared in 1902, the first edition of Schlatter's important and influential commentary on Luke was published in 1931, and so he had the potential advantage of drawing on Harnack's studies of Luke and Acts, which had been published close to the turn of the century. More significantly, the interval between the publication of Harnack's studies on Luke-Acts and Schlatter's commentary on Luke was one in which a number of ground-breaking studies of the gospels introduced new critical approaches, which significantly altered the landscape of biblical scholarship. Before discussing the work of Adolf Schlatter, it will be useful to review some of the most important general developments in NT scholarship during the first third of the twentieth century.

Albert Schweitzer's *Von Reimarus zu Wrede* (1906) came close to sounding the death knell to studies of the historical Jesus.[1] In a preface to the English edition, F. C. Burkitt said, "The book here translated is offered to the English-speaking public in the belief that it sets before them, as no other book has ever done, the history of the struggle which the best-equipped intellects of the modern world have gone through in endeavouring to realise for themselves the historical personality of our Lord."[2] This is not an overstatement, and even if Burkitt had had the foresight to include studies produced during almost a century after Schweitzer, he would have had no compelling reason to alter his judgment. The *Quest* serves not only as a guide to many of the issues in the study of the historical Jesus, but it also continues to serve the needs of those scholars who have an interest in theological and intellectual developments in the eighteenth and nineteenth centuries. If he did nothing else, Schweitzer succeeded in showing that scholars have not been able to isolate their studies of Jesus from their own culture. Schweitzer was able to show the ways in which various intellectual and theological positions, from rationalism to liberalism, affected the supposedly objective study of the historical Jesus.

The German title of Schweitzer's book called attention to the significance

of the work of William Wrede, and Schweitzer noted the remarkable coincidence of the publication, on the same day, of Wrede's work and his own sketch
of the life of Jesus.[3] Schweitzer characterized Wrede's position as "thorough-
going skepticism." Focusing on the theme of secrecy in the Gospel of Mark,
Wrede claimed that Jesus' commands to his disciples and others not to speak
about his Messiahship were not historical; rather, they came into the early
Christian tradition in order to explain the absence during Jesus' lifetime of any
association of him with messianic conceptions. Wrede found the key to the
meaning of this motif in Mark 9:9, where, after the story of the transfiguration,
Mark states: "As they were coming down the mountain, he ordered them to tell
no one about what they had seen, until after the Son of Man had risen from
the dead." The Markan motif, therefore, serves the purpose of explaining the
absence of an identification of Jesus with Messiahship during his lifetime. In
Wrede's judgment, it was only after the resurrection that such speculation
began to occur among the followers of Jesus, but Mark wanted the reader to
think that, although Jesus was supernaturally and correctly perceived to be
Messiah during his lifetime, open and public announcements were intentionally suppressed until after the resurrection. Schweitzer explains the concept as
follows: "The idea of a secret which must remain a secret until the resurrection of Jesus could only arise at a time when nothing was known of a Messianic claim of Jesus during His life upon earth: that is to say, at a time when
the Messiahship of Jesus was thought of as beginning with the resurrection.
But that is a weighty piece of indirect historical evidence that Jesus did not
really profess to be Messiah at all."[4]

Although he expresses appreciation for Wrede's insight, Schweitzer
points out that Wrede's argument depends on something that, from a historical
perspective, is quite incredible. It speaks of the resurrection of Jesus as a
historical event, which becomes the turning point in messianic speculation in
regard to Jesus. Schweitzer asks, "But how did the appearance of the risen
Jesus suddenly become for them a proof of His Messiahship and the basis of
their eschatology? That Wrede fails to explain, and so makes this 'event' an
'historical' miracle which in reality is harder to believe than the supernatural
event."[5]

In his own view, Schweitzer makes the historical life of Jesus dependent
upon his conception of himself as Messiah. The gospels represent a merging
of two representations of Jesus, one quite natural and human, the other supernatural and dogmatic. In the sheer conviction that he was God's Messiah,
Jesus proclaimed that the Kingdom of God would come at the time of the next
harvest. Schweitzer observes that Jesus' parables, such as the parable of the
mustard seed, emphasize a contrast between an initial fact and a coming miracle. In the seed parables, the initial fact is the sowing, and the miracle is the
harvest. Metaphorically, what had begun as a movement of repentance with
John the Baptist and Jesus will conclude with the miracle of the arrival of the
Kingdom of God. Indeed, according to Schweitzer, Jesus expressed his con-

viction about the future when he sent the twelve out on a mission to Israel and told them, "You will not have gone through all the towns of Israel before the Son of Man comes" (Matt 10:23). But when the twelve returned (Mark 6:30–31; Luke 9:10), it became clear that Jesus' prediction had not been fulfilled. So Jesus determined that he must go to Jerusalem and by being persecuted bring about the conditions that would lead to the coming of the Kingdom: "Jesus' purpose is to set in motion the eschatological development of history, to let loose the final woes, the confusion and strife, from which shall issue the Parousia, and so to introduce the supra-mundane phase of the eschatological drama."[6] But "instead of bringing in the eschatological conditions, He has destroyed them. The wheel rolls onward, and the mangled body of the one immeasurably great Man, who was strong enough to think of Himself as the spiritual ruler of mankind and to bend history to His purpose, is hanging upon it still. That is His victory and His reign."[7] Schweitzer concluded with the verdict, "There is nothing more negative than the result of the critical study of the Life of Jesus."[8] His long study had the effect of bringing a temporary halt to the publication of lives of Jesus, at least among scholars in the historical-critical tradition.

It is during this same period that *Formgeschichte,* or form criticism, developed as a method for reconstructing the oral tradition that is presumed to have been alive in the period between the life of Jesus and the first written gospel. Karl Ludwig Schmidt maintained that the first gospel, Mark, was composed out of the fragments of the Jesus tradition.[9] This tradition did not, according to Schmidt, produce a continuous story of Jesus, but rather consisted of a large number of individual narratives, which originated in the context of different religious, apologetic, and missionary interests. The framework for these individual narratives was supplied by each of the writers of the gospels. Although Luke alone among the evangelists aspired to write literature, he still belongs within this same process.

The first edition of Martin Dibelius's *Die Formgeschichte des Evangeliums* appeared also in 1919, the year in which Schmidt's *Rahmen* was published.[10] Dibelius agreed that the various materials about Jesus first circulated as independent units of oral tradition. But he wanted to concentrate on the forms of these units. The form is important precisely at those points where the personality and creative power of an author are of little importance. The development of oral forms is subject to definite rules, "for no creative mind has worked upon the material and impressed it with his own personality."[11] Dibelius was interested in tracing the development of the forms that lay behind the Christian gospels and in determining their original *Sitz im Leben* in the pregospel period. For the most part, the sayings of Jesus, some of which developed into paradigms, were kept alive in Christian sermons. And Dibelius maintained that "the nearer a narrative [or paradigm] stands to the sermon the less is it questionable, or likely to have been changed by romantic, legendary, or literary influences."[12] The tales of Jesus, however, which served to demonstrate the pre-eminence of Jesus and were useful in spreading the cult, stand at some distance from historicity. Legends, which attempted to satisfy curiosity about Jesus and the people who surrounded him, are even farther removed from history.

Dibelius also turned attention to Acts in an important essay first published in 1923.[13] He recognized that the genre of Acts was not the same as that of the gospels and that one could not readily import the method of *Formgeschichte* and apply it directly. Instead, he proposed the use of what he called, "style criticism," an undefined term that nevertheless makes use of insights from *Formgeschichte*. Dibelius thought that there was a sketchy narrative of the travels of Paul which Luke used in Acts 13–21, but that for the rest of the book the author was free to arrange various narratives to suit his own purposes. Dibelius also cited a number of narratives in Acts, which he identified as legends, such as the story of Cornelius in Acts 10:1–11:18.

The discussion of *Formgeschichte* was continued by Rudolf Bultmann in a major publication of 1921.[14] Although he agreed with Dibelius that the forms of the oral tradition behind the gospels developed without conscious creative activity, Bultmann disagreed with Dibelius's tendency to treat the sermon as the major context within which the original forms developed. Bultmann portrayed pregospel Christianity as engaging not only in proclamation but also in controversy, and he located the *Sitz im Leben* of many controversy dialogues, for example, "in the discussions the Church had with its opponents, and as certainly within itself, on questions of law."[15] Bultmann also provided a detailed classification of the primitive forms, described the components of the various forms, and discussed their history.

Although most of the leading scholars were forced to agree that it was no longer possible to speak with conviction about the historical Jesus, *Formgeschichte* seemed to provide a way to identify the elements in the Jesus tradition that probably originated in the earliest days of the Christian movement. And that period was only a step away from the historical Jesus. Even Bultmann declared, "The individual controversy dialogues may not be historical reports of particular incidents in the life of Jesus, but the general character of his life is rightly portrayed in them, on the basis of historical recollection."[16] *Mutatis mutandi,* Bultmann would be able to draw the same conclusion about other apophthegms.

The time between Harnack's studies on Luke-Acts and Schlatter's commentary on Luke was also a time that witnessed a remarkable expansion in knowledge about the world in which Christianity originated. Adolf Deissmann displayed the excitement of working with newly discovered papyri, inscriptions, and ostraca, and he emphasized the importance of social location in the study of early Christianity.[17] Almost simultaneously Richard Reitzenstein wrote on the Hellenistic mystery religions and their relationship to the NT.[18] In 1913 Wilhelm Bousset published the first edition of his study of Christian belief, in which he made use of the studies of Greco-Roman religions.[19] Bousset called attention to the central importance of ritual and cult in the formation of Christian belief.

Bousset had also published an important study of Judaism during the first centuries of the Christian era.[20] He drew mainly from Jewish apocalyptic literature and emphasized the affinities between Judaism and Hellenism. But the most influential resource for tracing the relationships between NT and Jewish documents was the six-volume commentary by H. L. Strack and Paul Billerbeck.[21] In the commentary, Billerbeck, who was in fact the sole author, juxtaposed rabbinic passages with what were thought to be the relevant NT verses. One could thus look up any verse in the NT and expect to find the rabbinic passages that help to interpret the verse. Stephen Neill's was a typical reaction: "In the dark days before Strack-Billerbeck we referred to Rabbinic matters cautiously, if at all; in this bright post–Strack-Billerbeck epoch, we are all Rabbinic experts, though at second hand."[22]

The massive study by George Foot Moore of Harvard stands in stark contrast not only to that of Bousset but to that of most preceding studies of early and rabbinic Judaism.[23] Moore was highly critical of Bousset's study and its concentration on the apocalyptic literature. Moore drew heavily on rabbinic literature in order to analyze what he called "normative Judaism." In this respect he joined a number of Jewish critics, who complained that a concentration on apocalyptic literature led Bousset to ignore those materials which became normative in Jewish religion. Moore wrote, "No account of Judaism would be complete which ignored the apocalypses and the kindred literature, but such incompleteness would not fundamentally misrepresent its subject as does an account based chiefly on them."[24] Although Moore's study has been outdated by the discovery of the Dead Sea Scrolls and other documents, as well as by more recent approaches to rabbinic literature, it retains its value not only by virtue of the author's acquaintance with the relevant literature but also by his use of an approach that does not require the denigration of early Judaism.

The relationship between the gospels and rabbinic sources was explicitly explored by the English-Jewish scholar C. G. Montefiore.[25] Montefiore was critically appreciative of both Jewish and Christian teachings. He was aware of the dangers of rabbinic legalism, but he insisted that a figure such as the Pharisee in Luke 18:9–12 must not be taken to represent the average Pharisee but, on the contrary, the perversion of rabbinic religion. Montefiore was also quite critical of the Billerbeck commentary, which he said frequently illustrated NT passages with quotations that denigrated Jews, instead of quotations that might bring the NT passages themselves into question. Montefiore's own study of the synoptic gospels constitutes one of the earliest such studies by a critical scholar who was deeply familiar with rabbinic literature.[26]

There was vigorous discussion of the historical value of NT writings generally and of Acts in particular during the early twentieth century. Although most critical scholars continued to raise serious doubts about its historicity,

Luke-Acts was not without defenders. Among them W. M. Ramsay is probably the best known to English-speaking readers.[27] Although he began with a
bias against the historical accuracy of Acts, Ramsay, led by his own geographical and historical studies, came to have great confidence in it. The commentaries on both Luke and Acts by Theodor Zahn[28] and the three-volume
history of early Christianity by Eduard Meyer[29] argue strongly for the historical reliability of these texts.

Without doubt, the most important study of Acts to appear in English during this period was the five-volume work *The Beginnings of Christianity.*[30]
Although the editors, F. J. Foakes-Jackson and Kirsopp Lake, were born and
educated in England, they were in America at the time these volumes were
published, and so the project is usually thought of as American. In addition,
many of the contributors were Americans, about whom W. Ward Gasque
writes, "The American contributions to the volume, above all those of H. J.
Cadbury, represent the very best of all the contributions by Americans to the
history of the study of the Book of Acts."[31] Indeed, Cadbury was arguably
the most significant American scholar of Luke-Acts in his generation. In a
careful assessment of his work, Beverly Gaventa writes, "Ranking Cadbury
among the leading twentieth-century American contributors to the study of
Acts amounts to an understatement."[32]

The importance of *Beginnings* does not rest on its exploration of a new
method of research. Ernst Haenchen is only partially correct in classifying it
as remaining "close in essentials to the outlook of Harnack's time,"[33] but he is
right to recognize its emphasis on linguistic, historical, and archaeological
matters.[34] The attention that the contributors to this project pay to such details
almost precludes a theological interest. Nevertheless, in connection with our
interest in treatments of Judaism in the critical study of Luke-Acts, the *Beginnings* project is notable. Volume 1, published in 1920, is a prolegomenon,
which deals with the Jewish, Gentile, and Christian backgrounds. The second
essay in the section on the Jewish world, "The Spirit of Judaism," was written
by C. G. Montefiore.[35] Montefiore, whose work was noted above, begins the
essay by recognizing that the author of Acts pays a great deal of attention to
diaspora Jews. But he cautions that "care must, however, be taken to distinguish between the Jewish *background* of *Acts* and the Jewish *religion* in the
years in which the story is set."[36] Here we have the expression of a critical attitude that most of the earlier students of Acts did not observe but which is to
be found over and again in the various sections of *Beginnings*. Montefiore's
essay is well balanced in its positive and negative statements about early
Judaism, but he does not shrink from facing issues that were widely discussed
among Christian scholars. He finds that, although there are expressions of lib-
erality in early Judaism, there was not a conception of a completely impartial
God. This is partly due to the scriptural background on which early Judaism
drew and partly due to Jewish experience: "Israel is oppressed by the heathen;
and reacts humanly towards the oppressor. He cannot pay him back in deed;

he can only pay him back in words and theory."[37] Montefiore addresses the question of legalism and admits that "there existed a certain tendency to look at righteousness and sin as if a man's character could be measured in the same manner as his weight. But the truth seems to be that though such a tendency existed, it was checked by other tendencies, more human, more healthy, more 'prophetic,'"[38] And Montefiore lays stress on the rabbinic concept of God's readiness to forgive, and his combination of mercy and justice. He questions the Christian "contrast of Righteousness for Judaism and Love for Christianity."[39] Serious attention to rabbinic literature should be sufficient to cause the abandonment of such a concept. Montefiore does, however, find that in the teaching of the gospels there is a distinctive emphasis on a form of love that seeks out the sinner and the enemy. He writes, "The summons not to wait till they meet you in your sheltered and orderly path, but to go forth and seek out and redeem the sinner and the fallen, the passion to heal and bring back to God the wretched and the outcast—all this I do not find in Rabbinism; *that* form of love seems lacking."[40]

Montefiore's essay is followed by one by the editors, Foakes-Jackson and Lake, "Varieties of Thought and Practice in Judaism."[41] The essay treats the usual groups of early Jews and is generally sympathetic both to those regarded as orthodox and the separated groups. One comment on Pharisees is worth quoting in connection with our interest in the critical appraisal of early Judaism: "The common view that Pharisees were a sect occupied in trivial matters of ritual, and making the Law intolerable by their traditions, is as erroneous as that the Sadducees were worldly men promoting scepticism in faith and laxity in conduct."[42]

Volume 2 of *Beginnings* is devoted to a number of essays on the composition and purpose of Acts and the identity of the editor of Luke and Acts. It also includes two very useful essays on the history of criticism, one on Germany by A. C. McGiffert and one on England by J. W. Hunkin. Volume 3 is a discussion by James H. Ropes of the text of Acts and is indispensable for textual critics. Volume 5, containing thirty-seven extended notes on various aspects of Acts, appeared in 1932.

Volume 4, published in 1933, is the translation and commentary on Acts, written by Lake and Cadbury. Gasque thinks that Lake was responsible for a greater part of this volume than was Cadbury. He bases this contention on his own comparison of the material in the commentary with Cadbury's other writings, but he also says that his impressions are confirmed by a letter from Cadbury himself.[43] Theological interests are peripheral in the commentary, which concentrates on lexical and historical questions. The editors are inclined to consider favorably Harnack's theory of sources for Acts. From time to time they raise questions about the historical accuracy of Acts, but they express rather moderate ideas and, where there is doubt, lean toward accepting the credibility of the text. The Paul of Acts is not often contrasted with the epistolary Paul, and at times there are efforts to harmonize them. Lake and Cadbury do, however, question the contention in Acts 22:3 that Paul had been a student of Gamaliel. The difficulty is "that the Pauline statement of the Jewish doctrine of the Law is so gross a caricature of anything which he could have learnt from Gamaliel."[44]

There is a clear recognition that one strong motif in Acts is the "malice of the opponents of the Church, especially of the Jews."[45] But at some points the editors question the ways in which Luke portrays Jewish concepts and practices. The comment on Acts 15:10, where Peter characterizes Torah as a burdensome yoke, may be cited as an illustration: "The question may legitimately be raised whether this is a fair statement. The following propositions may reasonably be defended. (a) Some Jews in the first century doubtless felt that the Law was a burden. But the majority found their 'delight in the Law of the Lord.' . . . (b) Jesus showed no desire to abolish or even to emend the Law, but was impatient with much of the current interpretation of it. (c) Paul objected not to any details of the Law, but to the whole concept of salvation by a code of conduct. . . ."[46] The comment continues by tracing the view of law in early Catholicism and in the Epistle of Barnabas.

The editors leave no doubt about the meaning of Paul's final statement in Acts 28:28, which they translate, "Therefore be it known to you that this salvation of God has been sent to the Gentiles; it is they who will hear."[47] And so we have the comment, "It is part of the author's purpose to show that the Christians have become the true heirs of Jewish promises."[48]

The first three decades of the twentieth century may thus be characterized as a period of remarkable productivity and creativity in NT studies, including the study of Luke-Acts. As we approach the scholarship of Adolf Schlatter, we must not forget that some of his work was undertaken in the late nineteenth and the early part of the twentieth centuries and so could not have benefited from these studies. But we must also note that much of his later work, including his commentary on Luke, was published after 1930, after the rise of *Formgeschichte,* after the growth in knowledge about early Judaism, and after the first several volumes of *Beginnings.*

Adolf Schlatter was born in St. Gallen, Switzerland, in 1852. His father, a pharmacist, had helped to found a free church, which he continued to support throughout his life. The mother and the children, however, remained in the Reformed Church. Schlatter began his university studies in 1871 in Basel but transferred to Tübingen in 1873, to study theology, primarily under Johann Tobias Beck. In 1874 he returned to Basel to complete his studies. About this period of education, Werner Neuer writes, "And so it happened that Schlatter completed his theological examinations in the spring of 1875 without having declared allegiance to any of the theological schools of the time or attaching himself to a loner like Beck."[49]

Between 1875 and 1880 Schlatter served pastorates in the Reformed Church of Switzerland, and in 1880 he was encouraged by a group of pietists to join the faculty at Berne, which he did, with little support from the predominantly liberal faculty. In 1888 he accepted a call to the University of Greifswald, Germany, in the same year that Harnack began teaching at Berlin. Many German pietistic and conservative Christians were deeply opposed to Harnack's liberal theology, and they called for the appointment of a professor whose theological views would balance those of Harnack. After Martin Kähler and Hermann Cremer declined the appointment, it was offered to Schlatter, who reluctantly accepted it. Thus, a five-year period of colleagueship between Harnack and Schlatter began, and by all available reports the two scholars got along quite well. Neuer comments that "the one man on the faculty who was most nearly Schlatter's theological opposite, the famous Adolf von Harnack (1851–1930), received him from the very start with unusual friendliness and openness!"[50] Nevertheless, when Schlatter received a call from Tübingen, he gladly accepted it and served on the faculty there from 1898 until his retirement in 1922. His best-known exegetical works on NT texts were written after his retirement, and his publishing activity continued almost to his death in 1938.

Adolf Schlatter takes his place among those scholars who assume the general historical reliability of Luke-Acts and the other writings of the NT. He was well equipped in philological studies as well as in the history of NT times. Martin Hengel has recently written that, next to Ferdinand Christian Baur, Schlatter was "the best known Evangelical theologian at Tübingen during the last two hundred years."[51] While not downplaying the great theological differences between them, Hengel notes the similarities between Baur's and Schlatter's emphases on serious exegetical and historical scholarship. Other assessments of Schlatter's scholarship call attention to the difficulty of classifying him, a difficulty that reflects Schlatter's own unusual position. Mark Noll, in the foreword to Neuer's biography of Schlatter, writes: "Schlatter was far too conservative in his approach to the New Testament, and to Christian theology in general, to win a reputation in the university world in which he labored so earnestly. Yet he was also far too scholarly in his approach to problems of theological method and far too willing to engage the leading thinkers of his day to make much of an impact on the popular pietism of the German-speaking world with which he shared so much."[52]

Peter Stuhlmacher also notes the obstructions that Schlatter met from the theological liberalism that dominated German and Swiss faculties during the late nineteenth and early twentieth centuries. But he also says that, after his installation in Berlin, Schlatter was opposed by some leading pietists, who attacked him as "an 'unbelieving critic' who lacked the proper respect for the verbally inspired Scriptures."[53] So Schlatter was something of a loner, who respected the accuracy of scripture but nevertheless practiced criticism. Stuhlmacher concludes: "In Schlatter's footsteps we would not need to avoid with fear the results of the historical and dogmatic criticism of holy writ (which is incumbent upon us, according to Schlatter), nor would we need to exaggerate those results with an enlightenment mentality. Rather, we would simply ponder them carefully, and in togetherness."[54]

Schlatter's studies of the NT and early Christian history rested not only on his general confidence in the accuracy of the ancient texts but also on his assumptions about the unity of the NT. In the introduction to his study of early Christian history he wrote, "Of course when these [NT] documents are used in historical reconstruction, their chronological order must always be taken into account. But chronological distinctions do not sever them from the undivided stream of events which gave the Church its life."[55] Similarly, Schlatter was not inclined to see the kinds of battle lines among early Christian parties that Baur had emphasized. He recognized the different practices among early Jewish Christians and early Gentile Christians, but he also stressed the efforts made by the leaders, Paul and James respectively, to preserve the unity of the church. As leader of the Jewish-Christian segment, James had no intention of destroying the harmony of the church, and he did in his sphere precisely what Paul did in his: "As James took care that the Jewish Christian should remain a Jew, and not turn into a Greek, so Paul insisted that the Greek Christian should remain a Greek and not pretend to be a Jew."[56] Schlatter recognizes, however, that some difficulties were inevitable, and he addresses some of the problems in his commentary on Acts, which we shall examine below.

Schlatter on Judaism

Adolf Schlatter was interested in second-Temple Judaism and well acquainted not only with the Hebrew Bible but with the later apocryphal and pseudepigraphical writings. In a study of Josephus published originally in 1932, he treated early Jewish theology directly.[57] In addition, he included analyses of early Judaism in a number of other writings on NT subjects. Of particular interest are his life of Jesus and his commentary on Romans.[58]

Schlatter's life of Jesus stresses the relation of Jesus to Israel but also his intention to distance himself from Judaism. At one point he writes: "He [Jesus] was united with Israel in life and in death, and the completeness of divine grace that authorized him to grant the requests even of Gentiles and Samaritans had its initial revelation in the fact that he called Israel."[59] But on the very next page we have, "From the very beginning, his work had led him on a course that separated him thoroughly from Judaism, since the latter had a strong interest in the public nature and greatness of God's rule."[60] Schlatter's treatment becomes confusing at a number of points but is partially clarified by a footnote that reads, "By 'Judaism' I refer to that form of Jewish piety that frames the relationship between God and the nation in such a way that the nation's preservation and glorification were God's purposes."[61] So Schlatter can speak not only of the Jewishness of Jesus, that is, his relationship to the people of Israel, but also of his separation from Judaism, that is, the religious system of the Jews. To be more precise, Schlatter understands Judaism as a system dominated by Pharisees, who stressed meticulous observance of Torah in all expressions of life. Thus Jesus attempted to gain freedom from the Pharisees. Schlatter writes, "[Jesus] initiated the struggle by freeing himself and his disciples from Pharisaic regulations and did this in clear awareness of the ensuing consequences. Since Pharisaism demanded from the entire community submission to its leadership and discipline, it considered Jesus to be sinning by eluding its jurisdiction. Jesus, on the other hand, was not content with justifying himself but conducted his defense by an attack that destroyed the entire Pharisaic piety."[62] Schlatter also insisted that Jews were guilty of the death of Jesus, despite the participation of the Roman governor.

Schlatter's commentary on Romans demonstrates a similar ambivalence toward Israel and Judaism. In his comments on Romans 9–11, which he titles, "The Revelation of God in Israel's Fall," he begins by stressing Paul's sense of grief over Israel: "Only the one who grieves over Israel's fall speaks correctly about it."[63] And, in a comment on Rom 11:16–22, he is able to make a significant application for Christians of his own time: "The arrogance that boasts about the Christian life and disdains the Jew, severs the bond that links them with kindness and thus eliminates them from God's people. Thereby the question of how the Christian community relates to the Jews receives its profound earnestness. If they deny the relationship with the fallen, they jeopardize their own existence, for they are only able to disfigure their relationship with the Jews into hatred if they hide the wonder of grace from themselves even though it granted them their share in God."[64]

Just two pages later, we have a more precise statement of Schlatter's position: "God's disposition toward Israel indicates to Christianity how Christians are to order their association with the Jews. They are not to relinquish their independence and must not be mixed with Judaism; instead they are to know that the Jews are their enemies. But at the same time they are to honor the glorious faithfulness of God that does not allow the Jews to fall. Neither in themselves nor in the Jews are they allowed to stir up unbelief that doubts the changeless grace of God, because they cannot forget that the Jews are beloved of God."[65] It is indeed difficult to know just what Schlatter means at this point. He wants to designate Jews as enemies of Christians but to encourage Christians to honor God's faithfulness to God's covenant with them.

Despite the ambivalence and even ambiguity that are present in some of Schlatter's writings about early Judaism, his descriptions leave no doubt about his conceptions of Jewish piety at the time of Jesus. It is a piety dominated by Pharisees, who are the authoritative interpreters of Torah and who, as such, demand the careful, meticulous observance of every aspect of it, no matter how small or how large it may be. Indeed, they place everything on the same level and allow no distinctions between the more important and less important demands of Torah. Their religion requires Jews to work out their relationship with God by way of works. Schlatter recognizes that faith plays a role in early Jewish thought, but he understands that even faith is regarded as a work. In his study of the history of early Christianity, Schlatter acknowledges that there is a connection between the Christian community and the Jewish, but he also finds it necessary to make a sharp contrast. Despite the connection between the church and Israel, "It remains true that faith was not the distinctive characteristic of the people of God in the old [sic] Testament. Because the important thing was what man accomplishes in his willing and doing—for a man's works determine his relation to God—Israel was not divided into 'believers' and 'unbelievers,' but into 'righteous' and 'unrighteous.' The rabbis also knew that faith is indispensable to the good life, and, indeed, extolled faith as the highest achievement. But the very fact that they considered it as an achievement shows that they included it in the category of human accomplishments."[66] Although Schlatter insisted on interpreting both Jesus and Paul as Jews, his conception of early Judaism differs little from those views that seem to be typical of Christian scholars of the nineteenth century. The liberal Harnack and the conservative Schlatter stood at opposite poles on most theological issues, but their conceptions of the nature of early Judaism are remarkably similar.

The issue of Judaism was not solely of academic importance for Schlatter, who, in his eighties, witnessed the rise of National Socialism and the ascendancy of Adolf Hitler as Chancellor of Germany. His biographer, Werner Neuer, points out that he was a member of an opposition political party, and he insists that Schlatter saw the danger of National Socialism from the very first and often, in letters to his son, raised objections to Nazi racial theories, totalitarianism, and the Führer cult. But Schlatter said little in public and was reluctant to lend his support to Dietrich Bonhoeffer and the other pastors who formed the Confessing Church. Even Neuer, whose biographies of Schlatter are highly apologetic, observes, "The value of Schlatter's brave polemic was weakened, however, by his failure to speak up for the German Jewish Party, which was at that time already at a severe disadvantage due to repressive legal measures. Schlatter did not recognize the danger that threatened the Jews."[67]

It is tempting to connect this failure with Schlatter's views about Jews, both ancient and modern. In his 1933 essay *Die neue deutsche Art in der Kirche,* he shows his awareness of antisemitism among Nazi youth but maintains that what they call Jewish is actually a way of life, life according to the flesh.[68] Judaism is for him a metaphor for materialism, and as such it can be found among Christians. We shall see that this concept appears also in Schlatter's commentaries on Luke and Acts.

Lenore Siegele-Wenschkewitz writes that Schlatter's views on Jews have no basis in any kind of exchange he might have had with living Jews but rather arise from traditional stereotypes that he held.[69] She points to a tract written in 1930 as an example, a document that served as a textbook for Christian missionaries to Jews.[70] Here Schlatter maintains that Christians must seek to have relationships with Jews, but it is clear that the goal must be their conversion.

In 1935 Schlatter published a now infamous tract titled *Wird der Jude über uns siegen?*[71] His son, Theodor, wrote that some forty thousand copies were published and distributed all over Germany.[72] The younger Schlatter also noted that the National Socialist party expressed a great deal of displeasure with the document. In it Adolf Schlatter objected to proposals to substitute the observance of the winter solstice for the observance of Christmas. Under these Nazi proposals Christians would continue to celebrate Christmas in their homes and churches, but a more secular observance would be instituted on public occasions. Actually, the argument against the public observance of Christmas was founded in part on an antisemitic basis, namely the contention that the celebration of the birth of Jesus connected him with his Jewish mother, an unacceptable fact to the Nazi leaders.

In the 1935 tract, Schlatter argues that Germany presents a very strange picture during the Christmas season, for now we see Christians and Jews marching together in a common cause. We have been able to banish Jews from the *Reichstag,* universities, government service, theaters, and newspapers, Schlatter observes, but now we have supported them in a most important matter. He maintains that to abandon the observance of Jesus' birth in public life would be tantamount to surrendering to the Jews in their opposition to the Christian belief in the virgin birth and the Messiahship of Jesus. Schlatter is also aware of the contention that, since Jesus came from Galilee, he was not Jewish but Aryan, an argument used by Schlatter's student, Walter Grundmann.[73] But Schlatter rejects this argument. Jesus counted himself as king of the Jews, and, says Schlatter, no Aryan would demean himself by counting himself as a Jew, king or not. Furthermore, the things that Jesus taught were from the spirit and had nothing to do with corporeal things, either Jewish or Aryan. But Schlatter also maintains that Jesus was the greatest adversary the Jews ever had, and he implies that his modern day disciples must follow him in this. And so, in this tract, Schlatter ironically contends that to adopt Nazi practices is to surrender to the Jews.

The booklet, a mere twenty-three pages, has been the subject of much recent discussion. In his popular biography, published in German in 1988, Werner Neuer referred to it as a "brave polemic."[74] In her critique, published in 1994, Lenore Siegele-Wenschkewitz seriously questioned this contention and considered Schlatter's booklet as supporting the Nazi program of de-judaization.[75] She called attention to Schlatter's claim that Christians were suffering more than Jews in Nazi Germany and pointed out that, although he was opposed to Nazi racism, Schlatter traced even this to a Jewish origin. In 1996 Neuer published a much more detailed and well-documented biography of Schlatter.[76] In this book he stresses Schlatter's objection to Nazi racism and his passionate defense of the independence of the church. But he also acknowledges the problems with Schlatter's booklet, the title of which he calls unclear and provocative. Neuer observes that, in view of the increasingly sharp anti-Jewish polemic of the Nazis, Schlatter's comparison of the anti-Christian stance of Jews with Nazi racial ideology misses the point. It ignores the fundamental nature of attacks by the powerful on the powerless. He says that

Schlatter assumed that Nazi Jewish policy had achieved its goal by 1935 and, of course, he could not then have foreseen the Holocaust, although many discerning German Jews had already feared worse to come.[77] But Siegele-Wenschkewitz forcefully expresses the irony: "In the third year of National-Socialist domination, after c. 70,000 Jews had emigrated from Germany in the face of the openly antisemitic policy of the state and party, two months after the notorious 'Nuremberg laws' were passed," Schlatter published *Will the Jew Overcome Us?*[78]

Walter Grundmann, a student of Schlatter and a leading figure in the de-judaization and germanization of Christian theology, claimed that Schlatter's theology paved the way for National Socialism.[79] In an important study of the German Christians, Reijo Heinonen considers this claim carefully.[80] He writes that Schlatter's studies of early Judaism and his maintenance of a religious basis to the concept of *Volk* were important for the concept of German unity. Schlatter ranked one's duties toward the state and to Christianity on the same level. He wrote, "We must live totally in the church in order to live totally in the state, and live totally in the state in order to live totally in the church."[81] And Heinonen comments, "Blind obedience to the state and Christian conviction arising from experience appear in Schlatter's view to be mutual demands."[82] It must be emphasized, however, that Schlatter did not equate the two entities, church and state, and was prepared to recognize tensions between them. But his metaphorical view of Judaism as a spiritual phenomenon brings him into close proximity to the German Christians, says Heinonen. Judaism for Schlatter is an ethical-metaphysical phenomenon, which can be found in the church as well as in the synagogue. He frequently uses the term "Jewish" to signify a characteristic that may have universal significance for religion, politics, life, and science. It is against such a concept that, in Schlatter's view, the church must fight, and the state becomes a fellow combatant with the church in this matter. This means that Schlatter's concept of Judaism is no more racial than is his concept of *Volk*. But Heinonen affirms that racist antisemitism can easily merge with the theological anti-Judaism of an Adolf Schlatter. Thus, although he ignores Schlatter's political opposition to totalitarianism, Grundmann may well be right in saying that Schlatter's theology paved the way for National Socialism.

With an understanding of Schlatter's cultural background and his views on early and modern Judaism in mind, we are now in a position to examine his major works on Luke and Acts.

Schlatter on Acts and Judaism

Schlatter included a commentary on Acts in his three-volume publication *Erläuterungen zum Neuen Testament,* addressed to a fairly wide audience of "Bible readers."[83] The commentary on Acts had been published separately in 1902 and was republished with only slight revisions in several editions, most recently in 1962.[84] There is no introduction, and there are only a few notes, almost none referring to other scholarship. Schlatter does not discuss the authorship, date, or possible sources. The commentary simply works from the beginning to the end of Acts and includes a translation of and notes on the various sections. It is not a verse-by-verse commentary, but every pericope receives some attention, and the comments mix explanatory notes and brief theological interpretations.

One gains some understanding of the ways in which Schlatter treats the issue of Israel by examining his comments on any of several pericopes in Acts. Some of the comments simply explain certain Jewish practices. For example, on Acts 3:1, where Peter and John go to the Temple at the ninth hour, the hour of prayer, Schlatter points out that the second sacrifice of the day was held at the ninth hour, that the ninth hour was three o'clock in the afternoon, that there was a congregational prayer at this time, and that consequently the ninth hour was called the hour of prayer.[85] The captain of the Temple (Acts 4:1) is a distinguished priest who has charge of the Temple guard, which is made up of priests and Levites.[86] On Acts 21:23–24, where James advises Paul to join four men in a ritual of purification and to pay their expenses, Schlatter notes that it had become a common practice for well-to-do Jews to pay the expenses for poor Nazirites engaged in their sacrifices.[87] No documentation is supplied for any of these notes, and in some cases one suspects that for Schlatter the only documentation needed is the book of Acts itself.

More significant for our interests are the theological comments that Schlatter makes at certain pregnant points in the commentary on Acts. One such point is the story of Stephen in Acts 6:8–8:3. Schlatter understands the story not solely as that of the first Christian martyr, but as a chapter in the history of Jewish hostility to the emerging Christian movement. At first, Christian preaching was forbidden, and then the apostles were charged with disobedience to God's law. "Now follows the first death sentence and the first persecution, which was directed against the entire community and attempted to destroy it."[88] The accusation against Stephen introduces the question of the relationship between Christ and the chief Jewish institutions, Torah and Temple. The accusation in Acts 6:13–14 "quickly makes the rift between Judaism and Christianity insurmountable."[89] Prior to this point in the narrative there has been no suggestion that the apostles preached against the law. They preached Christ and the word, but the Greeks who heard Stephen concluded that his preaching contained certain implications about law and Temple. Despite the fact that Schlatter points out that the accusation against Stephen was brought by false witnesses (Acts 6:13), he nevertheless characterizes Stephen's speech as a partial confirmation of the charge: "There have been two revelations, one through Moses, the other through Christ; which was the higher? Two sacrifices, through which reconciliation with God would occur, one at the altar, the other the death of Christ; which was effective? Two communities, since the priests and teachers opposed the preaching of Jesus; which would now finally [come] out of Israel? Stephen answered, as Jesus' word had prescribed for his disciples. How truly and seriously was his grace offered to Israel through the word of the apostle: he has already pronounced the judgment: the Temple must fall, no stone remains on another; the time of the old community is past."[90] Although it is not said that Jesus will destroy the Temple, it is said that the Temple must fall and that the revelation through Moses is no longer valid. Stephen's speech is intended to show that the ancient revelation of God to Israel did not affirm the eternal validity of either law or Temple. It is significant that the speech, which summarizes the early history of Israel, begins with Abraham rather than Moses. This means that Abraham, not Moses, is the father of Israel and that the ancient community was not constituted through law. Further, "Abraham himself observed only the commandment of circumcision, and so the patriarchs were born not under the law and Temple but only with the commandment of circumcision."[91] And the destruction of the Temple was itself foretold in scripture, which made it clear that God does not live in houses made by human beings (Isa 66:1–2): "So whoever trusts that the Temple will not fall denies the scripture."[92] And Stephen clearly and forcefully asserts that all the glory of the law and all trust in the works of law and justification by the law came to an end in the cross of Jesus.

Schlatter has shown that Stephen's speech essentially confirms the accusation of the false witnesses (Acts 6:13). So it is unclear how we should understand their witness as false. Perhaps their accusation was false at the time it was made, since Stephen had not previously made these kinds of statements. Of course, this is so only because Stephen had not previously appeared in the narrative. But Schlatter does not trouble himself with this problem. Rather he takes the speech of Stephen to be the first occasion in Acts for recognizing the fundamental difference between Judaism and Christianity. Judaism has wrongly focused attention on law and Temple; Christianity means freedom from these failing institutions. Schlatter's use of terms such as "works of law" and "justification" reveals a tendency to introduce Pauline terminology and concepts into the interpretation of a narrative that does not make use of these terms.

Another section of Acts that provides an opportunity for Schlatter to elucidate Luke's treatment of Judaism is Acts 15:1–33, which he titles, "The Confirmation of Gentile Christian Freedom from the Law by the Apostles in Jerusalem."[93] Here is the well-known story of the conference in Jerusalem at which a determination was made about the need of circumcision for Gentile Christians. Schlatter points out that the previous narratives about Paul's mission in Asia Minor showed why it was necessary to settle this question, since they showed how intensely the Jews were embittered against the gospel. He says that the major cause of Jewish opposition was the Christian inclusion of Gentiles, so that when Paul went to the Gentiles, work among Jews became impossible. But the speech of Peter at Jerusalem (Acts 15:7–11) shows that Jews did not keep Torah and that Torah did not produce any positive glory for Israel, but only transgression. Schlatter emphasizes that James's decision at this meeting (Acts 15:19–20), which forbids idolatry and adultery and requires the avoidance of blood and strangled things, was intended for Gentile Christians. Jewish Christians would continue to live as Jews. It was especially important for Gentile Christians to avoid bloody meat on those occasions when Jewish and Gentile Christians would eat together. Schlatter also draws attention to the discussion of eating food offered to idols in 1 Corinthians. Clearly he looks upon the apostolic decree in Acts as a kind of accommodation, which depends on the general separation of Jewish from Gentile Christianity. Gentile Christians must observe certain minimal food laws in order not to offend the Jewish believers. There is no sense in which the decree acknowledges the validity of Torah and no suggestion that Gentile freedom from Torah has been compromised.

Schlatter returns to the problem of the apostolic decree in his *Church in the New Testament Period*. After examining various suggestions about its possible interpretation, he declines to accept the decree as strictly ethical. The reference to things strangled stands in the way of such an interpretation. For the most part, says Schlatter, the prohibitions in the decree tell us that the church was unwilling to go in the direction of Gnostic antinomianism. But finally, Schlatter is here rather circumspect: "But whatever construction we place upon the decrees about 'blood' and things strangled, we must not forget that there is no conclusive evidence as to the reason behind these particular decrees. Our historical picture is, therefore, inevitably obscure, and we are thrown back upon conjecture."[94] The images of Judaism conveyed by Schlatter in these interpretations of Acts are consistent. Judaism in the book of Acts is a religion characterized by adherence to law and Temple. It involves a misreading of scripture, which, when rightly read, presents these institutions as impermanent. Despite their adherence to God's law, Jews have only succeeded in transgressing it. And they have bitterly opposed those who proclaim the revelation in Christ, which means freedom from law and Temple.

Although he takes note of the conversion of Jews as narrated in Acts, Schlatter clearly emphasizes Jewish rejection of Christianity. In the last meeting of Paul with Jews in Rome (Acts 28:23–28), Luke reports that some Jews in Paul's audience disagreed with him, while others accepted his message. But Schlatter simply says that the outcome of the meeting was negative: the Jews left. He understands this narrative to say that Jewry has rejected the gospel, which has been given to the Gentiles.[95]

Schlatter on Luke and Judaism

Schlatter included Luke, of course, in the *Erläuterungen zum Neuen Testament,* and these notes exercised an immense influence on Christian preaching, especially in Germany. But he also wrote a critical commentary on Luke (as well as on Matthew, Mark, and John), and it will be more fruitful for us to devote attention to this rather than to the more popular and less exhaustive work. The Luke commentary was first published in 1931.[96]

The subtitle of the commentary on Luke, *Aus seinen Quellen erklärt,* is to be taken quite seriously. In order to appreciate its significance and to understand the structure of the commentary, it is necessary to keep in mind Schlatter's approach to the problem of the relationship of the synoptic gospels to each other. It must be noted, however, that the literary problem itself was, for Schlatter, of secondary importance. What was important was the contact that each author had with the Jesus tradition. As Ulrich Luck points out, even the term "source" had a particular meaning for Schlatter. "'Sources' for New Testament history can, therefore, never be only literary or historical documents; they must always be in contact with their history, i.e., they must be contemporary witnesses."[97] So each of the evangelists is a witness of the Jesus tradition. Nevertheless, there is a chronological order to the writing of the synoptic gospels and a literary relationship. For Schlatter, as for Baur, Matthew was the first gospel. Matthew was a witness of Jesus as the Christ to his Jewish-Christian community in the midst of Israel. Mark, who wrote second and had the text of Matthew before him, is the evangelist for the Greeks. The author of this gospel is not himself Greek, however. He is, in fact, the John Mark of Acts 12:12 and comes from Jewish-Christian Jerusalem. Luke, who also wrote Acts, is the third of the synoptic gospels. This gospel contains substantial parts of Mark but in a new edition, and it also contains parts of an otherwise unpreserved gospel, from which the author took the so-called *Sondergut.* Finally, Luke included parts of Matthew.[98] Despite his use of a variety of sources, Luke produced a unified narrative of Jesus. In the foreword to the commentary, Schlatter states that his objection to the two-source theory, which had become predominant long before the publication of the Luke commentary, is that it results in an interpretation of Luke as full of contradictions.[99]

Schlatter's commentary on Luke is organized in accordance with his theory of sources. The first major section is called, "The New Edition of Mark," and it contains a commentary on those pericopes that Luke took over from the earlier gospel. The second section, called "The New Narrator," deals with the pericopes that are peculiar to Luke. The third section is called, "The Gospel of Matthew in Luke." Although there is a brief foreword that introduces the author's views about the sources of Luke, there is no introduction in the proper sense of the word. Thus the reader is not provided with a defense of the commentary's structure. There are no notes that would help to place the Gospel of Luke in a chronological or geographical setting and no explanation of its place in the development of Christian tradition. There are no footnotes, but there are several appendixes that provide information on the linguistic relationship of Luke and Acts to the writings of Josephus. In this connection, it should be noted that, in the comments on each of the individual pericopes, Schlatter has a section comparing the language of Luke with that of Josephus.

Schlatter includes a number of comments at various points about the ways in which Luke used his source materials. Luke was quite familiar with Mark, which was written for the Greek church with which, through his work with

Paul, Luke was also connected, and so Mark was Luke's basic source document. But Schlatter insists that this does not mean that Luke was negative about Matthew. This gospel had a great deal of value for Luke, as the collection of the words of Jesus. And for the most part Luke worked with the rule of two witnesses, so if a narrative appeared in both Mark and Matthew he used it. But Matthew was written for an entirely different audience from the one Luke needed to address. Matthew's church was still suffering pressure from the Rabbis and Pharisees and needed to give significant attention to the meaning of Jerusalem, the Temple, and the law. But the church for which Luke wrote was under a different kind of pressure from the Greek world.

In the sections of the commentary dealing with Luke's use of Mark and of Matthew, Schlatter traces the changes that, *ex hypothesi,* Luke made in his sources. In a number of cases he calls attention to Luke's tendency to downplay the Palestinian context of either Matthew or Mark. Typical is his comment on Luke 4:32. Mark 1:22 has, "They were astounded at his [Jesus'] teaching, for he taught them as one having authority, and not as the scribes." Luke uses this verse at 4:32 but omits the phrase, "and not as the scribes." Not only does Luke's version make it easier for a Greek reader to understand the situation, it fits better with Luke's aim. Schlatter comments here that, according to Luke, Jesus' adversary is not the rabbinic theological teaching or casuistry, although Luke knows that the Pharisees falsify judgment and hinder the fulfillment of the law. Jesus' adversary is rather the Mammon of the Pharisees.[100]

The second section of Schlatter's commentary, on "The New Narrator" (Lukan *Sondergut*), is clearly the most useful for exploring his conception of the Lukan treatment of Judaism. It is by far the largest section of the commentary.[101] We will, therefore, concentrate on this section in an effort to understand Schlatter's approach.

In a summary description of the New Narrator, Schlatter firmly states that this evangelist was not an opponent of Judaism: "The opponent with whom this evangelist wrestled was not the Rabbis but Mammon. He did not fight against the dominance of the law and against Jewish particularism."[102] The enemy of this evangelist was the way of life that was filled with concern for money. It was that culture that finds "the meaning of life in the acquisition of money."[103] But, as we have seen in the reference above to Luke 4:32, Schlatter believes that this attitude is also that of Luke himself. Although he thinks that Luke made some minor changes in his source at a few points, for the most part the viewpoint of the New Narrator and of Luke are the same. Thus it is justified to say that for both the New Narrator and Luke, the target for their opposition was not Judaism or Pharisaism, but Mammon.

Schlatter is convinced that the New Narrator and Luke were deeply concerned about those people whose lifestyles were determined by their love for possessions. At the very beginning of this section of the commentary, in a discussion of the expectation of the Christ, he emphasizes the connection between the Christian story and the Jewish community: "Israel waits for the Christ. With this the New Narrator creates a strong bond that connects the new thing that arises with Jesus with that which the Jewish community possessed before him."[104] But then he asks what it was that separated this Judaism from the community of Jesus. It was not rabbinism and Pharisaism: "The answer to the question, what caused the Jewish opposition to Jesus, this gospel gives with fresh earnestness: the enmity which separated and separates the Jew from Jesus is Mammon, trade, the lust for possessions and desire for enjoyment, kindled through Greek culture."[105]

But in many of Schlatter's comments the distinction between Mammon and Judaism is, to say the least, blurred. In addition, despite his denial, a number of statements are critical of things associated with Judaism that have little to do with the love of possessions.

In Luke 2:25–35, Simeon prophesied about the child Jesus that he was "destined for the falling and the rising of many in Israel, and to be a sign that will be opposed" (Luke 2:34). Schlatter asks why there has to be this falling and rising, why there could not rather be an overwhelming revelation of the lordship of God so that all would respond positively. And he answers that pious words and ritualistic customs hide the real condition of the people, which must be made known.[106] On the assumption that the real condition of the people is that they live lives governed by the desire for possessions, Jewish worship is a false covering of this condition.

In Luke 3:10–14, we have the requirements that John the Baptist gives to various groups who ask him, "What then should we do?" (Luke 3:10). One such requirement is that "whoever has two coats must share with anyone who has none" (Luke 3:11). Schlatter comments: "The Baptist's command is not, 'Whoever has taken a coat from someone must return it.' That would only be the old command which even Pharisees impressed on people. . . ."[107] The words of the Baptist are in line with the general ethical tone of this gospel, which calls upon people simply to give. But this is, according to Schlatter, very different from Jewish practices: "Against the Jewish Sabbath and against the Jewish interpretation of the love command, which only requires love for the neighbor, it is objected that it prohibits help, since the Sabbath makes it impossible and limiting love to the neighbor refuses it to the one who is far away."[108] Whence does this objection come? Apart from the fact that the text at hand does not explicitly suggest a contrast between the teaching of the Baptist and other Jewish teachings, it should be observed that Schlatter's interpretation constitutes a significant critique of fundamental Jewish concepts, a critique that he maintained was not part of the program of Luke or the New Narrator.

In Luke 5:1–11, there is the story of the miraculous catch of fish followed by the call of the first disciples. After the fish had been loaded, Simon Peter "fell down at Jesus' knees, saying, 'Go away from me, Lord, for I am a sinful man!'" (Luke 5:8). And again Schlatter takes the opportunity to comment on the contrast between Judaism and Christianity: "Out of what Israel possessed as revelation and law of God, there results for the guilty only the conclusion: Go away! The holy one is over against him. But Jesus reverses this rule; for he is bound with the guilty. The penitence which he effects and demands is that the sinner come to him."[109]

In Luke 10:25–37, a lawyer approaches Jesus to ask, "What must I do to inherit eternal life?" (Luke 10:25). Jesus responds by asking about Torah, and the lawyer says that Torah requires one to love God and to love the neighbor. Then to clarify the meaning of "neighbor," Jesus tells the story of the Good Samaritan. Schlatter comments that there is no significant difference between Jesus and the Rabbis on the question of what the law demands. It is not the interpretation of law that sets Jesus apart but one's behavior. The real question is, who is the neighbor? And in answering this question the rabbinic practice of casuistry begins. Thus it is rabbinic casuistry that creates the distinction with Jesus.[110]

But Jews are associated with material things. The section in Luke 11:37–52, which has Jesus' condemnations of Pharisees and lawyers, is, according to Schlatter, partially drawn from the New Narrator, although it overlaps with materials from Matthew 23. Although Luke 11:39 and Matt 23:25 overlap, Schlatter understands that for Luke's main source at this point the emphasis is on the Pharisaic tendency to be concerned about "outward" things. "Outward" things include, for Schlatter, one's possessions. And so he can say, in commenting on the cleaning of the outside of the cup, "Jesus is separated from the Pharisees, since they represent the usual Jewish morality in their valuing of possessions and stand with the opponents of Jesus."[111]

Schlatter recognizes that, in Luke, Jesus does not die because of the opposition of Pharisees. But Pharisees are nevertheless blind in regard to him. In Luke 13:31–33, some Pharisees come to warn Jesus about the danger of Herod Antipas. The pericope shows, says Schlatter, that it is Herod who is Jesus' enemy, not the Pharisees. But the Pharisees are, nevertheless, blind, since they do not see that Jesus must die in Jerusalem.[112]

In Luke 17:11–19, we have the story of Jesus' healing of ten lepers. In the story only one, a Samaritan, returns to thank Jesus for the healing. Schlatter entitles this section, "Jewish Ingratitude," and he suggests that ingratitude is a characteristic feature of Jews: "It [the narrative] shows the sin of the Jew, that he accepts God's gift without thanks."[113]

On the parable of the Pharisee and the publican in Luke 18:9–14, Schlatter calls attention to the Pharisee's boastful statement in 18:12. The Pharisee does not say anything about what he has done for the neighbor but what he has done for God. He observes two days of fasting each week, and he gives up a tenth of all his possessions. Schlatter focuses attention on the Pharisee's claim to tithe *all* his possessions. Here is an illustration of Pharisaic exactitude, to leave nothing out, and in this attitude is to be found the "never ending casuistry of the Rabbis."[114]

This selection of comments in the major section of Schlatter's commentary on Luke illustrates his treatment of the images of Judaism in this gospel. Although he insists that Jews and Judaism do not constitute the target for the New Narrator or for Luke, there are grounds on which this judgment must be questioned.

In the first place, there is a clear tendency in Schlatter's comments on Luke to associate Judaism with what he calls Mammon. In some contexts, the term appears to mean a concern for anything material; in others it is the love of possessions; and in still others it seems to be a morality that emphasizes external rather than internal considerations. But in every case these characteristics are associated with Jews. One may object that it is inappropriate to criticize Schlatter for these comments, since he is working with a book in which Jews are just about the only ones who people the narrative. There are virtually no "pagans" to condemn. But it is necessary to point out that, although Schlatter is inevitably bound to the narrative conditions of the Gospel of Luke, he is not compelled to invoke moral qualities as stereotypically characteristic of a group of people in the narrative.

In the second place, Schlatter frequently calls attention to characteristics of Jews, or Jewish groups, that have little or nothing to do with what he calls Mammon. We have noted his comments on Jewish reliance on ritual and Jewish ingratitude, on the limitations of Jewish interpretation of Torah, and on Pharisaic casuistry, blindness, and hypocrisy. If the target in question is not Judaism and Jews, then what is the relevance of these comments?

Adolf Schlatter published almost all of his biblical and historical studies after the turn of the century and a great deal of it late in his life. Certainly by 1931, when he published the commentary on Luke, he could have had the benefit not only of the studies of Harnack on Luke-Acts, but also the tremendously influential work of scholars such as Wrede, Schweitzer, Dibelius, Cadbury, and Montefiore. But there is little sign of their influence in Schlatter's studies of Luke and Acts. His work exhibits no awareness of problems about the historical Jesus, such as Schweitzer had analyzed. He seems not to have known the work of the form critics. And if he had read Montefiore's studies of the Pharisees and Judaism, he must have rejected them. For Schlatter, the NT speaks with a unified voice to reflect accurately the history, social conditions, and religious culture of the times. The history of NT interpretation in the early twentieth century is, for Schlatter, a story of roads not traveled.

We must not overlook Schlatter's insistence on the Jewishness of Jesus and Paul. But this insistence is compromised by his contention that Jesus was the greatest adversary the Jews ever had. Schlatter also counseled contemporary Christians to value God's covenant with Israel. But almost in the same breath he did not hesitate to refer to Jews as the enemies of Christians.

For Schlatter, the image of Judaism in Luke-Acts is, in almost every respect, negative and accurate. His understanding of Judaism in Germany in the twentieth century seems remarkably similar to his understanding of Judaism at the time of Jesus. In both cases Judaism is not so much an institution, alive in the present or an artifact of history, as it is an idea. For the most part, it seems to be identified with what Schlatter would think of as materialism, and as such it is opposed to Christian spirituality and is to be condemned. Under this definition, he finds Judaism just about everywhere, even in the church.

This recognition may provide some clue to help us understand the way in which Schlatter approached issues relating to Jews and Judaism in Luke-Acts. He maintained that Luke did not intend to attack Judaism but Mammon. But we have found that, in his commentary on Luke, the distinction between the two is blurred and that there are attacks on Judaism for reasons that have little to do with the love of possessions. But this situation becomes clearer if we conclude that, despite Schlatter's words to the contrary, for him Judaism and materialism are the same thing. The distinction between Mammon and Judaism is blurred because, for Schlatter, there really is no distinction.

CHAPTER 5

ERNST HAENCHEN (1894–1975) AND HANS CONZELMANN (1915–1989)

Many scholars today point to the work of Ernst Haenchen and Hans Conzelmann on Luke-Acts as constituting a formidable consensus of interpretation. In this consensus, Luke-Acts is read as a justification for the early Gentile-Christian movement. The Conzelmann-Haenchen consensus interprets Acts as maintaining that the Jewish refusal of the gospel formed the basis for the first Christian mission to the Gentiles. Presumably, if Jews had accepted the Christian preaching, there would have been no Gentile mission. Although both Haenchen and Conzelmann devoted serious attention to both parts of the Lukan double work, Haenchen is most noted for his commentary on Acts, and Conzelmann for his ground-breaking study of the theology of Luke. The terms of the consensus usually put Conzelmann first, but Haenchen was the senior of the two, and so he will be treated first here.

ERNST HAENCHEN

Ernst Haenchen began the study of theology in 1914 in Berlin, as a student of Harnack and Dibelius, but his studies were interrupted by World War I. He was wounded in combat in 1918 and lost his right leg. After the war he continued his studies in Tübingen. He contracted tuberculosis in 1928 and, for health reasons, lived in Switzerland for two years. In 1933 he went to teach systematic theology at Giessen. Ulrich Busse writes about Haenchen during the Nazi times:

> The time of National Socialism for Ernst Haenchen brought a period of temptation and probation. Prussian educated, a highly decorated participant in the war, he had risked his youth and health for the 'Fatherland,' had experienced and endured the Weimar Republic at first as a student—he financed his studies for the most part with tuition assistance—then as assistant and finally, though ill, as Privatdozent. The promise of a 'greater German Reich' and the promise of the German Christians to win back, with the help of a new ideology, many who had

left the church, must have been compelling when he got to know and respect Emmanuel Hirsch in 1931.[1]

In 1939 Haenchen was called to the University of Münster, but he spent only one term there before the German invasion of Poland in September. Most students and many faculty were drafted, and the university was closed in the summer of 1944. Haenchen then went back to Switzerland, carrying with him only a copy of the Nestle Greek NT text. This fact led him toward a second career, as a NT exegete. After his return to Münster in 1948, he published a commentary on Mark,[2] and a commentary on John was published posthumously in 1980.[3] His best-known work was his commentary on Acts, which was published in its first edition in 1956.[4] Haenchen died on April 30, 1975.[5]

Haenchen's struggle with Nazi ideology may be illustrated by an article he published in the first year of the Third Reich.[6] He noted that the new German state demanded total devotion, both in will and action. He asked if this demand was a gift for which one should thank God or political interference in the proper domain of God. His answer was based on the Reformation teaching that law is a gift of God in two forms: the law of God and the law of the state. The Christian, Haenchen wrote, owes a duty both to God and the state. The law of the state makes earthly life possible and forms a bulwark against the powers of chaos and destruction. In this respect it is an evidence of the love of God. Although it cannot be a substitute for God's law, nevertheless the Christian still stands under the concrete law of the state: "Even the 'born again' [Christian] still lives under the concrete law, of which we have just spoken. He remains a German. He does not flee from the state; he does not seek to withdraw his *Volkstum*. He remains a German."[7] And Haenchen adds that, for the Christian, the law has lost its horror, because he approaches it without self-seeking and with love for the neighbor.

In view of the history of the Third Reich, Haenchen's treatment of the law of the state is disappointing. He clearly is aware of the totalitarian claims that the state may make, but he seems to assume that, although they do not constitute divine law, they will not conflict with it. At some points he seems to speak the language of the National Socialist party, whose ideology emphasized the concept of *Volk*. He writes that the concept of *Volk* is central to the state and that it includes four aspects: blood, land, language, and history. History is, however, the most important, since blood is a matter of fate, and country and language are dependent on history. But history is the result of human decision. "History, experienced in community, is the hard hammer that shapes a population into a people."[8] But finally people-hood (*Volkstum*) is soul: "The German soul is a reality that totally rules the entire area of our earthly existence."[9] And Haenchen adds that blond hair and blue eyes do not make Germans; rather a certain inwardness, a certain soul, is demanded.

What is regrettable about the article is the lack of a vigorous critique of Nazi doctrines of *Volk* and law. To be sure, Haenchen was in no position in

1933 to foresee the further development of the Third Reich, but, to my knowledge, he never returned to these topics even in the postwar period. Clearly, he was struggling with problems of religious and political conflict, but he was too tied to Reformation concepts to break through to the kind of critique that showed itself in people such as Dietrich Bonhoeffer and Karl Barth.

Despite this lack, there is little sign of anti-Judaism in Haenchen's 1933 article. In his discussion of human responses to God's law, however, he lays out two options. Either one can be a confessing sinner or a Pharisee, i.e., a hypocrite. Clearly Haenchen is drawing on parables and sayings in the gospels at this point, including the parable in Luke 18:10–14.[10]

But the Lukan parable of the Pharisee and the publican (Luke 18:10–14) played an important role in one of Haenchen's early exegetical works, an analysis of Matthew 23, first published in 1951.[11] Here Haenchen attempts to separate the genuine Jesus material from that which comes from the Jewish-Christian community of Matthew, and he states, "We are looking here inside the polemic of the Jewish-Christian community of Jerusalem against Judaism."[12] He stresses a major distinction between this community and Jesus himself. Matthew is totally opposed to Pharisaism, without nuance and without exception, but we cannot ascribe this attitude to Jesus. Jesus engaged in controversy with scribes and was critical of Pharisees, but he did not think of them as hypocrites. Jesus' view, according to Haenchen, is better seen in the Lukan parable, in which the Pharisee is not pictured as a hypocrite, "but a human being who attempted, with all his might, to live according to God's teaching, which he had learned as the right and revealed way."[13] Haenchen insists that Jesus did not attack Pharisees for hypocrisy, but because they were in dead earnest about God's demands and did not help people to obey them. It would seem that Haenchen's exegetical study in 1951 led him toward a more carefully considered statement about Pharisees than he was able to make in 1933.

Haenchen did not publish a study of early Judaism that might give us insight into his general approach. His view may, however, be seen as expressed in fragmentary ways in his commentary on Mark.[14] It is only in incidental statements that we may discern something about his general feelings. And, for the most part, Haenchen's statements about Judaism or the Jewish people come as by-products of a theme that is, to him, far more important. Throughout the commentary on Mark he seems intent on showing ways in which Jesus differed from his contemporaries or challenged major aspects of his religious context. He points out that, for Jews at the time, the normal order of life was Torah observance, which required the pious to bring the sinner to divine judgment, but not to help the sinner: "Whoever helps the sinner is godless. He makes himself guilty; he becomes a sinner."[15] And later, "In a certain sense, Jesus saw God differently than did the pious among his people, not as a jealous, solicitous Lord to his select people, but as a shepherd who goes after the lost sheep and rejoices when it is found."[16] In commenting on the story in

Mark 3:1–6 in which Jesus heals on the Sabbath, Haenchen comments that Jesus is to be distinguished from the piety of his time. In Jewish piety one does not speculate about God's motives for giving a command, but Jesus requires an explanation for the Sabbath commands. Although Jesus is not a rationalist, he sees God differently: "He sees the heart of God, and they see only the regulations. So the word of God has become for them circumscribed, heartless, and godless."[17]

Although he is aware of some sayings of Jesus that have parallels in rabbinic literature, he downplays their importance. In a comment on Mark 2:27, he accepts the interpretation that Jesus understood the Sabbath to be given for the sake of human beings. He then cites a saying in the Mekilta on Exodus 31:13 that is substantially parallel to that of Jesus, but then he adds: "But in general the idea is that the Sabbath stands far above all human needs. . . . It is a holy pre-creation ordinance, which is for God's sake, not for humans'."[18] No documentation is provided for this general statement.

Haenchen's impressions of Judaism and Jewish people are largely products of his attempt to provide a contrasting portrait of Jesus, and so they are inevitably negative. But we should not leave the commentary on Mark without observing an important aspect of Haenchen's treatment of the trial of Jesus. In commenting on the so-called Sanhedrin trial in Mark 14:53–72, he maintains that the scene is not historically informed. Rather it is theologically motivated and intended to speak to Christians about Jewish guilt. I judge from this that, in Haenchen's view, Jews are not to be held responsible for the death of Jesus, but one might wish for a clearer statement on the subject.

Haenchen on Acts and Judaism

When Haenchen left Münster for Switzerland in 1944, he had with him only the Nestle Greek Testament. This fortuitous fact led him to examine the text of the NT more closely than he had before, and by 1946 he had begun work on a commentary on Acts. He comments that he was led by necessity to bypass the secondary literature and to experience the reading of the text firsthand. This work led to the publication, in 1956, of the first edition of his own commentary on Acts. It constituted the tenth edition of the famous series initiated in 1835 by Heinrich A.W. Meyer. Haenchen's commentary went through seven German editions, the fifth of which was translated into English in 1971.[19]

Haenchen's commentary on Acts is indeed a fresh reading of this text, but it is also in full conversation with the secondary literature. Indeed, one of its most helpful sections treats the history of scholarship on Acts from F. C. Baur to the time of Haenchen.[20] The importance of Haenchen's commentary cannot be too heavily stressed. In both German and English it has dominated scholarship for decades. No meaningful study of Acts can afford to overlook it.

Probably due to the influence of Dibelius, Haenchen was led to suspect the usefulness of source-criticism in the study of Acts. He devoted several pages to the history of source-critical studies of Acts in the introduction to the commentary, but most of his own comments were intended to show the deficiencies of this method. He admitted that the author of Acts made use of written source material, and at a few points in the commentary this fact becomes important. But for the most part his discussion emphasizes the creativity of the author in composing the various sections of the book. Despite the influence of Dibelius, Haenchen did not find form criticism to be useful in the study of Acts. Indeed, he noted that Dibelius himself had shown that form criticism was inapplicable to Acts. Haenchen wrote, "After all, Dibelius himself had let slip (p. 4) that in Acts—where Luke had not, as for the gospel, a ready-made tradition to hand—it was a question 'not of any Form-critical approach, but only of style-criticism.'"[21] But then Haenchen noted the positive outcome of Dibelius's form-critical studies, namely that they "gave due prominence to the New Testament author. No longer was Luke a mere 'compiler or transmitter,' but a writer with his own positive characteristics—and a theologian."[22] Clearly Haenchen's commentary forged new ground in emphasizing the role of the author of Acts, who manipulated traditional material and created entire episodes. Like Conzelmann's earlier study of Luke, Haenchen's commentary on Acts is a version of redaction criticism that itself opens the way for those later studies that call themselves literary or narratological.

For those who are interested in the issue of Judaism in Acts, Haenchen's commentary may be a disappointment. His commitment to study the text of Acts and the role of the author means that he has correspondingly less interest in the history that may lie behind the text. His approach affords him little opportunity to explore the relationship between the actual phenomenon of early Judaism and the portrait of Jews in the text of Acts. But Haenchen is certainly interested in the ways in which the author of Acts has treated this and related topics. Although the introduction to the commentary lacks a section specifically devoted to early Judaism, and most of the individual sections are without significant comments on this subject, the diligent reader will nevertheless gain a firm sense of the way in which Haenchen understands Luke's treatment of the relationship between Judaism and the new Christian movement.

In a section of the introduction titled "Luke the Historian in Acts," Haenchen pays special attention to this relationship as Luke presents it. He notes that the reader of Acts initially gains an impression of the steady problem-free growth of the Christian movement. The several summaries in Acts clearly present an ideal picture. But, says Haenchen, "in reality Luke the historian is wrestling, from the first page to the last, with the problem of the *mission to the Gentiles without the law.*"[23] He continues, "It is a problem with two aspects: a theological and a political. By forsaking observance of the Jewish law Christianity parts company with Judaism; does this not break the continuity of the history of salvation? That is the theological aspect. But in cutting adrift from Judaism Christianity also loses the toleration which the Jewish religion enjoys. Denounced by the Jews as hostile to the state, it becomes the object of suspicion to Rome. That is the political aspect. Acts takes both constantly into account."[24] Haenchen stresses that the problem of the Gentile mission without the law, although presented in Acts as a problem of the age of the apostles, is in reality treated as a problem of Luke's own time. For this reason one should not expect the Lukan Paul to resemble the Paul of the epistles: "The real Paul, as known to his followers and opponents alike, has been replaced by a Paul seen through the eyes of a later age, and . . . the primitive age of Christianity is not described here by one who lived through the greater part of it."[25] Similarly, the picture of relations between Jews and Christians is not that of the Pauline epistles. The problem that Luke wants to resolve is that of justifying the Christian Gentile mission as a necessary stage in the history of salvation and in continuity with Judaism and at the same time explaining why the greater part of the Jews did not respond positively to the Christian message.

Luke's solution, therefore, requires him to begin his narrative with stories of the initial success of the Christian mission among Jews. This is both a theological and a political necessity. And so there is great stress on the positive response to the apostles in Jerusalem and Judea in Acts 1–8. At a very early point, according to Haenchen, Luke provides an important signal that is to be developed in the later chapters of Acts. In the narrative of Peter and John before the High Council (Acts 4:1–22), Luke portrays the Sadducees as authoritative figures, who arrested people whose theology was different from their own. Haenchen questions the historicity of this approach and writes that "if the Sadducees had wished to proceed against all believers in resurrection they would have had to throw every Pharisee into jail."[26] He also notes that the Sanhedrin at that time was dominated by Pharisees. And so the opposition of Sadducees to the apostles is not historical, but does represent an important Lukan concept: "According to Luke, it is not Judaism and Christianity which confront each other as enemies, but only Sadducees and Christians. For Pharisee and Christian are at one where belief in resurrection, the nucleus of Christianity, is concerned (even if the Pharisees fail to draw the necessary conclusions in respect of Jesus' resurrection). Christianity is not a falling-away from Judaism; on the contrary, its doctrine of resurrection is the basic teaching of Israel, which only the αἵρεσις τῶν Σαδδουκαίων disputes."[27]

That Christianity is not a falling-away from Judaism is, for Haenchen, a fundamental Lukan axiom. But Luke nevertheless tells of times of persecution of Christians by Jews, beginning with the story of Stephen. Stephen's speech in Acts 7:2–53 was intended to show that Jews have "always resisted the Holy Spirit" (Acts 7:51). Haenchen recognizes that at this point there is an apparent problem, since Luke had previously shown that the Christians were popular among the Jews. This would seem to constitute a contradiction within the Lukan narrative. And Haenchen answers his own question, isn't this contrary to Luke's own conception?

Not in the least. What Luke is here depicting is the constant experience of his own community, of which Acts indeed tells a long enough tale: it is the Jews who unleash persecution upon persecution against the Christians; it is they who drive Paul from town to town and blasphemously reject the gospel again and again. At the time when Luke wrote, the Jews were the Christians' mighty and irreconcilable enemies; Jewry humbly open to receive the Word had become the dwindling exception, a merely theoretical possibility. And so these two images of Israel stand confronted, without any systematic comment on the part of Luke: on the one hand Israel with its task in salvation-history, the people of the patriarchs, of Moses and the prophets; on the other Israel, a people forever bent on the worship of idols and athirst for the blood of the prophets.[28]

Haenchen's insight that these two contrary images of Israel are both strongly maintained in Acts and are not fully resolved is an important one. Moreover, the location of the problem in Luke's time rather than in the time of the apostles provides an important key to the understanding of Acts. For if Luke is struggling with ways to present Christianity as of a piece with Judaism and as initially popular among Jews, he must nevertheless account for Jewish rejection. As Haenchen has observed, the fact of Jewish rejection, well known in Luke's day, must be shown to have been anticipated in apostolic times. Much of the narrative from Acts 7 on does precisely this.

Haenchen speaks more sharply and directly about Luke's conception of Jews and Judaism in an article published in 1963.[29] Here he reiterates many of the points made in the commentary, but he emphasizes the Lukan composition of the speech of Stephen and its anti-Judaic polemic. He maintains that "here Luke himself speaks, and not by any means in the costume of a person of the past who was friendly to Jews, but in the posture and voice of his own Gentile-Christian present."[30] Haenchen adds that the speech reveals that Luke's time was marked by a fundamental enmity between Judaism and Christianity.

Stephen's speech in Acts 7 prepares the way for Luke's explanation of Jewish rejection, but the narratives about Paul provide the details. According to Haenchen, the mission of Paul in Pisidian Antioch (Acts 13:13–52) forms a model for the entire Pauline mission: "Both the sermon and the resultant events are ideal or typical occurrences clothing in historical dress a host of similar crises constantly recurring. The whole Pauline mission—as Luke and his age saw it—is compressed and epitomized in this scene."[31] Here we have an initial approach of the Christians to the synagogue, then a second sermon to the populace as a whole, followed by Gentile acceptance and Jewish rejection. The most significant part of the pericope is Acts 13:46, where Paul and Barnabas announce to the Jews, "It was necessary that the word of God should be spoken first to you. Since you reject it and judge yourselves to be unworthy of eternal life, we are now turning to the Gentiles." Haenchen comments: "This is the moment of divorce between the gospel and Judaism: solemnly the missionaries declare that they will now turn to the Gentiles, who receive the word of God with jubilation."[32]

But Haenchen notes that this solemn announcement occurs twice more in

Acts (18:6; 28:28), and he acknowledges that after each of the first two announcements the missionaries return to preach in synagogues. Although each of these decisions to go to Gentiles may apply only to the local areas in which the announcements are made, Haenchen believes that they have a more general significance: "One may say, not without reason, that the decision of 13.46 holds only for Pisidian Antioch. That is correct. But at the same time the reader senses that these happenings bear a significance which surpasses the immediate occasion. This crisis of decision is representative of all later instances. The Jews who in Pisidian Antioch grow envious of the Christians are at the same time the Jews in general, while the ἔθνη attending the syna-gogue of Antioch are more than their actually very modest number: they are τὰ ἔθνη—all those multitudes of Gentiles who stream into the Christian Church and arouse the jealous rancour of the Jews."[33] Haenchen stresses the representative nature of the three announcements. In a comment on Acts 18:6, he says, "As in 13.46 and 28.28 this renunciation makes it clear to the reader that Israel by her own fault has forfeited salvation and made the proclamation to the Gentiles necessary, so that now Paul can go to them with a good con-science."[34] And Haenchen emphasizes the message that Luke intends for his readers by including these statements: "The repetition of these scenes is intended to impress upon the reader that it is not the fault of Christians or of Christianity that it has become a religion distinct from Judaism and standing hostile alongside it. So far as Paul was concerned (and he represents for Luke here Christianity in general!), the Christians had always remained within Judaism. It is exclusively the fault of the Jews if Christianity now appears as a separate community."[35] We shall see in later chapters that this is a contro-versial point. Critics of Haenchen will contend that the fact that the announce-ments of Acts 13:46 and 18:6 are followed by synagogue visits means that, for Luke, the mission of Christian preachers to Jews is not over.

Haenchen regards Acts 15 as the turning point of the entire narrative. It constitutes "the episode which rounds off and justifies the past developments, and makes those to come intrinsically possible."[36] Indeed, he is able to show that at this point a number of themes come together. But this story of the apos-tolic council should not be taken as historical. It is Luke's "imaginary con-struction," an attempt to legitimate the Gentile mission. At two points Haenchen's comments on this pericope have a distinct bearing on the issue of Israel in Acts.

First, in Acts 15:7–11, Peter speaks against the imposition of circumcision for Gentile believers. He recalls the incident of the conversion of Cornelius, narrated in Acts 10–11. Haenchen notes that this citation on Peter's part must mean that the Cornelius story is not historical, since, if it had occurred, there would not have been any subsequent debate about the requirement of circum-cision. But in Acts 15, Peter cites the incident and then, in drawing a conclu-sion says, "Now therefore why are you putting God to the test by placing on the neck of the disciples a yoke that neither our ancestors nor we have been able to bear?" (Acts 15:10). Here, in a rare move into historical criticism, Haenchen states that this cannot have been the viewpoint of the historical Peter, "for the strict Jew by no means regarded the law as an intolerable burden. Luke is rather portraying the image which Hellenistic Gentile Christians had of the law: a mass of commandments and prohibitions which no man can satisfy."[37] It is notable that in juxtaposing what is known about early Judaism with the Lukan viewpoint, Haenchen has not only shown the discrepancy between the two but has also countered a prevailing trend in Christian scholarship. Most of Haenchen's predecessors have emphasized the legalistic and casuistic character of Torah observance, while Haenchen himself has, at least at this point, questioned this characteristic.

Second, Haenchen pays special attention to the injunctions of the apostolic decree in Acts 15:20. He recognizes that these four prohibitions are distinctive among the ritualistic requirements of Mosaic Torah in that they are intended to be kept not only by the people of Israel but also by resident aliens living in Israel. These are the only such commandments: "Whereas in other respects the law applies solely to the Jews, it imposes these four prohibitions on *Gentiles also!*"[38] Therefore, the imposition of these four prohibitions on Gentile Christians forms the final part of Luke's justification of the Gentile mission free from the law. If a Jew should object that the Christian movement has forsaken the Mosaic law, then Luke is able to reply that "it is in full accord with Moses himself, who demanded just those abstinences of the Gentiles."[39]

The last several chapters of Acts are seen by Haenchen as an opportunity for Luke to solidify his portrayal of the relationship of Christianity and Judaism. The real issue in all of Paul's defensive speeches is the Gentile mission, not the fate of Paul. It is for this reason that the doctrine of the resurrection comes to the fore in these speeches, to remind the reader that this central tenet of Christian belief should forge a powerful link with the Pharisees. This point comes through clearly in Haenchen's comments on Paul's speech before the Sanhedrin in Acts 22:30–23:11. The speech, says Haenchen, is a creation of Luke, who is not so concerned about the immediate situation of Paul: "He [Luke] is concerned about something much higher, namely the truth that the bridges between Jews and Christians have not been broken. It is Luke's honest conviction that fellowship between Pharisaism and Christianity is in the end possible: the Pharisees also hope for the Messiah, await the resurrection of the dead. In this they are at one with the Christians. Their mistake is only that in this hope and faith they are not consistent where Jesus is concerned. The resurrection of Jesus, and his Messiahship thereby attested, are not contrary to the Jewish faith."[40] Haenchen consistently emphasizes this theme in his comments on the trials before Felix (Acts 24:1–23) and before Agrippa and Festus (Acts 26:1–32). In all these cases Luke is less interested in the immediate situation of Paul than in speaking to the reader about the contemporary situation in respect to Christianity and Judaism: "For in these chapters it is not simply a matter of Paul the man but of the cause of Christ. The new faith—

this is here again emphasized—is not a treason to the old. The hope of resurrection is the bond which holds the two together."[41] And Haenchen is no less attuned to the political purposes of Luke's narrative. In commenting on Paul's conduct in Roman courts, he draws on Dibelius in observing that Luke intended to provide a model for contemporary Christians who may find themselves in similar situations. And so he writes: "Hence Luke sees his task not in equipping the Church for martyrdom immediately before the end, but in securing for it the possibility of life within the Roman Empire. But with this very task Paul could help the Christians. How he, the Roman citizen, had been able to get along with the Romans—even in situations of conflict!—and to win their respect and trust. Why should Rome not tolerate the Christian 'Way'? Because the Jews up and down the country accused the Christians? They could be countered with the proof that precisely the strictest movement in Judaism, Pharisaism, agreed with Christianity in its belief in the resurrection. Luke emphatically presented this, especially in Chapters 23 and 26."[42]

The final scene in Acts (28:17–31) is the culmination of the story, but it follows the pattern that Luke has used throughout. Paul speaks to Jews, and although some respond positively, Luke has him repeat for the third time the solemn announcement directing the gospel to the Gentiles. Thus "the conclusion of the entire book agrees internally with the preceding description of the Pauline mission. The last chapter also is thus completely integrated into the total work in that it bases the justification of the Gentile mission on the refusal of the Jews."[43] Haenchen's detailed analysis of Acts is consistent with the judgment he makes in the introduction to the commentary: "For Luke the Jews are 'written off.' Acts 28.28 is not only a very effective conclusion of the book but also the expression of a conviction which already resounds in the Lucan account of the first sermon of Jesus of Nazareth [Luke 4:16–30]. . . ."[44]

Haenchen has, in this commentary, almost completely abandoned the attempt to use the Acts of the Apostles as a source for reconstructing the history of the first generation of the Christian movement. He has, for example, clearly shown that the Paul of Acts and the Paul of the epistles are quite dissimilar. In this respect he has parted company with those of his predecessors who read the NT text for information about the Jewish background. Only rarely does Haenchen reveal his own opinions about early Judaism. And so, for the most part his commentary asks only about Luke's views and intentions. And even here, Haenchen insists that Luke is writing for the people of his own day, even constructing whole scenes with the intention to provide his readers with an understanding of their own situation. But in so constructing his commentary, Haenchen has shown us a great deal about Luke's understanding of the Judaism of his day, even if he has not given us much information about the time of the apostles.

For Haenchen, Acts is from first to last an attempt to justify the Gentile mission without the law. And he insists that, in this context, it is fundamentally important for Luke to assert that Christianity is, at its base, continuous with

Judaism. And so, Haenchen's Luke, although he is aware of other parties, defines Judaism as resurrectionist Pharisaism, and this definition allows him to say that at heart Judaism and Christianity are one. In his portrayal, many Jews understood this and responded favorably to the apostolic preaching, but most did not, and God used Jewish rejection to open the way for the apostles to approach Gentiles. Thus Gentiles of Luke's day should feel no guilt about Jewish rejection, since it is perennial Jewish obduracy, clearly perceived by the prophets, that explains it. Furthermore, Gentiles are required to keep that part of Torah that, even in the Mosaic scriptures, was imposed upon both Jews and Gentiles. Finally, Christians may defend themselves in Roman courts by insisting on the continuity of their resurrection faith with Judaism, even if contemporary Jews have fallen away from authentic faith.

HANS CONZELMANN

Hans Conzelmann was just beginning his university-level education at the start of the Third Reich. Little is known about any public stands that he might have taken about National Socialism or about the program of genocide that led to millions of deaths in Auschwitz, Treblinka, and other camps. It is known that he had difficulties in obtaining his first faculty position, probably because of differences with the director of the Tübingen foundation, who seems to have been sympathetic with National Socialism. Conzelmann was a member of the Church Theological Society in Württemberg, which Dietz Lange describes as "a group corresponding to the confessing church elsewhere in Germany, and thus [Conzelmann] stood clearly in opposition to the current regime."[45] He was a draftee in the German military and was seriously wounded on the Western front in 1945. One leg had to be amputated. But after the war he taught at Zurich and then at Göttingen. He died on June 20, 1989, after suffering a number of serious health problems.

Conzelmann's major contribution to the discipline of NT studies was his analysis of Luke-Acts, *Die Mitte der Zeit*.[46] With its publication in 1954 and its subsequent translation into English in 1960, critical scholars were introduced to a new way of studying the gospels. Without denigrating the discipline of form criticism, as practiced by Dibelius and Bultmann, Conzelmann introduced the discipline of *Redaktiongeschichte,* or redaction criticism, which analyzed the text of Luke-Acts in its canonical form and asked questions about the intent of the final editor. The interest in redaction criticism was not directed to the history of Jesus or the forms of the Christian tradition in the pregospel period, but to the theology of the evangelist.

Before we examine Conzelmann's specific work on Luke-Acts, we need to explore his views on Judaism as expressed in other publications. There is not much to go on. He did not publish a comprehensive study of early Judaism, but we may draw on a number of remarks from publications on a variety of subjects related to the NT and early Christianity.

The article on grace in Kittel's *Theological Dictionary* was written jointly by Walther Zimmerli and Conzelmann, with the latter contributing the section on the meaning of the concept in Judaism. The article suggests that Conzelmann, at that time, followed the lead of the dominant school of German NT scholarship in picturing Judaism as legalistic and casuistic. For example, he acknowledges the use of the word "grace" in the rabbinic writings but points out the connection with law. On the uses of the term in rabbinic writings, Conzelmann writes, "The central problem is the relation between grace and works. The principle applies: 'One receives a reward only for an act,' . . . 'Grace is what thou hast done to us because there were no good works in our hands,' M.Ex., 3,9 on 15:13 (p.145,15). That is, grace arises only where there are no good works; it is supplementary."[47] And he concludes, "Basically, however, the concept of grace remains caught in the schema of the Law. In the understanding of grace no line can be drawn from the Synagogue to the NT. Judaism cannot accept the alternative of works or grace."[48]

Perhaps the fullest analysis of early Judaism by Conzelmann is to be found in his *Outline of the Theology of the New Testament.*[49] As a part of the introduction to this volume, Conzelmann devotes some three pages to the Hellenistic environment of early Christianity and thirteen to the Jewish, although he supports many of his contentions in this section by reference to the NT and often moves from Jewish to Christian ideas without warning. He introduces the section on the Jewish environment by noting that "Judaism not only provides the setting for Jesus and the primitive community, but is also their religion."[50] Conzelmann recognizes that Jewish thought and practice in the period before 70 CE was not a unity, but he nevertheless intends to concentrate on those points of general consensus. On the idea of God he repeats a frequently noted theme in critical NT scholarship, namely that Jewish thinking about God had emphasized transcendence and distance, as shown in the avoidance of the divine name and the reliance on intermediate beings. And in speaking of God as judge, he says that the idea of a double judgment has found its way into both Jewish and Christian eschatology from Persian religion. Then he writes, "The idea of an individual judgment means that the individual bears the whole weight of responsibility. . . . The idea of a general resurrection, however, makes it clear that the final victory falls to the good. This guarantees the certainty of salvation."[51] Then in the next paragraph, Conzelmann claims, "The view that man is justified only by his works is carried through consistently. There is no room for grace. The judge is bound by his own law."[52] In the section on "Man and Salvation," Conzelmann cautions against making "the Reformation's dogmatic judgment on the law as a means to salvation into a historical verdict on the Jewish understanding of the law."[53] He adds, "For Judaism, the law is not primarily a sum of precepts, but the sign of the election of Israel, the ratification of the covenant. It is not a burden but a delight (Paul: Phil. 2.4–6)."[54] But then he asks: "can obedience be achieved by legalistic casuistry at all?"[55] Attempts to obey law always involve casuistry, and not all things are covered by law. "There is also the limitation of all law; what is not prohibited is permissible."[56] But obedience to law can never suffice, says Conzelmann, because God demands the whole person, and by obedience to law, salvation can never be certain. And thus Judaism must resort to dependence on cult and apocalyptic expectation.

In what appears to be a much later revision of this section of the *Outline,* published in 1985, some different emphases and nuances are to be noted. It is, however, difficult to know in this case what specific contributions come from Conzelmann in this book and what come from his coauthor, Andreas Lindemann.[57] Near the beginning of this section there is a note on terminology, a vigorously discussed topic in Göttingen at the time. Conzelmann and Lindemann disavow both terms, "late Judaism" and "early Judaism": "Judaism of the NT era is often called 'late Judaism.' This is not a legitimate concept; it creates the impression that Judaism, existing alongside the church is an anachronism up to the present time. Equally erroneous is the apologetic designation 'early Judaism,' which creates the impression that the OT is not part of Judaism. It is best to speak of Judaism in late antiquity or of Judaism in the hellenistic-Roman era."[58]

In the section on law in Judaism, the authors emphasize the inaccuracy of the concept that Torah-obedience was considered to be a difficult burden, and they maintain that "the law is not to be construed as motivation for external legalism and, especially for the Jew, is not a nuisance. . . ."[59] In a paragraph that is remarkable when viewed against earlier statements by Conzelmann, the authors write: "Jewish obedience to the law must not be misinterpreted: The issue is not formal obedience but the attitude behind that obedience. What matters is not the human efforts alone, but the disposition to obedience. Even if one hopes for a reward for keeping the commandments, it is not permissible at all to use the law selfishly."[60]

The contrast between the teaching of Jesus and that of contemporary Judaism is emphasized in Conzelmann's article on Jesus in the third edition of *Die Religion in Geschichte und Gegenwart,* published in 1959.[61] Although even here Conzelmann did not provide an in-depth analysis of early Judaism, he characterized it as "dominated by the problems of law and eschatology."[62] And, as in traditional Christian writing about Judaism, law and casuistry go together: "For Judaism, the interpretation by which one can recognize and fulfill the will of God belongs to the law. This leads either to casuistry or to a heightening of the torah in the sense of the 'Rule of the Community' (1QS) at Qumran. . . . Over against this interpretation and practice, Jesus places a new and peculiarly dialectical method of exposition. He assumes the law is intelligible by itself and needs no interpretation at all. Such interpretation is the work of men and obscures the matter; it is a question of getting back behind the human precepts to the commandments themselves."[63] For Conzelmann, this is an explanation of the conflict between Jesus and the scribal community: "This understanding of God and law must lead to a conflict with the entire scribal casuistry in which, according to Jesus, God's will is not explained but distorted (Mark 7:6–7) and to a protest against the division of outer and inner which is unavoidable in legalism."[64] Thus the differences between the teaching of Jesus and the teaching of the scribes inevitably led to conflict. Indeed, Conzelmann maintains, "It is immediately obvious that this preaching had to lead to a fundamental conflict with *all* the trends within Judaism."[65]

In this same article, Conzelmann is emphatic and clear in denying that Jesus was put to death by Jews: "It is established that Jesus was executed by the Romans (and not by the Jews) since crucifixion is a Roman form of capital punishment and not a Jewish one."[66] Anything beyond this is speculation, and, although he does not deny that there was a session of the Sanhedrin involved in the proceedings against Jesus, he concludes that the reports in the gospels cannot be used to reconstruct the actual history. About the NT report of the Sanhedrin trial he says, "Methodologically it is misleading to interpret the present report as such a record [of the trial of Jesus]. It is a witness of faith."[67] Conzelmann is consistent in making this point about the death of Jesus. In an article on the passion narratives of the synoptic gospels, published in German in 1967, he makes the point quite directly. On the historical substratum of the narratives, he says, "The assured core is that Jesus was crucified. From that we can conclude that he was arrested and that a court proceeding followed (and, to be sure) a Roman one. Crucifixion is a Roman, not a Jewish, means of capital punishment."[68] He adds in the next paragraph, "All the rest in the course of events is debatable."[69] It is clear, however, that Conzelmann's chief interest in this article is in theology rather than history: "A contemporary approach to the passion narrative is not to be gained from single facts but only from the interpretation."[70] Granted that his main interest is in the interpretation, it is understandable that he does not want to engage in a sustained discussion of the historical substratum of the gospels. This means that, despite the fact that any historical conclusion beyond the contention that Jesus was crucified after a Roman trial is a debatable matter of speculation, the inclusion of a Jewish trial of Jesus in the synoptic gospels is part of the interpretation of his death. And so Conzelmann includes the narratives about Jewish involvement in the death of Jesus as part of the interpretation. What is surprising, however, is that he makes no effort in this article to call attention to the anti-Jewish character of this interpretation. It is simply Christian interpretation, which as he says is "not a secondary addition to primary facts of salvation."[71]

Conzelmann did, however, come closer to addressing this question in a paper delivered in New York at the meeting of the Society of Biblical Literature in 1964. In this paper he demonstrated an acute awareness of what he called the "historical consequences of this charge [about the death of Jesus] against the Jews and the sufferings of the Jewish people caused by a perverted understanding of the creedal formulations. There is no excuse for crimes Christians committed against Jews."[72] Conzelmann points out, however, that the original debates, reflections of which made their way into the NT, were between two groups of Jews, "Jews of the old and Jews of the new faith," both of which maintain "that they are the true people of God, the true Israel."[73] He also felt it important to point out that, at this time and in this context, the Christian Jews constituted the weaker group that felt itself to be persecuted by the majority.

In one of his last books, written in 1981 but not translated into English until 1992, Conzelmann produced an exhaustive study of antisemitism in the ancient period, as seen in the literature of Greco-Roman writers, Christian writers, and Jewish apologists.[74] The discussion of the ancient sources, admirable and helpful as it is, appears to have a subtext in which Conzelmann expresses words of caution about contemporary Christian-Jewish dialogue. As early as the introduction, he attacks the tendency in such discussions to picture Jesus as a Jew and to use this picture as a mediating device between Christians and Jews.[75] At a later point he makes it clear that the continuing history of the Jewish people has no theological significance for Christians.[76] After a discussion of anti-Judaism in the earliest Christian writings, Conzelmann judges that the conflict between synagogue and church was inevitable: "The conflict is inherent in the existence of the church itself. It will last as long as church and synagogue exist side by side."[77] At the end he repeats that the "only issue between Jews and Christians is the issue of faith."[78] And he concludes, "All are justified before God in exactly the same way, by faith alone, which Paul in Rom. 3:30 bases on the confession that God is *one*."[79]

Scholars who knew Conzelmann well insist that it is a misunderstanding of his remarks to perceive them as anti-Jewish. His main intent was to raise questions about a kind of Christian-Jewish dialogue that blurs the real distinctions between the two groups. Christians should be Christians, and Jews should be Jews. Indeed, Conzelmann, while discouraging the attempt to find religious agreements between Christians and Jews, encouraged attempts for them to come together on human grounds. He wrote, "But instead of attempting to find a basis for religious agreement, it is thoroughly possible to attempt a rapprochement on human grounds, since Christians stand under the commandment of love, which is the end of the law."[80] I take this to mean that Christians should respect those things that make Jews different from Christians and should love them, because to do so is to observe the command of Jesus. Nevertheless, there is a certain unresolved tension between the "human" and the "theological" concerns that Conzelmann offers. The concluding statement of the book about the justification of all humans must be considered carefully: "The Jews cannot be seen as some special *eschatological* category. Within this definition, all human beings, Christian and non-Christian, are directly confronted by God. . . . They are confronted by this Word not as Jews or Gentiles, Greeks or barbarians, but simply as human beings, i.e., as sinners who must renounce all boasting before God, including boasting that they are Christians, since the renunciation of all such boasting is inherent in faith. All are justified before God in exactly the same way, by faith alone, which Paul in Rom. 3:30 bases on the confession that God is *one*."[81] The stress on monotheism and the absence of Christology in this statement, as well as in the Romans reference, should be noted. Conzelmann would appear here to be affirming the validity of all monotheistic faith.

Conzelmann's *Theology of Luke*

Conzelmann wrote *Die Mitte der Zeit* in 1954 as his *Habilitationsschrift*.[82] The significance of his work, as a demonstration of the possibilities of redaction criticism, was praised by European and North American scholars alike. The German title focuses attention on one of Conzelmann's main contentions about Luke's theology, namely the conviction that, for Luke, the time of Jesus was not to be perceived as an eschatological sign. According to Conzelmann, Luke understood the history of salvation as a process that took place in three ages. The age of Jesus was the second of the three ages, and so the ministry of Jesus was not a precursor of an imminent kingdom of God. The three ages in the history of salvation were that of Israel, that of Jesus, and that of the church. The effect of seeing Jesus in the middle of this history is, for Luke, to understand that the period of the church, in which the reader of Luke-Acts is situated, is to be an indefinite and not necessarily brief period of time, and to expect that the consummation of all things will occur in a distant future. Conzelmann regards Luke's primary achievement to be his way of addressing the problem that is frequently called the "delay of the Parousia." What should one make of the interval between Jesus and the end? Conzelmann writes, "In Luke however—and this is the measure of his great achievement—we find a new departure, a deliberate reflection: he confronts the problem of the interval by interpreting his own period afresh in relation to this fact; in other words, the treatment of his main problem is the result of coming to grips with his own situation."[83] Writing at a time when the period of Jesus was already well in the past, Luke thus intended to discourage any expectation of a dramatic event that would herald the early end of history.

In this same book Conzelmann introduced redaction criticism as a new way of studying the gospels. Acknowledging the contributions of form and source criticism, he distinguished his own contribution as an attempt "to elucidate Luke's work in its present form, not to enquire into possible sources or into the historical facts which provide the material."[84] He understood the process by which the gospels were formed as one of the filling in of a basic kerygma, i.e., a proclamation of Christian faith about Jesus, with materials drawn from the traditional lore of Jesus' teachings and from the narrative material about him. Form criticism had clarified the first phase of this process by focusing attention on the primitive oral materials that made up this collection of teaching and narrative material. "Now a second phase has to be distinguished, in which the kerygma is not simply transmitted and received, but itself becomes the subject of reflection."[85] And so Conzelmann presents his study of Luke's theology as dependent on the results of form and source criticism but going beyond them to ask questions about the gospel in its present form.

A clarification in terms of method must be made at this point. Conzelmann maintains from the beginning that his work is not, "for the most part," dependent on a particular source theory: "This study of St. Luke's theology is, by its approach to the problems, for the most part not dependent on any particular literary theories about St. Luke's Gospel and the Acts of the Apostles, for it is concerned with the whole of Luke's writings as they stand."[86] But in this same opening paragraph, Conzelmann acknowledges a significant dependence on source theory: "A variety of sources does not necessarily imply a similar variety in the thought and composition of the author. How did it come about, that he brought together these particular materials? Was he able to imprint on them his own views? It is here that the analysis of the sources renders the necessary service of helping to distinguish what comes from the source from what belongs to the author."[87]

Clearly, Conzelmann accepts the two-document hypothesis, i.e., the view that, in his gospel, Luke made use of Mark and Q, and this theory undergirds his redaction criticism at a number of points. In regard to Acts, however, he, like Haenchen, is much more circumspect about source theories. In both cases it is important to distinguish between Conzelmann's redaction criticism and narratological or literary approaches that have more recently been utilized.[88]

After the introduction, Conzelmann's study is divided into five major sections: (1) "Geographical Elements in the Composition of Luke's Gospel," (2) "Luke's Eschatology," (3) "God and Redemptive History," (4) "The Centre of History," and (5) "Man and Salvation: the Church." The first section is probably the best demonstration of the significance of redaction criticism. Actually, Conzelmann develops this section with little or no methodological discussion, but it should be observed that he is at this point dependent on the results of form criticism, which maintained that the geographical and chronological settings of primitive narratives and teaching materials did not constitute a part of the original form. This would mean that the evangelists had a certain discretion in the use of geographical and chronological references. In order to produce a coherent narrative, Luke would find it necessary to arrange his materials in a particular sequence and provide locations for them.

Thus Conzelmann finds significance in Luke's choices of locations and chronological references. An important geographical element is to be seen in Luke's separation of the territories of John the Baptist and Jesus. Conzelmann does not think that Luke had any exact knowledge of Judea, Galilee, or Samaria, but that he was intent on making a geographical separation between John and Jesus. He writes, "Thus the locality of the Baptist becomes remarkably vague. Luke can associate him neither with Judaea nor with Galilee, for these are both areas of Jesus' activity."[89] Similarly, Luke makes a chronological distinction between them. Jesus does not make a public appearance in Luke until after the imprisonment of John (Luke 3:20). John stands on the threshold of the second period of salvation history, but he does not belong to it.

For Conzelmann, the key to the division between the epoch of Israel and that of Jesus is to be found in Luke 16:16: "The law and the prophets were in effect until John came; since then the good news of the kingdom of God is proclaimed, and everyone tries to enter it by force." This verse "provides the key to the topography of redemptive history. According to this passage, there is no preparation before Jesus for the proclamation of the Kingdom of God, that is, of the 'Gospel' in Luke's sense."[90]

With this general scheme in mind, I will now focus on some specific sections of Conzelmann's study that provide us with an understanding of Luke's treatment of Jews and Judaism. Initially, one might suspect that an analysis of the first period of salvation history, the epoch of Israel, would be useful for this purpose. In fact, however, Conzelmann says next to nothing about this period. He assumes that it is characterized by "law and prophets" (see Luke 16:16), and it obviously is intended to be coterminous with the history covered by the Hebrew Bible. But beyond this, Conzelmann has no interest in describing the period of Israel. On his assumption, this is a period that continues up through the time of John the Baptist, and so the reader of Luke should be able to assume that the evangelist covers at least some part of the period of Israel in the opening chapters, or up to the point where Jesus makes his first public appearance.

The opening chapters of Luke, including the birth and infancy narratives of Jesus and John in Luke 1–2, constitute a veritable mine of impressions of Jewish religious life. Here, if anywhere, Luke has a significant opportunity to describe Jewish religious life apart from and prior to Jesus, and the remarkable thing about the description is its positive character. Although the evangelist shows no intention of providing a full description of Jewish religious life, Luke 1–2 focuses the reader's attention on a number of devout Jewish people whose piety is described in positive fashion. Zechariah and Elizabeth are described as "righteous before God, living blamelessly according to all the commandments and regulations of the Lord" (Luke 1:6). Simeon is said to be "righteous and devout, looking forward to the consolation of Israel, and the Holy Spirit rested on him" (2:25). Anna "never left the temple but worshiped there with fasting and prayer night and day" (2:37). These characters are noted not only for their powerful convictions and expectations, but for their quiet devotion, their observance of Torah, and their engagement in prayer and fasting. Nothing emerges from these chapters about a religion that is drying up in enthusiasm or suffering the agonies of legalism and casuistry.

But Conzelmann entirely omits any discussion of these opening chapters of Luke. The one paragraph in *The Theology of St. Luke* in which he discusses Luke 1–2 is brief enough to be quoted in full:

> The introductory chapters of the Gospel present a special problem. It is strange that the characteristic features they contain do not occur again either in the Gospel or in Acts. In certain passages there is a direct contradiction, as for example in the analogy between the Baptist and Jesus, which is emphasized in

the early chapters, but deliberately avoided in the rest of the Gospel. Special motifs in these chapters, apart from the typology of John, are the part played by Mary and the virgin conception, the Davidic descent and Bethlehem. On the other hand there is agreement in the fact that the idea of pre-existence is missing.[91]

Conzelmann's refusal to take account of the birth narratives has been frequently noted and criticized. H. H. Oliver claimed that not only are there images and concepts in the birth narratives that are consonant with the rest of Luke-Acts, but also that attention to these narratives tends to support the theology of salvation history that Conzelmann sought to explicate.[92] Oliver disagrees with Conzelmann about the portrayal of John the Baptist and claims that the nativity account agrees with the rest of Luke in seeing John as part of the period of Israel. Paul Minear approaches the matter from a different perspective. He says that, had Conzelmann taken account of the birth narratives, his theology of Luke would have taken a very different turn.[93] Minear begins by displaying evidence for the integrity of Luke-Acts. He includes an impressive list of words and phrases "which appear both in the birth narratives and in the rest of Luke-Acts, and which are found more often in these two books than in the rest of the New Testament."[94] He also points to a number of syntactical elements that tend to tie the birth narratives to the rest of Luke-Acts.[95] There are pervasive interests and themes as well, such as the use of the historiographical style, the use of speeches, citations and hymns, common ecclesiological conceptions, allusions to liturgical usage, reliance on epiphany and angels, the theme of promise and fulfillment, and other themes found both in the birth narratives and in the rest of the gospel and Acts. Conzelmann is then taken to task for his "minimal use of the nativity stories."[96] Minear claims that "if Conzelmann had taken full account of the nativity stories, I believe his position would have been changed at several points."[97] Indeed, says Minear, "I believe that it is only by thus ignoring the birth narratives that Conzelmann can appear to establish his thesis that Luke visualized the story of salvation as emerging in three quite distinct states: the period of Israel, the period of Jesus' ministry, the period since the ascension. . . ."[98]

Conzelmann was, of course, aware of the Proto-Luke hypothesis developed by B. H. Streeter and Vincent Taylor.[99] This hypothesis states that, in its earliest form, the Gospel of Luke consisted of the non-Markan sections of canonical Luke, that is, those sections that, according to the two-document hypothesis, were drawn from Q and Luke's *Sondergut,* the source of material found only in Luke. Only at a later point did the author of the Third Gospel discover Mark, and when he did he supplemented his own gospel with those sections of Mark that seemed to be useful. Thus, according to this hypothesis, the Gospel of Luke was produced in at least two rescensions, Proto-Luke and canonical Luke. Actually, however, there was an intermediate stage, according to Taylor. Luke 1:5–2:52 is classified by him as a non-Markan section that appears to stand apart from everything else in the gospel.[100] And so Taylor is able to designate Luke 3:1 as the original beginning of Proto-Luke, and he notes that this carefully constructed setting of time is an appropriate beginning of a historical or biographical narrative. Taylor supplies a number of arguments to support his position. In Luke 3:2, for example, John the son of Zechariah is introduced as if he had not been mentioned earlier, and in Luke 7:19 he asks a question the answer to which was known to his mother. Although Conzelmann explicitly rejected the Proto-Luke hypothesis of Streeter and Taylor, he nevertheless was convinced that "the authenticity of these first two chapters is questionable."[101] And so he determined not to consider them.

It is difficult to ignore Paul Minear's contention that, if Conzelmann had considered Luke 1–2 as carefully as he did the rest of the gospel, his conclusions would have been quite different. And what is surprising is the absence of any compelling argument against the authenticity of these chapters, especially since Conzelmann announced at the beginning of the book that his concern was "with the whole of Luke's writings as they stand."[102] In the absence of such an argument it is inappropriate to presume the reasons that may have led Conzelmann to neglect these narratives. But the neglect clearly affects his treatment of the images of Judaism in Luke-Acts. The omission of any attention to Luke 1–2 means that Conzelmann forfeited an opportunity to discuss a section of canonical Luke that would support a positive image of Judaism at the time of Jesus. More problematic from his own point of view, neglect of these chapters means that there is no significant discussion of what Conzelmann thought Luke meant by the period of Israel. Although it is characterized as a period of law and prophets, there is no description of the period of Israel from Luke's perspective. The result is that Conzelmann is able to draw on the rest of Luke-Acts to show that this evangelist's portrait of Jews and Judaism is totally negative.

And it is a negative picture indeed. Conzelmann's analysis of the Lukan narrative shows that Luke took special pains to remove responsibility for Jesus' execution from Rome, where it belonged historically, and point it toward the Jews. He notes that Pilate pronounced Jesus innocent more than once in Luke's version of the Roman trial and that he did not condemn him: "Jesus does not die by the decision of the Roman judge—he is killed by the Jews to whom he is 'delivered' by the Roman (xxiii, 25)."[103] Conzelmann reads the narrative in Luke as saying that Jesus is not executed by the Romans, since Pilate plays only a passive role in the story: "In so far as there is any suggestion that the Romans take part, it is a survival from the sources and is not part of the plan of Luke's account, but rather, contradicts it."[104] Luke draws on the earlier tradition but develops it in a one-sided way to "put all the blame on the Jews."[105]

In Luke's theology, the guilt of the Jews in putting Jesus to death results in a forfeiting of their election. Still, in Conzelmann's view of the perspective of Luke-Acts, they are offered an opportunity "to make good their claim to be 'Israel.' If they fail to do this, then they become 'the Jews.'"[106] So, although Luke establishes the guilt of the Jews in the death of Jesus, the Christian sermons in Acts concede that they acted in ignorance (see Acts 3:7), and they are given another opportunity. They nevertheless refuse to repent and accept the Christian message, and so through most of Acts they are called "Jews." The terminology is important for Conzelmann, who emphasizes the claim that, in Luke-Acts, because of their guilt in the execution of Jesus and their unrelieved obduracy and opposition to the Christian preachers, the Jews have forfeited the right to be Israel.

Although Conzelmann notes that the idea of the "true Israel" had not yet developed in Christian thought, he nevertheless insists that, according to Luke-Acts, the church takes over "the inheritance of redemptive history."[107] He emphasizes the links that the earliest community had with Israel, in that it observed the law and occupied the Temple. The fact that the first generation of Christians observed the law does not mean that subsequent generations must follow this model. It is only necessary for the first generation to observe Torah in order to provide a link between the church and Israel: "The fact that the primitive community keeps the law . . . is proof that it is bound up with Israel."[108] Moreover, it is significant that loyalty to the Temple continues on into the Christian period. Conzelmann maintains that, for Luke, the Temple had ceased to be an institution for Jews, "because since Jesus' occupation of the Temple they [the Jews] have no right to possess it."[109] Conzelmann is quite clear about Luke's judgment on the Jews: "The idea of tradition is applied to Israel only in the general sense, that the Church is now the people of God."[110]

Conzelmann's Commentary on Acts

Ernst Haenchen published the first edition of his commentary on Acts in 1956.[111] Conzelmann wrote a favorable review of the 1959 edition,[112] and in 1963 he published his own commentary on Acts.[113]

To readers of Conzelmann's *Theology of St. Luke,* the commentary on Acts contains few surprises. He understands the book of Acts as a continuation of the gospel and as a filling in of the history of salvation in its third period, the period of the church. Conzelmann lays out this theology in the introduction, but he concedes that the three-age pattern of salvation history is clearer in the gospel than in Acts, where the theology is presumed rather than developed.

There are, however, important points at which the theme of salvation history is explicit in Acts. One such point is Paul's speech at Pisidian Antioch (Acts 13:16–41). About the speech, Conzelmann says, "The content of the speech is a fundamental encounter between church and synagogue, based upon salvation history. . . . The survey of salvation history replaces the usual introductory scriptural quotation. It establishes the continuity between Israel and the church."[114] Also at the end of this speech the reader finds the first of three announcements by Paul seemingly about the end of the Jewish mission and the turning of the missionaries to the Gentiles (Acts 13:46). Conzelmann comments, "Here a basic principle within salvation history is formulated and from this perspective subsequent scenes are formed. . . . Thus to the end of the book the decision remains one which belongs to Israel."[115]

In terms of the attitude expressed toward the Jews, Conzelmann notes two apparently opposing expressions: "Against the Jews, Luke reproaches Jews for their intrigues against Christians, even during his own time. But he never denies the connection between the church and Israel in terms of salvation history; indeed, he develops this theme."[116] We have already observed the contention that, in Luke's view, the church, by its observance of Torah in the first generation, forged a link with Israel, thereby allowing subsequent generations to be Israel without the burden of Torah observance. For Conzelmann, this is not a recognition that Luke has ambivalent attitudes toward the Jews, but only a reiteration of the role of the church in taking over the place of Israel as the elect of God. It is especially after the actions of Jews against Paul and Barnabas at Pisidian Antioch (Acts 13:44–50) that Jews are cast in the role of the enemies of Luke's heroes. From here to the end of the book, it is "the Jews" who are the enemies. Conzelmann comments, "The use of οἱ Ἰουδαῖοι, 'the Jews,' is pregnant: after they have rejected the gospel, they are 'Jews' in a qualified sense (cf. 14:1–2)."[117]

Conzelmann agrees with Haenchen in treating Acts 15 as the center of Acts and the major turning point in the narrative. For Conzelmann this narrative relates the transition from the beginning of the church to Luke's own generation: "From this point on the apostles disappear, even in Jerusalem itself. . . . In Jerusalem continuity is represented by James, in the Gentile Christian church by Paul."[118] Thus the dividing line between the first and subsequent generations in the history of the church is described in Acts as a council of the apostles, which determined that Torah was not to be imposed on Gentile Christians. In Acts 15:7–11, Peter characterizes Torah as a difficult burden, "which neither our fathers nor we have been able to bear" (15:10). The comment by Conzelmann on Acts 15:10 is notable: "The concept of the Law as an unbearable burden is neither the common Jewish view (the Jewish expression, 'the yoke,' does not imply something unbearable and impossible to fulfill) nor is it Pauline. It expresses the view of a Christian at a time when the separation from Judaism already lies in the past. On this basis we can also understand why Luke does not draw the conclusion which logic demands, that this yoke should also be removed from Jewish Christians. For Luke Jewish Christianity no longer has any present significance, but it is of fundamental significance in terms of salvation history."[119] It is significant that both Haenchen and Conzelmann were aware of aspects of Jewish religious life that turn out to be more positive than those emphasized by Luke, and that both call attention to them.

One of the most controversial claims made by Conzelmann, as well as by Haenchen, is that, in Acts, the Gentile mission came about as a result of the refusal of the Jews to respond to the Christian preachers. Conzelmann finds this point enunciated in Acts 22:17–21. Here Paul tells of his experience while praying in the Temple. On this occasion Jesus appeared to him to warn him to flee from Jerusalem, "because they will not accept your testimony about me" (Acts 22:18). And then Paul hears, "Go, for I will send you far away to the Gentiles" (22:21). Conzelmann comments that this concept had already been elucidated in Luke 14:16–24, the parable of the great banquet.[120] He adds, "In comparison with Paul (Romans 9–11), we note that the hope for the conversion of Israel before the end of the world is absent. Israel's turning away from salvation is final, as is clear in Paul's concluding statement in [Acts] 28:8 [*sic;* the reference should be to Acts 28:28]."[121] And Conzelmann is clear in understanding Acts 28:28 as the final turning of Paul from the Jews toward the Gentiles. He recognizes that Acts 28:24–25 says that there was a division in Paul's Jewish audience at Rome, but he does not agree that this text implies any continued hope for the conversion of the Jewish people. "The picture of Judaism divided within itself is presented here for the last time. Luke no longer counts on the success of the Christian mission with 'the Jews.' In οἱ μὲν ἐπείθοντο, 'some were convinced,' the emphasis is not that, nevertheless, some were converted (cf. 23:9). The scene has been constructed with the express purpose of conveying the impression that the situation with the Jews was hopeless."[122]

Thus Paul's solemn third declaration about turning toward the Gentiles in Acts 28:28 (cf. 13:46; 18:6) is final. The obdurate refusal on the part of the Jewish people to accept the Christian message has finally issued in the announcement that this mission has ended and that, hereafter, the Christian missionaries will go to Gentiles, who will listen.

The similarities between Ernst Haenchen and Hans Conzelmann, in their personal histories and in their scholarly methods, are remarkable. Here are veterans of the German military in two world wars, both of whom were wounded in combat and both of whom had serious life-long illnesses. In respect to their critical scholarship on Luke-Acts, it would be fair to say that together they changed the future direction of scholarship on these texts. Recent scholars have understandably and appropriately spoken of a Conzelmann-Haenchen consensus in regard to Luke-Acts. This consensus includes the contention that the author of Luke-Acts emphasized the Jewish rejection of the Christian gospel and believed that the mission to the Jews ended with the experience of Paul. Further, it involves the claim that, in Luke's view, the rejection by Jews opened the way for the early Christian missionaries to go to the Gentiles. In the chapters that follow we shall examine the views of certain scholars who reject this approach to Luke-Acts, but it is important to note at this point that their assessment of the consensus as forged by Haenchen and Conzelmann is accurate. Whether or not the consensus is an accurate portrayal of Luke-Acts is a separate question, to which we shall return at the end of this book.

Yet another similarity between the work of these two great scholars should be noted, and that is that both of them adopted the method of redaction criticism and so concentrated on the meaning of the text as we have it. They paid little attention to putative sources or to historical reconstructions. Thus, in their work on Luke-Acts there are few comments about the actual character of early Judaism. In some of their other writings, to be sure, both scholars speak of early Judaism in traditionally negative terms, emphasizing casuistry, legalism, materialism, and externality. These writings reveal that the tradition of critical Christian scholarship carried over long after the horrors of the Holocaust had become common knowledge.

We must not, however, fail to observe a number of features in the work of these two scholars that, when compared with earlier scholarship, constitute important differences in respect to the images of Judaism to be found in Luke-Acts. Both Haenchen and Conzelmann stress what they take to be Luke's sense of the continuity between early Judaism and early Christianity. Haenchen in particular emphasizes Luke's understanding of resurrection as a possible point of agreement between the Christians and the Pharisees. Both scholars call attention to the apostolic decree of Acts 15 as rooted in common Jewish practice. Both also make it clear that Jews at the time of Jesus probably did not regard Torah as a burden, and thus they concede that Acts 15:10 does not present an accurate view of early Judaism. Conzelmann is clear and convincing in his contention that the Lukan portrayal of the trials of Jesus is unhistorical. He is certain that Roman authorities bear the responsibility for Jesus' death and that Luke intentionally turned the guilt toward the Jews. Haenchen, although less clear at this point, probably agrees.

Despite these important observations, our two scholars have found a profound anti-Judaism in the writings of Luke. This is to be seen not only in the Lukan portrayal of the passion of Jesus, but also in the stories of Jewish rejection of Jesus and the Christian preachers. In their judgment, Luke's view is that the Jews have forfeited their right to be called Israel and that they are responsible for the separation between them and the Christians. Haenchen said that Luke had "written off " the Jews.[123] Although Conzelmann does not use this language, he nevertheless stresses what he takes to be a similar belief, namely that the church has taken over the role of the people of God.[124] Indeed, he was convinced that, in Luke's version of salvation history, the age of Israel came to an end with Jesus. It appears that Conzelmann's own theology conforms with Luke's at this point, since he maintained that the continued existence of Israel in the twentieth century has no theological significance for Christians.[125]

Finally, we must return to Conzelmann's decision to exclude from consideration the Lukan infancy narratives in his analysis of the theology of Luke. We have examined his stated reasons for this exclusion and remarked on their weakness. The omission of these chapters is particularly regrettable in view of the fact that they provide the only significant material that gives the reader clues about Luke's portrayal of the character of pre-Christian Judaism, i.e., that period that Conzelmann calls the age of Israel. The Lukan infancy narratives also provide relatively positive images of Judaism, giving the reader glimpses of pious, Torah-observant Jews and their devotional life. Whatever may have been the reason for Conzelmann's neglect of these chapters, the result of his decision is that his theology of Luke must do without any real description of the period of Israel, beyond the general characterization of it as a period of "law and prophets." In Conzelmann's study, Luke's view of Judaism is at the same time less complex and more anti-Jewish than many later scholars have found. The chapter that follows will direct attention to one of the most important of Conzelmann's critics.

CHAPTER 6

JACOB JERVELL (1925–)

The Conzelmann-Haenchen consensus in regard to Luke-Acts was widely accepted among critical scholars, but it did not go unchallenged. Indeed, the Norwegian scholar, Jacob Jervell, mounted a full-scale attack on the consensus, challenging it at almost every point. Jervell's approach to Luke-Acts proposes to constitute a revolution in understanding the ways in which this ancient author assessed the significance of Judaism for the early Christians.

Jervell was born on May 25, 1925, in Fauske, Norway, the son of a Lutheran pastor. He was educated at Lund, Oslo, Heidelberg, and at Göttingen, where he studied under Joachim Jeremias and Ernst Käsemann. He held the position of professor of biblical theology in the Faculty of Theology at the University of Oslo from 1960 to 1988. He also held positions as visiting professor at Lund (1964), Yale (1970), and Aarhus (1973). He published articles and books in a variety of NT areas, including Pauline studies and the Gospel of John. But most of his attention has been devoted to Luke-Acts, and since his retirement from the University of Oslo he has continued these studies, which now culminate in the publication of his commentary on Acts in the Meyer series. It should be noted that this volume, published in 1998, is the seventeenth edition of the Meyer Acts commentary and the successor in this series to those of Ernst Haenchen.[1]

In his doctoral dissertation, Jervell demonstrated competence in a wide range of literature that emerged from the period surrounding the writing of the NT.[2] In it he proposed to understand the interpretation of the *imago dei* and Genesis 1:26ff. in the Pauline letters, but he was convinced that what is found in Paul is not a repristination of Genesis and cannot be understood without an extensive analysis of the Apocrypha, Pseudepigrapha, Philo, Gnostic literature, and early rabbinic materials.

In 1962 Jervell published, in Norwegian, a book on critical studies of the historical Jesus.[3] This book has all the hallmarks of being addressed to a non-scholarly audience but nevertheless displays some of the author's deepest convictions at that time. Jervell first explains the present situation regarding scholarly quests of Jesus and notes the significance of the work of leading scholars, including Schweitzer, Wrede, and Bultmann. He explains that, in the post-Bultmannian era, there has been a reopening of the quest, based upon a renewed appreciation of the connection between Jesus and the church. Then

Jervell turns to some positive statements that he thinks can be made about Jesus. He employs a version of the criterion of dissimilarity, usually associated with the name of Ernst Käsemann.[4] Jervell's version puts it this way: "If the saying can be traced neither to Judaism nor to the primitive church, it is genuine."[5] And he hastens to add, "Of course, this does not mean that other sayings cannot have been spoken by Jesus. He said many things which might have appeared in Jewish books. It only means that, from a scientific point of view, we can speak with some certainty."[6]

This book contains evidence of a positive appreciation for early Judaism that distinguishes Jervell's work from most other critical NT studies of the time. On the Pharisees, for example, he says: "Our somewhat one-sided picture of the Pharisees as a pack of hypocrites will not stand up in the face of historical scrutiny. As a class, the Pharisees stood for high moral and religious standards."[7] But on the use of the Aramaic term, *Abba,* Jervell shows the influence of Joachim Jeremias.[8] He concedes that Jesus' use of the term was not unique. But he maintains: "Still there is something special in the way he uses this word. . . . He addresses God directly as Father in his prayers. A Jew could never do this. It was being too familiar with the honor of God. It was disrespectful and a profanation of the God who was transcendent and infinitely exalted."[9] And, although Jervell is clear that Jesus did not speak of himself as Messiah, he nevertheless stresses that Jesus thought of himself as acting for God and that, in Jewish eyes, this would have been blasphemy. Consider the following: "Jesus constantly demands to be regarded as one who in a special way acts in the place of God and with his plenipotentiary powers. This is most sharply expressed in the many sayings where Jesus asserts that a person's judgment or salvation depends upon the attitude he takes toward his preaching and person. Not that he is an example or an ideal. The Gospels contain no such idea. Rather, he possesses the ultimate authority, and in him men are confronted with God's final and decisively valid will for their lives. Therefore he can act in a manner which in Jewish eyes was reserved for God."[10] On this basis, Jervell is able to maintain that leading Jews determined to do away with Jesus on the charge of blasphemy. But, thinking that the Romans would not take this religious charge seriously, the Jewish leaders transmuted it to a political charge before Pilate.

Jervell concludes the book on the historical Jesus with a section on the relationship between history and theology. In view of a contention that he will strongly maintain in his later work on Luke-Acts, Jervell's conclusion to this section is significant: "The New Testament reflects something we could call a change of election. By that we mean that God replaced the chosen nation, the Jews, with a new people. These new people of God are those who have received the Gospel of Christ; in other words, the old people of God are replaced by the church."[11] Jervell intends this to be a warning to the church of his own day: if Christians are unfaithful, God may replace them. But we shall see that he totally abandons this form of supersessionist theology in his work on Luke-Acts.

Challenging the Consensus

It was precisely on the definition of the people of God that Jervell presented a challenge not only to the Conzelmann-Haenchen consensus but also to his own previously expressed views. Most English-speaking scholars first became aware of Jervell through his book, *Luke and the People of God,* published in 1972.[12] The book is actually a collection of seven essays, four of which had previously been published, one as early as 1962.

The essay, "The Divided People of God: The Restoration of Israel and Salvation for the Gentiles," previously published in 1965, is probably the seminal essay of the book.[13] Here Jervell maintains that Luke uses the term "Israel" in its meaning as "people of God," strictly and solely for Jews. This is the case in Lukan references both to the time before Jesus and the time after. According to Jervell, the function of Jesus in the Gospel of Luke was to begin the process of dividing the Jewish people into the repentant and the obdurate. The repentant Jews remain as part of the people of God, as Israel, but the obdurate Jews have excluded themselves from this body by their refusal to repent. This division of the people, including the elimination of the unrepentant, is a fulfillment of scripture, as shown by the quotation of Deut 18:19 in Acts 3:23. In Luke's view, then, it is the Jewish Christians who now constitute the people of God. The non-Christian Jews are simply called "Jews."

Jervell is quite aware that he is going against a strong body of scholarly opinion. He writes, "The interpretation of Luke's theology of mission most widely advocated today may be described as follows: Luke describes the rejection of the Christian proclamation on the part of the Jewish people. Only after and because Israel has rejected the gospel, and for that reason has itself been rejected, do the missionaries turn to Gentiles."[14] Jervell identifies this "widely advocated" view specifically with Ernst Haenchen, but he himself is impressed with the theme in Acts that emphasizes the acceptance by Jews of the Christian message. He calls attention to the reports of mass conversions of Jews in Acts 2:41; 4:4; 5:14; 6:1, 7; 9:42; 12:24; 13:43; 14:1; 17:10ff.; 19:20; 21:20. Jervell comments that these notes are clearly from Luke himself and must have been intended for a specific function. And so he can reverse the view of Haenchen: "One usually understands the situation to imply that only when the Jews have rejected the gospel is the way opened to Gentiles. It is more correct to say that only when Israel has accepted the gospel can the way to Gentiles be opened."[15] Jervell insists that Luke never thinks of the church as the new Israel, does not use this terminology, and does not use the term "Israel" in connection with the Gentile church. It is those Jews who accepted the Christian message who constitute the people of God, and this is a large group. Those who think of the great bulk of Jews as rejecting Jesus and the apostles may be historically correct, but they are also reading their historical knowledge into the text of Luke-Acts.

Jervell calls special attention to Acts 21:20 as evidence of sizable Jewish acceptance of the Christian message. He notes that what is most striking about the large numbers mentioned here is that the people are all Torah-observant

Jews. This verse is found in the pericope that describes Paul's reception when he arrives in Jerusalem for the last time in Acts. The pericope is one of the "we" sections of Acts. Paul and his party have arrived in Jerusalem, and they go to visit James and the elders, who welcome them warmly. But James reports that there may be problems, and he says to Paul, "You see, brother, how many thousands [πόσαι μυριάδες] of believers there are among the Jews, and they are all zealous for the law" (Acts 21:20). And then James says that these Jewish believers are actually concerned about Paul, because they have heard that he teaches diaspora Jews to abandon the observance of Torah. What is most notable at this point is the uncontested report by a reliable character of a large number of Jewish believers, all of whom observe Torah. And so Jervell maintains that "it is those Jews who are faithful to the law, the real Jews, the most Jewish Jews, that become believers."[16]

What then can one say about the mission to the Gentiles in Acts? Again, the usual critical interpretation of Acts holds that Luke is describing a movement that, indeed, started among Jews but was led by God to break out of the limitations imposed by Torah and to find among Gentiles the freedom from law and casuistry that came to characterize the Christian tradition. Jervell agrees that Luke describes a divinely led mission to Gentiles, but he insists that this is no departure from basic maxims that find their roots in the Hebrew Bible. The inclusion of Gentiles as an associate people along with the repentant Jews is a standard feature of Jewish expectation. Besides, Jervell claims in a later article, Acts does not describe a mission to "pure" Gentiles, but only to God-fearing Gentiles.[17] He conceives of three groups of Gentiles: proselytes, God-fearers, and pure Gentiles. The last named would be those "pagans" who have never had an association with the synagogue. Jervell claims that Luke never describes a successful mission to the "pure Gentiles," but only among proselytes and God-fearers. Cornelius is the prime example of the God-fearer. He is described as a devout and generous man, who feared God (Acts 10:2). To be sure, the narrative of Paul and Barnabas in Lystra (Acts 14:8–20) may be regarded as a mission to pure Gentiles, but Jervell calls attention to the fact that this mission does not end in any conversions. The people mistake the missionaries for Zeus and Hermes, and they prepare to make a sacrifice to them. So Jervell concludes, "Such idolaters do not belong to the church."[18] The situation at Athens (Acts 17:16–34) is similar in Paul's lack of success. There are only two named converts, and Jervell claims that they are God-fearers (Acts 17:34; cf. 17:17). So when Paul announces that hereafter he is going to Gentiles (Acts 13:46; 18:6), this does not mean that he has abandoned the mission to Jews; nor does it signify a mission to "pure" Gentiles. It means that Paul is going to preach to God-fearers. It is only after Acts 28:28 that a mission to "pure" Gentiles is envisioned, although not described.

These observations provide a basis for a fundamental maxim, namely that the church that Luke describes is the "restored Israel," composed of repentant Jews and those Gentiles who had previously been associated with them.

According to Jervell, the main concerns for Luke in writing Acts were "(a) to narrate that tens of thousands of pious Jews have become believers (21:20) and (b) to show that the converted Gentiles were 'God-fearers,' i.e., men who were previously related to Israel. The Gentiles of the synagogue accept the gospel."[19]

Luke's well-known interest in Samaritans is further evidence of the theme of the "restored Israel." Jervell maintains that Samaritans are "the lost sheep of the house of Israel" and that Luke understands them as Jews. Thus, a Samaritan mission is not a transition to a mission among "pure" Gentiles, but a part of the mission to Jews. The mission begins with a rejection of Jesus in Luke 9:51 but ends with the successful mission by Philip in Acts 8. The inclusion of Samaritans is necessary to produce a restored Israel: "To put it another way, at the Apostolic Council in Jerusalem James can speak about the restored Israel in which the Gentiles will also be included (15:16ff). This can only be accomplished after the Jews in Samaria have been included in God's promises and their fulfillment."[20]

Jervell's treatment of the Lukan conception of the people of God directly affects his interpretation of a number of additional aspects of Lukan thought, including the conception of Torah. Here also Jervell goes against the grain of contemporary critical studies, which largely maintained that Luke in Acts is describing the history of a movement that progressively distances itself from Torah-observance and Jewish restrictions. But Jervell maintains quite the contrary, that Luke views Torah as fully valid for Jewish Christians and partially valid for God-fearing believers.

The full validity of Torah for Jewish Christians is made most clear in Acts 21:20, a verse we have previously discussed. Here, late in the book of Acts, we learn that there are thousands of Jewish believers and that they are all zealous for Torah, i.e., fully observant and obedient. In addition, Jervell notes that Luke goes to great lengths to deny that Paul taught Jewish Christians to abandon Torah, as some had suspected (Acts 21:21). Jervell describes Luke as having "the most conservative outlook within the New Testament, because of his concern for the law as Israel's law, the sign of God's people."[21] Indeed, Luke does not separate the moral from the ritual parts of Torah, but actually emphasizes the ritualistic and ceremonial aspects: "The law is to him not essentially the moral law, but the mark of distinction between Jews and non-Jews. The law is the sign of Israel as the people of God, which is evident from Luke's overall perspective and from individual passages."[22] In Lukan theology it is necessary to maintain Torah in order for the church to be the continuation of Israel.

But Jervell also shows that there is a distinctive view of Torah throughout Luke-Acts. Not only do we have in the infancy narratives of Luke 1–2 a description of pious Jews who await the fulfillment of God's promises to Israel and do so as fully observant of Torah, but the child Jesus himself is shown to be "an apprentice of the law, a rabbinic disciple in the temple, 2:41ff."[23] There

is in Luke no summary of the law in one central commandment, as there is in
Mark. The saying on divorce in Luke 16:18 avoids the disavowal of Moses
that appears in Mark 10:5. The section of Mark dealing with ritual cleanliness
(Mark 7:1–23) is missing in Luke, and Luke does not have Jesus declare all
foods clean as in Mark 7:19. Jervell maintains that in the Lukan version of
Jesus' disputes about the Sabbath, there is no conflict with the law. He
observes that "Luke records no less than four disputes, and he is concerned to
show that Jesus acted in complete accordance with the law, and that the Jewish leaders were not able to raise any objections."[24]

In 1972 Jervell published the article "The Circumcised Messiah."[25] He
called special attention to the fact that only Luke has a narrative about the circumcision of Jesus, and he regards this as especially important: "Within the
framework of the prehistory this indicates that for Luke Jesus is the true bearer
of the promises to Israel. He bears the 'sign' of Israel's identity."[26] The circumcision of Jesus in Luke 2:21 is yet another indication that Luke intends to
preserve Torah as the sign of God's people, and so this verse "indicates that
the legitimacy and right of Jesus to speak and act in the name of the God of
Israel for salvation on behalf of the people and the nations is beyond doubt."[27]

Torah-observance is therefore the sign of God's people both before and
after Jesus. The Jewish Christians, who constitute the needed continuity with
Israel, fully observe the law, but what about the Gentiles? They should be
treated in precisely the way Torah describes; that is, no more and no less
should be imposed on the Gentiles than Moses required. This point is made at
the apostolic council described in Acts 15 and specifically enunciated in Acts
15:20. The God-fearing Gentiles must refrain from idolatry, food offered to
idols, ritual fornication, and blood. Jervell, aware of the vigorous controversy
surrounding the apostolic decree, does not regard it as embodying moral commands but ritualistic requirements: "The apostolic decree enjoins Gentiles to
keep the law, and they keep that part of the law required for them to live
together with Jews. It is not lawful to impose upon Gentiles more than Moses
himself demanded. It is false to speak of the Gentiles as free from the law. The
church, on the contrary, delivers the law to the Gentiles as Gentiles."[28] Jervell
insists that the idea of Gentiles as an associate people with Jews as constituting Israel is not a new idea. What is new, however, is the inclusion of Gentiles
as uncircumcised.

Jervell paid significant attention to the apostolic decree in an article on the
topic published in 1995.[29] He announced his thesis at the beginning of the article: "The law of Moses as the law of the people of God signifies for Luke a
confession of the one God of Israel as well as opposition to idolatry. The
decree binds the Gentiles to the law and to Israel and, through the four rules,
requires them to avoid idolatry and preserve the purity of the people of God."[30]
Actually, Jervell believes the decree to be historical. He notes that its original
meaning may have signified a release from the law but that Luke did not
understand it that way. For Luke, it was the way to incorporate God-fearing

Gentiles into the people of God, to preserve the purity of Israel, and to oppose idolatry. In Lukan theology, the chief function of the law is to oppose idolatry. Israel has not been faithful to the law in this respect, but those Jews who responded to Jesus have, and in order to keep Israel pure and avoid idolatry, the uncircumcised Gentiles must adhere to that part of Torah meant for them. But the apostolic decree, says Jervell, does not abolish the distinction between Jews and Gentiles, since circumcision is not required for Gentiles: "The decree makes it clear that the distinction between Jew and Gentile still stands. The Jew remains Jew and the Gentile Gentile. The latter cannot become Jew, and there is never any talk of a 'third race.' The object of the decree is clear: the purity of the people of God, so that the church can remain the people of God."[31]

Jervell's considerations about Lukan theology lead him to a reconstruction of the history of early Christianity. He knows that the church in Jerusalem was composed of Jewish Christians, but he thinks there was at an early date an element in the church that was open to Gentiles and "liberal" on Torah observance: "The church in Jerusalem was originally of a 'mixed' composition, partly 'liberal' on questions of law and temple and open-minded regarding to uncircumcised [sic]. Later we find a theological severity on these points. A strongly Jewish imprint on theology and ethics is not there from the very beginning but develops later. This is not so much a part of Luke's concept but is inherent in the material which he treats in a faithful manner."[32] Despite the fact that Luke did not invent this concept, the growing dominance of the conservative wing of Jewish Christians may nevertheless be traced in Acts, and the apostolic decree is one of the main signs of it. According to Jervell, the conservative Jewish Christians did not become active and theologically articulate until about the time of the apostolic conference, which he dates c. 48 CE. At that time the Jewish Christians were able to compel the leaders to demand that Gentile Christians be required to abide by the Noahide regulations: "No matter how we value the apostolic decree it imposes demands on the Gentile Christians, demands which were not there from the beginning."[33] After the council, this group, still associated with the church in Jerusalem, became dominant: "And we find outside Jerusalem and in connection with the church in Jerusalem a very self-conscious Jewish Christianity."[34] And then, in the postapostolic period, the Jewish Christians constituted a "mighty minority" in the church: "The minority, that is, Jewish Christianity in the second part of the first century, remained in the church throughout the century, not *a* but *the* great power, determining the thinking, the theology, and the preaching of the Christian church."[35]

Here again Jervell quite consciously goes against the consensus in reconstructing the history of Christianity in the first century. The usual view is that Jewish Christianity all but died out after 70 CE. Jervell, however, thinks that it became more powerful, although not numerically dominant, within the church as a whole. This reconstruction explains the greater conservatism toward the end of the century, and it explains a phenomenon related to the composition of Acts. Paul in Acts is shown to be a conservative Jewish Christian, a Pharisee, who believes everything written in the law and the prophets, and who claims to be on trial for a distinctively Pharisaic belief, belief in the resurrection. Why is it necessary for Luke to portray Paul in this way, apparently in contrast to the Paul of the epistles? Jervell's answer is that, given the growing conservatism, Paul had become a problem, as represented in the comments of James in Acts 21:21: "They have been told about you that you teach all the Jews living among the Gentiles to forsake Moses, and that you tell them not to circumcise their children or observe the customs." Luke clearly regards this as a false charge against Paul, but one made by powerful people, and so he must defend Paul by showing him to be meticulous in his observance of Torah and a loyal Pharisee who believes the scriptures.

In Acts, Paul is actually "the teacher of Israel." In an essay first published in 1968 and titled "Paul, the Teacher of Israel: The Apologetic Speeches of Paul in Acts,"[36] Jervell asks about the purpose of the speeches in Acts 21–28. He notes that it has been difficult to find a convincing reason for the inclusion of these speeches in Acts. Dibelius's contention that Luke meant them to support Christians under threat of persecution meets with the problem that the speeches are very heavily biographical, i.e., they fit only the Pauline situation. The idea that they are meant as political apologetic is also difficult to maintain, since Roman governors are not presented in a very good light in these chapters. Jervell's view is that the apologetic speeches are meant to defend Paul against the criticisms that powerful Jewish Christians brought forward late in the first century. He says that the charges against Paul that are reflected in Acts deal with Paul's teaching Jews, not Gentiles, and have nothing to do with Roman politics: "Further, just as the Gentile mission is not cited as the basis for the accusations against Paul, so also it does not appear as a theme in Paul's apologetic speeches. The main point is not what Paul teaches Gentiles, nor is it that he preaches to them; rather, it consists in what he teaches Jews and that he is precisely the one who appears as the teacher of Israel."[37]

At one point Luke portrays James as Paul's champion. James must have been known to Luke's readers as an indisputable authority, whose "orthodox" Judaism was well known. In Acts he actually makes more controversial statements on the law than Paul does: "But since Luke knows the 'historical' James and his faithfulness to the law, and since Luke can assume that his Jewish Christian readers regard James as an incontestable authority, he can attribute to him certain daring viewpoints. James needs no defense, but he can be used in the defense of Paul."[38] All of this is evidence for Jervell that, even as late as the writing of Luke-Acts in the 80s, conservative Jewish Christians constituted a powerful, respected, and influential element in the church. And Luke wrote "for Christian readers who are under fire from their Jewish neighbors because of Paul."[39]

But Jervell goes a step farther to claim that the Paul of Acts is not unhistorical. Going consciously against a strong scholarly consensus and objecting especially to the contentions of Philip Vielhauer,[40] Jervell reminds us that the letters of Paul were occasional letters, which do not require full biographical information. He writes, "As such they [the Pauline letters] obviously conceal parts of Paul's preaching and activity, since it was not necessary to treat such in a letter."[41] The Paul of Acts is "the unknown Paul," the Paul who emerges from the shadows of the letters. In his essay on "Paul in the Acts of the Apostles: Tradition, History, and Theology," first published in 1979 and republished in his collection of essays under the title, *The Unknown Paul,*[42] Jervell announces his thesis: "My thesis is as follows: The Lukan Paul, the picture of Paul in Acts, is a completion, a filling up of the Pauline one, so that in order to get at the historical Paul, we cannot do without Acts and Luke."[43] Jervell does not insist that every detail of the Acts portrait should be regarded as historically correct. Rather he emphasizes the Lukan treatment of Paul as a practicing Pharisee. And Jervell calls attention to those places in the Pauline letters where Paul claims to have lived as a Jew—Rom 9:7; 11:2; Gal 2:15; 2 Cor 11:22, and especially 1 Cor 9:20. In general these references in Paul's letters certify the context in which he saw himself. The reference from 1 Cor 9:20 speaks of Paul's practice: "To the Jews I became as a Jew, in order to win Jews. To those under the law I became as one under the law (though I myself am not under the law) so that I might win those under the law." Jervell notes that in first-century Judaism orthopraxis is more important than orthodoxy, and so he can conclude that the Lukan Paul's claim to have lived as a Jew means that, in his own practice, he observed Torah: "But Paul adheres to the law as a Jew and as a Christian."[44] And it is as a Pharisee faithful to Torah that Paul is represented in Acts. He has Timothy circumcised in Acts 16:3 and provides support to men fulfilling a vow in Acts 21:22–26. The latter story "emphasizes that Paul is a Jewish Christian, and as such is a venerator of the Mosaic torah."[45] Jervell concedes that Luke has built his portrait of Paul "on material to be found in the marginal notes in Paul's letters."[46] But the Acts picture can be harmonized theologically with one of Paul's letters, actually a single section of one of Paul's letters, namely Romans 9–11.[47] Here Paul emphasizes the irrevocable covenant of God with Israel and projects the expectation of the eventual inclusion of all Israel in the believing community. And Jervell concludes, "I am therefore inclined to assert that what Luke writes on the subject of Paul is historically correct, even if not in detail—and we have in Luke of course not the whole of Paul. But the practicing Jew Paul, the missionary of Israel and to Israel, the theologian for whom Israel's salvation is the goal of his work—all these important Lukan views can be found in Paul's letters."[48]

Further, Jervell writes, "I do not for a moment doubt that the author of Acts knew Paul well, if not personally."[49] In one of his most recent books, Jervell asserts that the author of Acts is Luke, the companion of Paul mentioned in Col 4:14, 2 Tim 4:11, and Phm 24. He recognizes the problems pointed out by critical scholars but maintains that the Luke mentioned in these passages is the author. After all, the letters of Paul give us a one-sided view: "You can find all Pauline theological conceptions in Acts, even if sometimes in a rudimentary form. And all the concepts of Paul in Acts can be traced to the Pauline letters, but there more in the background and in the shade, without significant theological importance. What we find in Acts is the average, unpolemical theology, which characterizes Paul apart from his most polemical letters in the times of his hardest controversies."[50] Jervell admits that Luke made some biographical errors, but he says that so did Paul: "And in biographical matters Paul is not always the one who presents the correct version. When it comes to the Apostolic Decree, never mentioned by Paul, Luke is obviously correct. . . . But Paul did not see the decree as binding for himself."[51]

One of the apparent conflicts between the Pauline letters and Acts on the characterization of Paul has to do with the question of Paul's apostleship. It is well known that Paul emphatically defends his status as an apostle (see, e.g., Galatians 1). It is also well known that Paul does not meet the criterion for being an apostle as set up in Acts 1:21–22 and that he is not listed as an apostle in Acts 1:13. In only two verses is Paul (along with Barnabas) referred to as an apostle, indirectly in Acts 14:4 and directly in Acts 14:14. Jervell addressed this problem in a paper delivered to the Society of New Testament Studies in 1985.[52] Here he referred to the Lukan Paul as *Überapostel,* or "Super-Apostle." He claimed that in Acts Paul is not portrayed as being an apostle alongside the others, and he cited four supportive indications. First, Paul's call is based on an incomparable revelation, which shows that his standing in the church does not come from an apostolic tradition but from God himself. Second, Paul is the only world-apostle or world-witness in Acts. Third, only Paul has a farewell discourse (Acts 20:17–38). Fourth, there are a number of parallels between Jesus and Paul, which prompt the reader to think of them together. So Luke refrains from granting Paul the title, apostle, because he thinks of him as ranking well above those who have the title.

Before the publication of Jervell's commentary on Acts, his critics could claim that his innovative solutions to problems in the Lukan corpus lacked a firm exegetical basis. The Acts commentary, which appeared in 1998, neutralizes this criticism. It serves as the culmination of Jervell's work on Acts. For one who is familiar with his previous scholarship, there are no surprises, but in its more than 600 pages it provides a consistent and comprehensive reading of the text that promises to be a major guide to future generations of critical scholars.

Jervell's approach to the authorship and historical validity of Acts is conservative. He believes it was written by a coworker and fellow traveler with Paul, that the "we sections" and other reports constitute eye-witness testimony, and that Luke was in touch with others of Paul's coworkers and drew on the information they were able to supply. Luke was, according to Jervell, a Jewish Christian, perhaps born as a Gentile but a God-fearer who had deep roots in Hellenistic-Jewish Christianity. Luke's intention in writing was "to demonstrate to his readers that the church is really Israel, that the promises are now being fulfilled and so salvation is given."[53]

An interesting theme to trace in Jervell's commentary is that of the conversion of God-fearers. He never departs from his insistence that Acts does not describe conversions of "pure" Gentiles but only of those Gentiles who were already associated with the synagogue. One such is the Ethiopian eunuch in Acts 8:26–40, who is a proselyte. Cornelius in Acts 10:1–11:18 is a God-fearer, as all commentators agree. Sergius Paulus in Acts 13:4–12 is not explicitly described as a God-fearer, but Jervell thinks he could scarcely be otherwise, for the following reasons. First, Acts 10:35 shows that the mission among non-Jews is a mission among God-fearers. Second, argues Jervell, the characterization of Sergius Paulus in Acts 13:7 suggests this. He is described as *synetos,* which Jervell interprets to mean, "understanding, pious, God-fearing."[54] Third, he wants to hear the word of God, which for Luke always means the Scriptures, and, fourth, he has a Jewish prophet in his court. The Gentile converts at Pisidian Antioch (Acts 13:13–52) and at Iconium (Acts 14:1–7) are said to be God-fearers, since they are, supposedly, in the synagogue with Jews. One probable exception to Jervell's rule is in the narrative of the jailer in Acts 16:29–34, who confessed faith in Jesus and was baptized. Jervell makes no comment on this character.

The last section of Acts is devoted to the trial of Paul, and here Luke includes a number of speeches intended to defend Paul against Jewish, but not Roman, charges. Jervell's comments on the conclusion of Acts (28:17–31) are among the most important in the entire commentary. He notes that many interpreters think it remarkable that when Paul arrives in Rome, he turns to speak to Jews and not to Christians. They also find it surprising that the appeal to Caesar is not mentioned, despite the fact that the appeal constituted the legal reason for Paul's being in Rome. But Jervell finds the scene to accord with Luke's earlier treatment of Paul as missionary to Jews, and so he says that only by speaking to Jews in Rome is Paul able to complete his missionary work. In a comment on Acts 28:24 he chastises those commentators who try to weaken the meaning of ἐπείθοντο. Jervell claims that it has the same meaning here as it has elsewhere, namely that they believed: "Thus a portion of Roman Jews has been selected as believing and repentant. The point here is no more that of a total rejection than elsewhere in Acts."[55]

Jervell is convinced that Paul's closing words in Acts mean to signify to the reader that the Christian mission to Jews has come to an end. The quotation of Isaiah here does not mean "that now the time of Gentile Christianity has broken in. . . . But the time of unrepentant Israel is past."[56] The previous judgments against unbelieving Jews (Acts 7:51–53; 13:46; 18:6) had geographical limitations. "But now the judgment is valid for the whole of unrepentant Judaism. All Jews throughout the world have heard the gospel. Now it is directed to Rome and the West, and with that the fate of universal Judaism is sealed. So we arrive at the turning point of history. The mission to Jews has ended, the commission of Acts 1:8 fulfilled. For 1:8 is intended to be an answer to the question about the future of Israel. A future conversion of Israel, as in Romans 11, is excluded."[57]

Assessing the Challenge

Jervell once noted that his work had been largely overlooked by German scholars: "It is perhaps no coincidence that of the reviews of my work, 90% have been in English and French, 10% in other languages, and none in German."[58] He might also have added that few of the English-language reviews appeared in those journals usually associated with mainline critical scholarship.

Most of the reviews of *Luke and the People of God* and *The Unknown Paul* expressed appreciation for Jervell's work, while questioning some of the specific aspects. John Carroll thought Jervell's reassessment of the Jewish character of early Christianity was salutary but that he assigned a too high degree of veracity to popular traditions in Acts.[59] His generalizing assessment is fairly typical. After a careful review of *The Unknown Paul,* he says that Jervell's work, while "provocative and refreshing . . . is also exaggerated and one-sided."[60] Earle Ellis doubted that Luke would have been able to portray James as artificially as Jervell claims: "Since James was a widely known figure [at the time Luke wrote], a Lukan apologetic about him that was not historically defensible to some reasonable degree would be self-defeating, discounted from the outset."[61] A number of reviewers questioned Jervell's assessment of the strength of Jewish Christianity toward the end of the first century. Schuyler Brown noted that Jervell based his argument about the role of the Jewish Christians on the stress in Luke-Acts on the Jewish connection of the early Christian movement.[62] But Brown said that such a theology would have been relevant not only to Jewish Christians but also to those Gentile Christians who saw in Judaism the "antiqua religio" that provided the historical character that the Christian movement needed in the Roman world.[63]

Several reviewers have called attention to resemblances between the work of Jervell and that of F. C. Baur, noting that both scholars saw conflict in early Christianity between a Jewish-Christian branch and a Pauline-Christian branch and understood Acts as a conciliatory document. C. K. Barrett made this point, not in a book review but in a perceptive article, "What Minorities?" published in a Festschrift for Jervell in 1995,[64] and he added: "Everyone knows that F. C. Baur based his understanding of early Christian history on the existence of controversy (if that is a strong enough word). Baur's account of the history has been widely abandoned; understandably, since Baur set it out in relation to the dates that he ascribed to New Testament documents. Since Baur's time many of these dates have been shown to be mistaken and with them Baur's whole view of New Testament history has been jettisoned— understandably, but in error."[65] Barrett inclines toward a view that would support Baur and Jervell but without Baur's dates or Jervell's historical reconstruction: "Acts is best explained as the honest but not always accurate product of an age of consensus, written at a moment of peace when the old conflicts were no longer understood and new ones had not yet broken out."[66]

Although not all reviewers expressed appreciation for it, Jervell has made a significant contribution to the understanding of Luke's treatment of Judaism and the Jewish people. Not only does he challenge the scholarly consensus, he also offers for consideration a significantly different alternative interpretation. In his paper delivered to the SBL Seminar on Luke-Acts in 1991, he correctly noted, "One of the pressing problems in the theological interpretation of Luke-Acts today is what may be called the Jewishness of Luke's work. There is today no serious question about the existence of this Jewishness, even if it was forgotten or overlooked for years."[67] As evidence of Luke's Judaism, Jervell points to the author's Christology, ecclesiology, soteriology, and use of Jewish customs and concepts. It would not be far from the mark to say that, for Jervell, the main contention of Luke-Acts is embraced in a saying that he quotes: "Luke knows that *extra Israel nulla salus est,* that Israel is the one and only people of God destined for salvation."[68] To my knowledge, Jervell is the first to attribute this motto to Luke, and one has the impression that he would adopt and adapt it in his own theology.

It is especially important to recognize the contribution that Jervell has made to the understanding of Judaism in Luke-Acts and the implications of his assessment. As we have seen in previous chapters of this book, the overwhelming emphasis in critical scholarship has been on the alleged negative character of Judaism in the Lukan texts. Although there have been significant modulations in the literature we have examined, it is fair to say that Jervell's is the first scholarly study of Luke-Acts to provide the reader with anything like a positive view of first-century Judaism and of the ancient author's perception of it.

In our studies of previous scholarship, we have seen that three factors are frequently interrelated: (1) the scholar's view of first-century Judaism, (2) the scholar's view of modern Judaism, and (3) the scholar's view of Luke's treatment of first-century Judaism. In the case of Jervell, we have few explicit statements on the first two topics. His focus has been almost exclusively on the Lukan text. In his published dissertation, *Imago Dei,* he exhibited his competence in handling rabbinic materials and recognized the diversity within them. But there is little else. Jervell's studies have, nevertheless, contributed to a reappraisal of first-century Judaism by insisting on an interpretation of Luke-Acts that stresses a strong historical and theological relationship between early Judaism and early Christianity. The positive attitude toward Torah that Jervell finds in the Lukan text contrasts sharply with its appraisal in earlier scholarship.

There is also little evidence of Jervell's views on contemporary Judaism or Jewish-Christian relations. In the last chapter of a recent publication, *The Theology of the Acts of the Apostles,* he addressed the topic of the significance of Acts for today but said nothing about modern Jewish-Christian relations. He noted that the church of Luke had problems because it consisted of Jews and non-Jews and that Luke had a way of dealing with these problems. Then he added, "Our problems in the church of today in this field are not the relations between Jews and Gentiles, but those between different groups coming from various nations, cultures, political backgrounds etc."[69] But, again, Jervell's work has had a significant impact on scholars who perceive a relationship between Christian views of Judaism and modern expressions of antisemitism. As we shall see, several of them have found in Jervell's work a basis for a new kind of scholarship on Luke-Acts, scholarship that is no less sound than that of earlier critics but is more explicit in its social awareness.

Central to Jervell's program is his contention that, for Luke, the church derives credibility only from its Jewish foundation. Several considerations support this central argument, and some of these considerations now require our examination. Although a number of facets of Jervell's work might be addressed, we shall limit our examination to four interrelated topics: (1) the definition of Israel, (2) Jewish acceptance of the Christian message, (3) the role of the God-fearers, and (4) Luke and anti-Judaism.

(1) The Definition of Israel

Jervell is right to point out that Luke never uses the term, "new Israel," to refer to the church and probably correct to say that Luke has no such concept. Jervell is, however, willing to use other terms, such as "restored Israel" and "true Israel," terms that may carry many of the same connotations as "new Israel." Moreover, there is some confusion that results from inconsistent definitions of Israel in Jervell's work. In some cases, he uses Israel to refer to all Jews, but in other cases it means only the Christian Jews. Consider the following: "In Acts, 'Israel' continues to refer to the Jewish people, characterized as a people of repentant (i.e., Christian) and obdurate Jews."[70] But later in the same paragraph we have, "'Israel' does not refer to a church that is made up of Jews and Gentiles, but to the repentant portion of the 'empirical' Israel."[71] Of course, one may distinguish between the empirical Israel and something else, perhaps, 'spiritual' Israel, but this language is not consistently employed in Jervell's work. Later Jervell explicitly states that "Israel" includes the excluded, that is the non-Christian Jews. "After the completion of the mission to the Jews, the time of the Gentile mission, as predetermined in the history of salvation, began; and this is the time of Luke. In this way Luke is able to explain why *there still is an Israel alongside and unrelated to the Christian church,* to which the church is not obligated. The reason is that *this Israel includes the Jews who were excluded from the people of God* on account of their rejection of the gospel and who have no right to the name 'Israel.'"[72] In any event, Jervell's basic insistence is that the Jewish-Christian portion of the early church is the continuation of Israel and that the unrepentant Jews are being eliminated from Israel.

Jervell describes the ministry of Jesus and the mission of the apostles as that of dividing Israel into the two groups: the repentant and the obdurate. Another way to express this is to say, "The unrepentant Jews do not represent Israel, but are being extirpated from the people (Acts 3:23)."[73] Jervell insists that this dividing of the people is in accord with scripture, and he calls on Luke's quotation of Deut 18:19 in Acts 3:23 as support. But Acts 3:23 does not accurately quote either the Hebrew or the Greek of Deut 18:19. Neither version speaks of a separation from the people, but only of undesignated punishment or recompense. It is generally thought that Luke has here combined Deut 18:19 with Lev 23:29. The Leviticus passage says that anyone who does not properly observe the Day of Atonement shall be cut off from the people. C. K. Barrett says that there may be several reasons to account for the combination of the two texts in Acts: "This may have been because Luke was quoting from memory; it may have been because he was using a collection of *testimonia* in which the OT passages had already been combined. . . ."[74] It seems equally plausible that Luke himself created the combination of verses in order to support his own theological convictions. Jervell might have reflected the situation more accurately if he had said that Luke intended to suggest that the concept of extirpation was rooted in scripture, rather than claiming that it was in fact based on scripture.

Although Jervell insists that the result of the ministries of Jesus and his immediate followers is a division of the people into the repentant and the obdurate, he pays very little attention to the latter group. Those people who have refused to accept the Christian proclamation, i.e., refused to repent, are, for Jervell, no longer a part of Israel. But how does Luke speak of them? He calls them "Jews." And in Acts, the term, "Jew" almost always denotes the opponents of the Christian missionaries. The narratives that tell of their hostility and their strategies of opposition are prominent. Jews contradict Paul at Pisidian Antioch (Acts 13:45); they stir up and poison the minds of Gentiles at Iconium (Acts 14:2); they turn the crowds against the missionaries in Lystra (Acts 14:19), Thessalonica (Acts 17:5), and Beroea (Acts 17:13); they bring charges against Paul in Corinth (Acts 18:13) and speak against him at Ephesus (Acts 19:9); and on and on. At one point Luke is able to use the terms, "Jews" and "apostles" to designate opposing factions: at Iconium "some sided with the Jews, and some with the apostles" (Acts 14:4). In connection with the trials of Paul in Acts 21–26 we read of fierce Jewish opposition, plots, and intrigues. Of course, Paul and the other Christian preachers meet opposition from non-Jews as well, but some of this opposition is, according to Acts, fomented by Jews, and in no case can it be compared with the opposition of Jews in terms of covert intrigue, repeated occurrence, and sustained hostility.

Throughout his commentary on Acts, Jervell notes that when Luke tells of this opposition to Paul he means to signify that the opposition comes from the unrepentant portion of the Jewish people. On Acts 12:3, for example, he observes that the term, "the Jews" is used in a negative sense for the first time here. And he adds: "Israel is split into believing and unbelieving, and Luke here calls the unbelieving 'Jews'"[75] And on Acts 14:4, he writes: "'Jews' here means the non-believing Jews, who are here just regarded as 'the Jews.'"[76] Of course, by definition, those Jews who refused to repent at the preaching of the Christian missionaries are unbelieving Jews, i.e., they do not believe what they have heard from the missionaries. But the problem is that Luke does not use language that makes this distinction but calls them simply, "Jews." Jervell has correctly assessed the logic of the passages in Acts but has failed to judge the rhetorical force of Luke's language. It is difficult to avoid the conclusion that, at least in the narratives about the preaching of Paul, Luke does not call the reader's attention to a division among the Jewish people but to a division between the Christians and the Jews.

(2) Jewish Acceptance of the Christian Message

As a result of his interpretation of the narratives in which Jews play roles as opponents, Jervell insists that Acts does not describe a rejection by Israel of the Christian message. He also cites the several statements in Acts about the growth of the church and the many stories of mass conversions, and he insists that, for the most part, these narratives involve Jews. He counts in Acts fourteen narratives about mass conversions, eleven of which are conversions of Jews, and he states, "There is not a single report of a mass conversion of Gentiles."[77]

But is it clear, in the eleven cases cited by Jervell, that the account is of Jewish, and only Jewish, conversions? He cites the following references in Acts: 2:41; 4:4; 5:14; 6:1, 7; 9:42; 12:24; 13:43; 14:1; 17:10ff.; 21:20. Some of these, in context, clearly speak of Jewish conversions or Jewish Christians, certainly including those in Acts 1–5 and 21:20.[78] If one agrees that Cornelius is the first non-Jewish convert in Acts, then all conversions described in Acts 1–9 would be those of Jews, but this interpretation is controversial. Acts 6:1 is not so clear, since it speaks of a division—between Hebrews and Hellenists. The two divisions may designate Hebrew-speaking and Greek-speaking Jews, but the meanings of these terms have been widely debated.[79] The reference in Acts 9:42 comes within a narrative about Peter's raising of Tabitha in Joppa, and it refers to "many" who believed as a result of Peter's act, but Luke does not specifically state who the "many" were. Acts 12:24 is another summary verse about the growth of the church. It follows the narrative about the death of Herod (Agrippa I), a story that implies the presence of a mixed audience, and it would be difficult to maintain that 12:24 designates a totally Jewish response to the Christian message.

References to the conversion of diaspora Jews in Acts 13:43; 14:1; and 17:12 are never references to the conversion of Jews alone. All speak of Jews together with others: πολλοὶ τῶν Ἰουδαίων καὶ τῶν σεβομένων προσηλύτων, "many of the Jews and of the worshipping proselytes" (Acts

13:43); πιστεῦσαι Ἰουδαίων τε καὶ Ἑλλήνων πολὺ πλῆθος, "a great number of both Jews and Greeks believed" (Acts 14:1); πολλοὶ μὲν οὖν ἐξ αὐτῶν
ἐπίστευσαν καὶ τῶν Ἑλληνίδων γυναικῶν τῶν εὐσχημόνων καὶ ἀνδρῶν
οὐκ ὀλίγοι, "many of them therefore believed, including not a few Greek
women and men of high standing" (Acts 17:12). The coupling of believers
among Jews and non-Jews is significant in indicating a transition from a
purely Jewish to a mixed community of believers.

More significant is the fact that all three of the references cited above
(Acts 13:43; 14:1; 17:12) form part of a pattern that calls the reader's attention
to Jewish opposition to the Christian movement.[80] In each of the pericopes we
have essentially four stages: (1) the preaching in the synagogue, (2) acceptance by Jews and others, (3) Jewish opposition to the preaching, (4) results of
the Jewish opposition. The story of Paul and Barnabas in Iconium (Acts
14:1–7) may serve as an example of this important literary pattern. (1) Paul
and Barnabas begin by preaching in the synagogue (Acts 14:1a). (2) Many
Jews and Greeks become believers (Acts 14:1b). (3) Unbelieving Jews stir
people up against Paul and Barnabas (Acts 14:2–5). (4) Paul and Barnabas go
on to Lystra and Derbe, where they preach (Acts 14:6–7). Although Jervell is
right to call attention to the often-overlooked acceptance by Jews in Acts
14:1b and other passages, it is difficult to agree with him that Jewish acceptance is the main point of these narratives. Jewish rejection (Acts 14:2–5) is at
least equally important here as well as in other narratives (see, e.g., Acts 13:45;
17:13).

In almost every pericope that deals with the Pauline mission, Acts tells of
Jews who reject and oppose the Christian message, and this motif is an important factor in the narrative. Jervell's failure to treat seriously that component
of Israel that rejected the Christian message and opposed the missionaries provides an unbalanced view of Luke-Acts. Jervell acknowledges that some Jews
opposed the Christians, just as he notes that some Jews no longer belong to
Israel, but this fact seems to carry little weight for him. Indeed, it is almost as
if the unbelieving Jews had fallen below the horizon of consciousness.

(3) The Role of the God-Fearers
Yet another contention that is important to the case that Jervell wants to make
is his claim that Luke tells only of the conversions of God-fearers and not of
"pure" Gentiles. His comments on the mission to Lystra (Acts 14:8–20) seem
to be on target. He says that this is an attempted conversion of "pure" Gentiles
(note the idolatry and the proposed sacrifice) and that no conversions are
recorded in this pericope. The narrative about Athens (Acts 17:16–34) also
involves a mission to "pure" Gentiles, but the results are meager at best.[81]
More questionable, however, is Jervell's assertion that, in the solemn
announcements that the missionaries make about going to Gentiles (Acts
13:46: 18:6), the meaning is that they are going to God-fearers. Support for

this view is found in the fact that the narratives following these announcements show the missionaries once again in synagogues, but the contention rests only on an inference that Jervell draws from the narratives rather than from any specific statements in the text.

Jervell's contention also rests on his interpretation of a series of verses that, according to him, tell of the conversion of God-fearers. He lists the following: Acts 11:21, 24; 13:43; 14:1; 17:4, 12; 18:8, 10.[82] Some of these references form parts of narratives that tell of the Christian missionaries speaking in synagogues, and Jervell asks what kinds of Gentiles would one find in synagogues and answers that they would have been God-fearers. But Luke does not call them God-fearers, and since we are largely dependent on Acts for the definition of this term, it would be prudent to be cautious at this point.[83] What do we actually find in these verses that Jervell cites?

- Acts 13:43 refers to the conversion of Jews and worshiping proselytes in Pisidian Antioch (πολλοὶ τῶν Ἰουδαίων καὶ τῶν σεβομένων προσηλύτων), and we are led to think of Gentile converts to Judaism.
- Acts 14:1 tells of the conversion of Jews and Greeks (Ἰουδαίων τε καὶ Ἑλλήνων πολὺ πλῆθος) in the synagogue at Iconium.
- Acts 17:4 tells of the conversion of Jews and Greeks in the synagogue at Thessalonica.
- Acts 17:12 tells of similar conversions in Beroea.

In none of the references above does Luke designate the non-Jews as God-fearers, although the synagogue setting may imply it. Others of Jervell's citations are more questionable.

- In Acts 11:21, Luke tells of a great number of believers who turned to the Lord, and in context the believers are designated as Hellenists (Ἑλληνιστάς) in Antioch.
- In Acts 11:24, Barnabas brings about the conversion of a large but unspecified crowd in Antioch.
- In Acts 18:8, we hear of the baptism of many Corinthians, who hear Paul preach in the home of a God-fearer.
- In Acts 18:10, the Lord speaks to Paul in a vision and tells him, "there are many in this city who are my people."

Jervell is certainly correct to refer to the narrative of Cornelius in Acts 10:1–11:18 as a model conversion of a God-fearer, for Luke's description of him makes this manifest. But Jervell's interpretation of the other notes of Gentile conversions requires a forcing of the evidence in Acts. The varying terms used—Greeks, Hellenists—and the indefinite designations—crowds, people—hardly suggest that Luke is depicting a special class of Gentiles that elsewhere he has been very careful to describe exactingly (see Acts 10:2).

(4) Luke and Anti-Judaism

One final question must be raised: Does Jervell's work demonstrate that Luke is free from anti-Judaism? To be sure, Jervell has given no indication that he intended to address this question. But in view of the history of NT scholarship, it is appropriate for us to ask about the implications of his work. We shall also see that several recent scholars have found Jervell's work to be liberating precisely at the point of assessing ancient Christian attitudes toward Jews.

At one level, Jervell's scholarship suggests that Luke himself is free from anti-Judaism. To accept Jervell's major contentions is to recognize that, according to Luke, there is no salvation outside Israel, that Torah was not rejected by the early Christians, that the Jewish element in the early church was powerful, and that even Paul was an observant Christian Pharisee. Israel is the people of God, and the church is not the "new Israel." A writer who holds these views does not give aid and comfort to anti-Judaism.

But there is another level to be considered. In Jervell's interpretation of Luke-Acts, the church is not the "new Israel," but it is the "restored Israel." It is in continuity with the Israel from before the time of Jesus, but *it is the only continuation*. Jervell makes this point quite clear in a number of comments: "The promises to Israel are fulfilled in the only Israel of which Luke is aware, the Jewish Christians."[84] "The identity of the church, then, is clear: it is Israel, the one and only. The Christians are heirs of the promises to Israel, and they are so as Jews."[85] Further, Jervell affirms that at the end of Acts, the divine rejection of the people Luke calls "Jews" has become clear: "Israel is divided into believers and unbelievers, and the unbelieving Jews are judged and rejected by God through the scriptures, since in fact they have denied Judaism."[86] With the proviso that the first-century church included a substantial number of Jewish converts, indeed, a "mighty minority" by the end of the century, Jervell's view of the Lukan church as the "restored Israel" and his conviction about the divine rejection of the unbelieving Jews constitute a form of supersessionism, perhaps more subtle than earlier forms, but a form nevertheless. It is still the case that the promises of God to Israel have been fulfilled, not among the people Luke calls Jews, but among the Christian believers.

Despite the reservations discussed here, it is important to observe that Jervell has managed an important redirection in Lukan studies. He has successfully shown that Luke stressed the continuity between Israel and the church, even if he has at some points overstated the case and at others left some loose ends. The positive picture of early Judaism that results contrasts markedly with those portraits found in the scholarship that we examined in previous chapters, and the positive images of Judaism in Luke-Acts have been given their due recognition.

CHAPTER 7

LATE-TWENTIETH-CENTURY AMERICAN SCHOLARSHIP

Scholarship on Luke-Acts in the last quarter of the twentieth century has been especially vigorous. The interests of Lukan scholars have been as wide-ranging during this period as in earlier times, although many authors of commentaries and monographs have expressed little interest in the issue of Israel.[1] But as our knowledge of early Judaism increased so did interest in the early history of Christian anti-Judaism. Granting that interpretations of the NT have historically been predominantly anti-Jewish, scholars at the end of the twentieth century have been especially interested in the pro-Jewish or anti-Jewish character of the NT itself. Do documents such as Luke-Acts promote or inhibit Christian anti-Judaism? This question, in regard to Luke-Acts, has been debated extensively, and the answers have ranged from categorical affirmatives to total denials.

Gerhard Lohfink maintains that Luke-Acts provides a predominantly positive image of Jews and Judaism.[2] He agrees with Jacob Jervell that Luke describes the gathering of Israel, and he stresses the Lukan concept of the church as continuous with Israel. He notes that, for the most part, the Jewish people are treated positively in Luke-Acts until Acts 5:42. In the first five chapters of Acts we have what Lohfink describes as a "Jerusalem springtime." But the story of Stephen marks drastically changed conditions. Then follow persecution, scattering, and the spread of the gospel. Why is there this change? "In the time of the first apostolic preaching, the true Israel is collected out of the Jewish people! And that Israel that still persists in rejecting Jesus loses any claim to be the true people of God—it becomes Judaism."[3] Lohfink thinks that Luke was writing at a time when the separation of his community from Judaism was clear and that Luke signaled this separation by his use of language. The rule is: "When Judaism is still spoken of as a matter of salvation history, the term is generally Ἰσραήλ and not Ἰουδαῖοι,"[4] and Lohfink notes that the latter term predominates in the latter half of Acts. Despite the differences in the perception of the historical context of Luke-Acts, Lohfink agrees with Jervell that the Gentile mission can occur because the true Israel has been gathered not because of Jewish rejection.

Matthias Klinghardt emphasizes the role of Torah in the Lukan writings.[5] He points out that Jesus' controversies with Pharisees about the Sabbath are mostly attempts to legitimate Christian practice, not to challenge the concept of Sabbath observance. The apostolic decree in Acts 15:20 is an indication of the importance of "Jewish purity laws in a form that is very close to certain Stoic-Encratite traditions."[6] This shows that Luke does not think of a strict separation between Jews and Christians but rather stands in a continuing process of separation. Klinghardt concludes that the Lukan community, like Qumran, was governed by some ritual Jewish laws and by the observance of the Sabbath. He thus agrees with Jervell that, at the end of the first century, there was a strong Jewish-Christian component in the church, although he thinks the community was more highly differentiated than Jervell had assumed. In Klinghardt's view, Luke-Acts provides evidence that the question of Torah was still being debated by Christians at the end of the first century.

Especially in his commentary on Acts, Luke Timothy Johnson emphasizes Luke's positiveness toward the Jewish people.[7] He proposes that Acts be understood as an apology, but an apology for God, thus a theodicy. The very success of the Gentile mission has "created a serious problem of confidence in the very God who accomplished it. The Gentiles have been converted only, it seems, because the Jews have rejected the Gospel."[8] Luke "will show *by the sequence of events in the story* how God in fact did offer the blessings to Israel in the first proclamation of the good news in Jerusalem, and that great numbers of Jews actually accepted the message and received the blessings of Abraham. . . ."[9] So Luke cannot evade the fact that the majority of Jews rejected the Christian message, but he refrains from portraying Jewish rejection as total. He emphasizes the popular reception of Jesus in the gospel and tells of Jewish conversions by Paul. Even when Paul meets Jewish rejection and says that he is turning to Gentiles, he returns to preach to Jews: "Even after his repeated rejections by his fellow Jews which caused him to turn to the Gentiles (13:46–47; 18:6), even after their seeking to kill him in Jerusalem by treachery (23:12–15), and cooptation of the Roman system (25:1–5), Paul still seeks out his own people. The reason is not his personal heroism but God's fidelity to the promises. They have still another chance to respond."[10]

James D. G. Dunn also stresses the continuity between Judaism and Christianity in the Lukan writings:[11] "It is important to recognize that for Luke these are the three most fundamental features—(the name of) Jesus, (the power of) the Spirit, and continuity with Israel—which mark out the movement whose beginnings he records and which define its identity most clearly."[12] Luke's primary concern in defining earliest Christianity is to maintain "that Christianity can only understand itself in relation to the people of the law and the prophets as well as by means of their message; and that the salvation which this Christianity proclaimed is also for the other nations as well."[13] On the conclusion to Acts, Dunn writes:

The mistake of those who see here the account of an irretrievable breakdown between Christianity and Judaism has been to assume that the third report of such a denunciation by Paul of his fellow Jews was intended to be the final. On the contrary, Luke was well aware that the real history continued beyond the limits of his narrative (cf. 1.11!). That was no doubt why he allowed the final scene to fade out with the image of Paul secure in Rome and preaching and teaching all who came to him openly and unhindered. That is to say, what Luke records is not so much a final scene as a definitively typical scene—the ongoing debate between believers in Messiah Jesus and traditional Jews as definitive for Christianity; the debate continues, some Jews being persuaded, other disbelieving.[14]

Despite the differences among the writers mentioned above, they are similar in their attempts to understand Luke-Acts as positive toward Israel and as stressing the continuity between Judaism and Christianity. Other scholars have, however, not been so positive in their treatments of Judaism in Luke-Acts. Robert Maddox, for example, finds Luke to be predominantly anti-Jewish.[15] He understands the purpose of Luke-Acts to be to assure Christians about the significance of the tradition in which they stand. He thinks this assurance is necessary because Christian doubt has been raised by the recognition of Jewish rejection. Christians would be thinking, "How could non-Jews hope to find any value in something which has its roots in Judaism, yet seems to be repudiated by the leaders of the Jews?"[16] In providing this assurance, Luke stresses two things: "first, that in principle there exists the possibility of agreement between Pharisaic Judaism and Christianity; but secondly, that on the whole this possibility has not been realized, because the Jews have refused to accept the plain evidence which indicates the fulfillment of their own hopes and expectations."[17] The main reason for Jewish rejection is that the leaders opposed the gospel, but Luke emphasizes the unbelieving nature of the Jewish community: "This is well exemplified in the final scene, Acts 28:17–28, where Paul calls 'the leading people among the Jews' to a discussion with him (v. 17), but at the end he quotes Isaiah's words to 'this people' (v. 26), which is contrasted with the Gentiles, who 'will actually listen' (v. 28)."[18]

François Bovon recognizes that Luke appreciates the Jewish heritage of the early Christian movement, but he also maintains that Luke has no interest in continuing the demands of the Mosaic law.[19] Luke represents a form of Hellenistic Christianity, and, although he stresses the Jewish practices of the first apostles and other witnesses, he does this as a historian, underscoring the historical roots of Christian faith, but not making a theological demand that subsequent Christians also follow Torah. For Luke, the Christian ethos is determined by the commands of the gospel, especially the double love command, not by the Mosaic law.[20]

S. G. Wilson struggles with what he regards as an ambivalent posture in Luke-Acts on the question of Torah.[21] He thinks that the Gospel of Luke exhibits little sign of any reflection on Mosaic law and that this means that, for

Luke and his Gentile-Christian readers, Jesus' attitude toward Torah was not a significant problem. But in Acts, which Wilson thinks was written some time later, things are different. When Acts was written it had become necessary to defend Paul against charges that he intended to annul the law. These charges came from Jews and Jewish Christians, so that Luke's readers "experienced non-Christian Judaism as a hostile force, and may have known of Jewish-Christian anti-Paulinism as well."[22]

M.-E. Boismard's three volumes focus almost entirely on the sources for Acts,[23] and his source theory permits him to explain Lukan ambivalence in a different way. Boismard thinks that the canonical book of Acts went through three redactions, which he calls Acts I, Acts II, and Acts III. Behind these redactions lie certain ancient documents, including a travel journal written in the first-person plural and a "Johannite" document, which maintained that the Baptist was Elijah. In Acts II, the mission to the Gentiles is regarded as essential, and to serve this end, there must be a break with Judaism on some points. In particular, strict adherence to the Mosaic law must be relaxed. But Acts II does not forget the relation of the believers to Judaism, and the author avoids condemning the Jews in block. Acts III, however, accentuates the guilt of the Jews and emphasizes their role in the death of Jesus. Jews are opponents of Paul, who call for his death and refuse God's plan to extend salvation to Gentiles. For Boismard the ambivalent attitude expressed toward the Jews in canonical Acts is the result of the combination of previous sources or redactions.

Although the scholars noted above and others have devoted attention to the issue of Israel in Luke-Acts, three recent studies by American scholars have focused special attention on this issue and created something of a "storm center." W. C. van Unnik used this term in reference to the scholarship on Luke-Acts in the mid-sixties,[24] but it is perhaps even more appropriate to use it again at the end of the century. The three, Jack T. Sanders, Robert L. Brawley, and Robert C. Tannehill, offer distinctive approaches to the problem that deserve significant consideration on our part. Analysis of their works should help us to focus attention on the most important aspects of the current discussion.

Jack T. Sanders

Jack T. Sanders, who recently retired as professor of religious studies at the University of Oregon, has worked for a number of years on Luke-Acts and has given special attention to issues relating to Luke's treatment of Judaism. His most systematic and extensive reflections on these topics are in his book *The Jews in Luke-Acts,* published in 1987.[25] In his preface, Sanders tells his readers why he is interested in this problem. The study, he says, is prompted partly by the lack of a scholarly consensus and "in part by what seems, at first reading, to be confusion in the mind of the author of Luke-Acts as to whether he is friendly or hostile to Jews."[26] But there is another aspect to Sanders's interest, "for antisemitism—and with it Christian antisemitism—is one of the more pressing social issues of our day."[27]

Sanders addresses the issues in two major sections of his book. First, he has a thematic investigation, in which he analyzes Luke's treatment of the Jewish leaders, Jerusalem, the Jewish people, the Pharisees, and what he calls the periphery (outcasts, Samaritans, proselytes, and God-fearers). Then he gives the readers a systematic analysis, first of Luke, then of Acts.

According to Sanders, the Jewish leaders in Luke-Acts, not including Pharisees, are consistently portrayed as enemies of Jesus and the church: "In the Gospel of Luke, the Jewish religious leaders are a cohesive group capable of manipulating the Roman authorities toward the end of getting rid of Jesus for very murky reasons."[28] Luke's narrative is intended to show that "the Temple authorities carried out the crucifixion of Jesus (allowed, grudgingly, by Pilate), and that they possessed the personnel so to do, captains and soldiers."[29] Sanders maintains that the soldiers who in Luke 23:36 carried out the crucifixion were Jewish soldiers, a contention that is exegetically permissible. In context, Luke tells about the two criminals, presumably Jewish, with whom Jesus was crucified (Luke 23:34), the actions of the (Jewish) leaders and the (Jewish) crowd (Luke 23:35). And so, in 23:36 we hear about the (Jewish) soldiers. Sanders notes that Luke "has sprinkled his narrative with Jewish military personnel from the beginning,"[30] and so the reader should not be surprised to find them here in the act of putting Jesus to death.

Jerusalem is for Luke "the *locus classicus* of hostility to God, to his purposes, to his messengers."[31] "If the first Jerusalem scene [Luke 1–2], then, provides only the precondition for the later hostility, the other three Jerusalem scenes express it. In scene 2 Jesus is killed, in scene 3 Stephen is killed, and in scene 4 Paul comes as close to being killed as possible without actually losing his life."[32] Sanders acknowledges that both the gospel and the Acts begin with scenes that have positive images of Jerusalem and the Jewish people. But he stresses that this "Jerusalem springtime," to use Lohfink's phrase, serves as a way for Luke to make two important points: "one, that Christianity has not broken with the ancient Israelite religion, and that, rather, a direct line of continuity runs from Moses and the Prophets to the church; and, two, that it is not Christianity that has rejected Judaism, but Judaism that has rejected Christianity."[33]

Sanders calls the problem of the Jewish people in Luke-Acts a "sticky wicket." As he lays it out, the problem is that of determining whether Luke condemns the Jewish people in their entirety, or only that portion of the Jewish people that rejects the Christian message. The former view sees Luke as considering the Jewish people without distinctions among them. Sanders identifies this view initially with Franz Overbeck and sees Ernst Haenchen as a more recent advocate of it. The other view emphasizes the concept of the divided Israel, a concept we saw treated prominently by Jervell. But Sanders also associates this view with Harnack and Conzelmann. He proposes a fresh attempt to solve the problem but acknowledges that "we shall also want to keep in mind that a successful negotiation of the thicket will be likely to bring us out upon one of two clearings: that which allows us to see that Luke thought that all Jews are perverse, or that which provides a perspective showing that he intended to represent only those who reject Christianity as perverse."[34] In other words, the solution is likely to be one of the two proposed candidates.

The key to the noted ambivalence, or confusion, of Luke in regard to the Jewish people is not to be found in his use of diverse sources, but in the difference between speech and narrative in the two texts. In brief, narrative portions of Luke-Acts show distinctions among the Jewish people; some are repentant and accepting of the Christian message, while others are obstinate and rejecting. In the speeches, however, these distinctions disappear, and all the Jews are condemned. This process begins with the speeches of Jesus in the gospel: "As the Gospel approaches its climax, the Lucan Jesus begins increasingly to use parables to voice the condemnation of the Jewish people."[35] Sanders cites the parable of the banquet (Luke 14:16–24), the rich man and Lazarus (Luke 16:19–31), the parable of the pounds (Luke 19:11–27), and the parable of the wicked tenants (Luke 20:9–19). The process of condemnation continues in Acts with the accusation that the Jewish people killed the prophets and Jesus. Luke, of course, knows that diaspora Jews, those addressed by Paul, had nothing to do with the death of Jesus, but "when Jews in Paul's Diaspora mission reject the gospel they fall under the same condemnation that is pronounced against those in Jerusalem (13.27) who actually carried out the deed."[36] Even in the first speech of Peter in Acts 2, Sanders sees a condemnation of all Jews: "The point must be made again, even at the risk of a charge of repetitiousness: it is not the priestly leadership, nor Jerusalemites, nor even Judahites or Palestinian Jews alone whom Peter accuses of 'doing away with' Jesus; it is a representative group of Jews from all over the world."[37] The speeches of Peter, Stephen, and Paul contain wholesale condemnations of the Jewish people. And so Sanders concludes:

> Thus, with the unlikely exception of Jesus' statement at the conclusion of the Zacchaeus story, Jesus, Peter, Stephen and Paul present in Luke-Acts, *in what they say on the subject,* an entirely, completely, wholly, uniformly consistent attitude towards the Jewish people as a whole. That attitude is that the Jews are and always have been willfully ignorant of the purposes and plans of God expressed in their familiar scriptures, that they always have rejected and will reject God's offer of salvation, that they executed Jesus and persecute and hinder those who try to advance the gospel, and that they get one chance at salvation, which they will of course reject, bringing God's wrath down upon them, and quite deservedly so.[38]

Sanders insists that the differences between speech and narrative in Luke-Acts are not to be explained by reference to a source theory but that both genres are the work of a single mind. He claims that "only one mind is responsible for the narrative and for the speeches, that the apparent disharmonious juxtaposition of the good Jewish people in the narrative and the bad Jewish people in the speeches is quite deliberate and serves a definite purpose, and that our author finally—and quite skillfully, one might add—brings the two together in a successful resolution."[39] Sanders notes the progression of the narrative and calls attention to mounting Jewish opposition to the mission of Paul, which ends finally in Rome:

> Thus, for all that Luke has sketched a variegated portrait of Paul's mission, he has also drawn a picture of *increasing Jewish hostility and opposition to the gospel.*[40]

> Paul is done in not by the religious authorities alone and not by Diaspora Jews alone but by THE JEWS.[41]

> By the end of the Acts the Jews have *become* what they from the first *were;* for what Jesus, Stephen, Peter and Paul say about the Jews—about their intransigent opposition to the purposes of God, about their hostility toward Jesus and the gospel, about their murder of Jesus—is what Luke understands the Jewish people to be in their essence.[42]

In other words, although Jews are treated somewhat more favorably in the earlier narratives of Luke-Acts than in the speeches, by the end of Acts the narratives and speeches agree in a totally negative judgment about the Jewish people.

Sanders rightly pays special attention to the end of Acts, which has the last of three Pauline statements announcing an end to the Jewish mission. He points out that Luke's narrative of Paul in Rome takes essentially the same form as the earlier ones, except that Luke is careful to avoid saying that some of the Roman Jews believed. He will say only that some were persuaded (Acts 28:24), and Sanders notes that Luke has elsewhere used the verb πείθω to suggest something short of conversion (cf. Acts 13:43). In any event, this verse is followed in Acts by Paul's quotation of Isa 6:9–10 and his announcement about the Gentiles. Sanders's comments here are worth quoting in full:

> Luke does not have Paul say here that he will never any more seek to convert Jews, and he does not say it himself editorially; and in this fact some modern authors find hope. These interpreters see that the same themes are present in this concluding speech as in Paul's earlier statements of turning to the Gentiles, in the episodes in Antioch and in Corinth, and they prefer to think of Luke as having created an alternating pattern of rejection and mission, a circle of going repeatedly to the Jews. But the Book of Acts is here at an end, and so is the cycle.

Jervell has seen this plainly, and it is regrettable that others who would like to ally themselves to his position have not been so clear-sighted.[43]

One of Sanders's more intriguing proposals relates to the treatment of the Pharisees in Luke-Acts. Many scholars have noted that the Pharisees in these texts constitute something of an anomaly, since there appears to be no consistently applied principle to account for both negative and semi-positive treatments. Sanders, however, concentrates on this apparent difficulty and offers a unique solution. As he had done in his analysis of the treatment of the Jewish people, again here Sanders calls attention to the differences between speech and narrative. Thus he observes, "If we leave aside for the moment, taking a clue from the preceding chapter, what Jesus says to or about the Pharisees and confine our attention to their behaviour in the narrative, we see that, quite strangely, Luke has omitted nearly all the instances of Pharisaic hostility towards Jesus that appear in Mark and Matthew and has substituted his own."[44] Sanders then notes that, in the gospel, Luke is careful to confine controversies between Jesus and the Pharisees to points of Torah observance. In the Acts, the situation is more complex, because here Luke has made some distinctions among Pharisees. Non-Christian Pharisees, such as Gamaliel, are presented in a favorable light, while Christian Pharisees, such as those who demand the circumcision of Gentile Christians in Acts 15:5, are portrayed negatively.[45] Sanders writes, "It seems that Luke has portrayed the Pharisees in this strange way in order to let them represent the position within Christianity of traditional Jews, with the added nuance that the friendly Pharisees in Acts help him to demonstrate the continuity between ancient Judaism and Christianity."[46] We thus have three groups of Pharisees: those who contend with Jesus in the gospel; the friendly Jewish Pharisees in Acts; and the Christian Pharisees who oppose the Gentile mission.

Sanders's analysis of the apostolic council in Acts 15 is especially pertinent to his argument. In the Lukan account of this incident, it is the Pharisaic Christians who demand that Gentile Christians be circumcised and commit themselves to the observance of the Mosaic Torah (Acts 15:5). The apostolic council considers this demand and agrees that only the four requirements listed in Acts 15:20 will be imposed on the Gentiles. Sanders calls special attention to Acts 15:21, which seems to serve as a defense for the imposition of the four requirements. About Acts 15:21, Sanders writes, "The meaning of this last statement seems to be that the laws prescribed for Gentile Christians in the preceding verse are nothing new and that Gentiles being converted to Christianity come under no obligation to obey any additional laws in the Torah that were not already obligatory for them in their pre-Christian state."[47] Thus, he can conclude that the result of the apostolic council of Acts 15 was a defeat for the Christian Pharisees. There is no compromise here, no attempt at reconciliation between two opposing Christian groups, as F. C. Baur had maintained, because the Pharisaic group gains nothing. Luke's position is no reconciliation; it is an invalidation of the Jewish-Christian position. Although Sanders and Jervell assess the force of the apostolic decree in similar ways, their descriptions of its function form polar opposites. Jervell maintained that the use of the apostolic decree is evidence that the church still conceives of itself as Jewish. The Jewish members continue to observe Torah, and the Gentiles observe that part of Torah intended for them. Thus , for Jervell, the Acts community is a group of Jewish Christians plus some added Gentiles. In Sanders's view, Jervell had "the relationship between Jewish and Gentile Christians reversed."[48] The rejection of the Pharisaic-Christian viewpoint in Acts 15 shows that, for Luke, the attempt to combine Jewish adherence to Torah with faith in Christ is misguided, indeed hypocritical: "When Christianity comes to be viewed as a religion separate and distinct from Judaism, which is the way Luke viewed it, then someone who tries to be both is, from a dispassionate descriptive point of view, an anomaly, but from a partisan religious viewpoint a hypocrite."[49]

Sanders's assessments of the ultimate fate of the Jewish leaders and people are sufficiently clear, but what about the Pharisees? Does Luke hold that the hypocritical Jewish Christians, who insist that Gentile Christians must circumcise their sons and observe Torah, suffer the same fate as other Jews? And what about Pharisees such as Gamaliel, who seems to be supportive of the movement? Perhaps Pharisees form something of an in-between group. The friendly non-Christian Pharisees provide a link between the Christian movement and its beginnings within Judaism. Christian Pharisees provide for the reader a signal of the way not to go. They stand for an inauthentic Christianity, but should they be grouped with the Jews who are rejected at the end of Acts? Sanders understands this to be the "most difficult question of all; for can it be that Luke intends his readers to understand that even those Pharisees who became Christians are without hope of salvation?"[50] The answer finally is yes. Luke acknowledges that they are believers (Acts 15:5), but their belief has not issued in true contrition, but in a continued attempt at self-justification. Thus they are to be called hypocrites: "The Christian Pharisees of Acts 15.5 stand, in the view of the author of Luke-Acts, under the charge of hypocrisy (Luke 12.1) because, while seeming to be 'believers,' they are in reality promoting self-justification and self-exaltation. Thus the truly contrite sinner 'goes down to his house justified instead of' the Pharisee—yes, instead of even the Christian Pharisee."[51] Under this interpretation, Jesus' warning about the leaven of the Pharisees (Luke 12:1) becomes especially apt, for Pharisaic hypocrisy is to be understood as a danger that arises from within the church. Near the end of his book, Sanders gives credit to Étienne Trocmé for the recognition that what binds both non-Christian and Christian Pharisees together is their opposition to the inclusion of Gentiles in the same movement with Jews. Sanders says, "Trocmé, however, may well have laid his finger on the issue that gives coherence to Luke's hostility towards both non-Christian Jews and Jewish Christians; for is not, in fact, the Jewish opposition to and hostility toward Christianity and Jesus, as Luke presents the matter, from first to last over the issue of the inclusion of Gentiles?"[52]

Sanders's analysis of the views about Jews in Luke-Acts forms a dramatic contrast with that of Jervell, which we considered in the previous chapter. The most fundamental questions are answered in diametrically opposite ways. For Jervell, Luke's church lays hold of the right to be Israel because it has been remarkably successful in converting large numbers of Torah-observant Jews. Gentiles are added as an associate people, but it is only Jewish Christians who have a right to be called the people of God. For Sanders, the link between Luke's church and pious Judaism is important, but the real issue for Luke is the inclusion of Gentiles, to which the Jewish Christians are opposed, except on terms that are unacceptable to Luke and his church. The church of Luke's day, therefore, can only look back upon a history which began among Jews but, despite the best efforts of leaders such as Paul, was forced into a separation. Authentic Christianity for Luke is Gentile Christianity, free of Torah.

Some scholars who prefer the interpretations of Jervell have reacted to Sanders's contention on the grounds that it is an excessively harsh overstatement.[53] It should be borne in mind, however, that he and Jervell are in complete agreement that Luke allowed no room for a continuing mission to Jews after the end of Acts. In this sense, although Jervell would strongly object to the language, both scholars conclude that, at the end of Acts, Luke has written off the Jews, understanding "Jews" to mean those who have remained unrepentant and have rejected the preaching of the apostles and Paul. This point will be contested by certain scholars whose views we shall examine later in this chapter.

A second area of agreement between Jervell and Sanders is to be seen in the understanding that both scholars have of Luke's view of the link between Christianity and Israel. That link has been well recognized in Jervell's work, but is rarely acknowledged in Sanders's. It is true that Sanders did not emphasize this in the way that Jervell did, but it is important to his work. His comments on the infancy narratives in Luke 1–2 make this point quite clearly: "In every way possible Luke informs us that Christianity did not seek an exodus out of Judaism but was rather squeezed out by the Jews. The infancy narratives play their part in that pattern, for they show how totally immersed the Christian beginnings were in good Jewish piety."[54] Sanders also observes that the beginning of Acts is similar to the beginning of Luke and that one function of this motif is to show "that Christianity has not broken with the ancient Israelite religion, and that, rather, a direct line of continuity runs from Moses and the Prophets to the church. . . ."[55] Both Jervell and Sanders would agree that the Lukan church stands in continuity with the religion of ancient Israel.

But there are important differences that must be faced. Sanders denies that

Israel was simply divided by the ministry of Jesus and the apostles. He does not see Jesus as "gathering Israel." And, without question, he perceives the darker aspects of Luke's portrayal of Jews. Some of the difference is to be laid to Jervell's failure to give sufficient consideration to what he termed the unbelieving part of Israel and by Sanders's concentration on this element. Sanders's darker picture results partly from his considerations about the roles of the Jewish leaders and people and partly from his assumption about the Lukan context. Two matters are fundamental to Sanders's project. One is the distinction he draws between speech and narrative; the other is his description of the Pharisees.

There is no problem with the formal distinctions Sanders draws between speech and narrative. Further, although one may quibble at some specific interpretations, it may be granted that the images of Jews and Judaism in the narratives do not always conform with what is said about them in the speeches. Sanders may be right in claiming that the differences between speech and narrative in Luke-Acts have produced a situation in which scholars have been unable to agree on the interpretation of Luke's views about Judaism. His refusal to account for the differences by resorting to a source theory means that he does not want to take a relatively easy alternative. He is also right to claim that, in the final analysis, a source theory does not offer a sufficient explanation, since it provides no way to account for the activity of a final redactor who brought conflicting sources together. But is Sanders's explanation any more credible? Under his interpretation we are called upon to believe that the author quite consciously used different literary genres to express different theological views, while carefully manipulating the narrative so that it progressively represents what the speeches have been claiming all along. Sanders applauds this procedure and calls attention to the author's remarkable literary skill. He might also have congratulated the reader who would have had the skill to discern the meaning of this procedure. What Sanders claims is possible, but one wonders if there is not a more plausible explanation, one that would not make such severe demands on the intended reader.

Sanders's discussion of the Pharisees in Luke-Acts may well be unique. As we have seen, he finds three groups of Pharisees in Luke-Acts: (1) those who are frequently in controversy with Jesus and are condemned by him, although he often enjoys social intercourse with them; (2) those who, like Gamaliel, are somewhat protective if not supportive of the church as well as those members of the Sanhedrin who agree with Paul about resurrection; and (3) those who become believers but oppose the Gentile mission as Luke conceives it. But this pie may be sliced differently and allow for only two pieces, since Sanders also argues that the Pharisees in the gospel are actually surrogates for the Christian Pharisees, or Jewish Christians, in Acts.

In any case, this is a very complex kind of characterization for a first-century author. Could Luke have expected an audience to be able to keep the different kinds of Pharisees apart, recognizing the similarities and differences as well as agreeing to the varying degrees of evaluation? This seems highly doubtful.

Further, we may ask if Sanders has built a convincing case for his contention that the Pharisees in the gospel are surrogates for the Christian Pharisees in Acts? In the Gospel of Luke, the Pharisees and Jesus are shown to be in controversy over points of *halakah*. On Luke 5:33, for example, Sanders comments, "The issue is practice, *halakah;* and the Pharisees are consistently shown to be following petty rules, whereas Jesus pays attention to significant issues."[56] Sanders also notes that Luke does not associate the Pharisees with the Jewish leaders, who bring about Jesus' death. He has this comment on Luke 9:22: "We thus see how systematically Luke has kept the opposition to Jesus from the Jerusalem leadership, which culminates in Jesus' death, separate from the disagreements with the Pharisees over practice, which disagreements do not preclude acts of overt friendliness towards Jesus (and, later on, towards the church) on the part of the Pharisees. It is this kind of distinction that points to the Torah-observing Jewish Christians of Luke's own day as the people whom he wishes to criticize by his portrayal of the Pharisees."[57] Although Luke distinguishes between the Pharisees and the Jerusalem priests and never directly implicates the former in the death of Jesus, it is not at all clear how this indicates that these Pharisees are surrogates for the Jewish Christians of Luke's own day. Is the reader to understand that noninvolvement in the death of Jesus is somehow suggestive of or tantamount to being a believer in him?

In addition, what must we make of the claims of the Lukan Paul about his own identification with Pharisees? Sanders calls the statement in Acts 23:6 a Pauline "ploy": "Saying in the Sanhedrin that he is a Pharisee is therefore like telling his Philippian jailers that he is a Roman (Acts 16:37); it is just a way of getting out of trouble."[58] A similar Pauline claim in Acts 26:5 is meant simply to show that Paul has been a good Jew and to remind the reader that some Pharisees (Jewish ones) are good to the church. Of course, Sanders is right at one level: the Pauline claims function as his defenses. But there seems to be another level, where Luke is bringing together the preaching of Paul, the belief in resurrection, and some relation with Pharisees. This aspect of Luke's project, which is stressed in a number of interpretations, is barely acknowledged by Sanders, although he notes that Luke wanted to call attention to certain links between Christian faith and that of the non-Christian Pharisees. Indeed, one might be inclined to suggest that Sanders should add to his list of Pharisees one more type: the Pauline Pharisee, who believes in resurrection and the mission to the Gentiles. This would add complication to an already complex interpretation, but it would at least acknowledge another important Lukan theme.

Sanders has often been associated with the view that Luke "has written the Jews off," a phrase he quotes from Ernst Haenchen[59] in connection with his description of the position that Luke condemns all Jews without distinction.[60]

Notably, he acknowledges that both this view and that of a divided Israel—the
view of Harnack, Conzelmann, and Jervell—find support in Luke's text, since
the speeches and the narratives sometimes go in different directions. But he
argues that the speeches and the narratives come together at the end of Acts
and that the result is that the Jews have become what the various Christians
from Jesus to Paul said they were—unheeding, unhearing, blind, and obstinate. And so Paul announces the end of the Jewish mission, an announcement
that, according to Sanders, is intended to have finality. In the sense that Luke
anticipates no further mission to the Jews by Christians, he has written them
off.

    In the last paragraph of *The Jews in Luke-Acts,* Sanders states his concep-
tion of Luke's view quite clearly: "In Luke's opinion, the world will be much
better off when 'the Jews' get what they deserve and the world is rid of
them."[61] Lest he be understood as endorsing this view, Sanders adds: "The
modern reader of Luke-Acts is now forced to ask whether Luke's polemic
against 'Jews' has not become the leaven within Christianity—and within
Western society—against which we must all and eternally be on guard."[62]

Robert L. Brawley

Robert L. Brawley, professor of New Testament at McCormick Theological
Seminary in Chicago, sees himself in deep opposition to the views expressed
by Jack Sanders and others. In the introduction to his book on Jews in Luke-
Acts he announces his position: "I am adding my voice to a growing chorus of
scholars who are protesting the notion that Luke depicts the triumph of gentile
Christianity at the expense of Jews, and who are formulating a construct of
Luke's thought in relation to his life in an environment where inner Jewish
questions are still viable."[63] Sanders's and Brawley's books were published the
same year, and although neither was able to cite the other's book, their basic
viewpoints had been made known in selected articles.[64] In a number of ways,
Brawley's position is similar to Jervell's. It is necessary only to comment on
those contributions of Brawley that seem distinctive.

    Brawley's fundamental argument is that Luke does not portray a Gentile
Christianity that is opposed to Judaism. The Lukan Paul and the Gentile mission are, instead, accommodated toward Judaism, at least toward Judaism as
Luke understands it.[65] Brawley writes: "Therefore, the standard paradigm for
understanding Luke's view of the relation between Christianity and Judaism
should pivot 180 degrees. That is, rather than setting gentile Christianity free,
Luke ties it to Judaism. And rather than rejecting the Jews, Luke appeals to
them."[66]

    Brawley's distinctive contributions may be seen in his contention (1) that
Acts tells the story of Paul rather than the story of the Gentile mission;
(2) that Pharisees are treated positively and with respect in Luke-Acts; and
(3) that the end of Acts does not announce the rejection of the Jews. We shall
comment on each of these points.

(1) Acts tells the story of Paul rather than the story of the Gentile mission.
Brawley pays particular attention to certain legitimizing techniques that he
finds in Luke-Acts. Following the lead of Charles Talbert, he understands that
one of the major purposes of Acts is to identify the legitimate exponents of the
Jesus movement after the time of the founder.[67] Paul is one of the authoritative
successors of Jesus, but he is not to be understood as a symbol of Christianity
or of the movement to the Gentiles. As he did with Jesus in the gospel, so also
in Acts Luke makes a special effort to legitimate Paul, and he does so in terms
of conventional Hellenistic techniques: "Luke uses at least six major cate-
gories of legitimating techniques, all of which have remarkable parallels in
Hellenistic literature: (1) divine approval, (2) access to divine power, (3) high
motivation, (4) benefiting others, (5) possessing a high level of culture, and (6)
adhering to an ancient tradition."[68]

Brawley thus maintains that the latter half of Acts is the story of Paul, not
the story of the Gentile mission. Luke knows of a number of other missions,
to which he alludes, but his interest is in the story of Paul: "He knows of
Philip's mission to Samaritans, to the Ethiopian eunuch, and to Phoenicia. He
is aware of the evangelization of Phoenicia, Cyprus, Antioch, and Damascus
by those who were scattered from Jerusalem by persecution. He summarizes
the mission of Barnabas and Mark after the former separates from Paul. He
mentions the work of Apollos at Ephesus and Corinth. Luke alludes to Christians in Rome who greet Paul on his arrival there. But the story of the extension of Christianity does not occupy center stage for Luke. Rather, he places
Paul in the limelight."[69] Brawley further maintains that Paul does not fulfill
the prediction of Acts 1:8 by going to Rome. Rome is not, for Acts, the end of
the earth, and Jerusalem functions as the goal for Paul rather than Rome. His
arrival in Rome is "anti-climactic," and it occurs as the result of a legal appeal.
Brawley suggests that, if Luke had meant to describe the Christian mission to
the Gentiles, he had the materials to do so. But, instead of filling out his narrative with descriptions of missions to a number of places in the Gentile world,
he chose instead to tell the story of Paul.

The point that Brawley wants to show is that Luke does not stress the
Gentile mission at the expense of the Jews. His contention that the latter half
of Acts is a biography of Paul rather than an account of the Gentile mission is
intended to support this claim. So Brawley stresses the point that Jews are
never definitively rejected by Paul. He acknowledges, against Jervell, that
Paul reorients his mission toward Gentiles as a result of Jewish unbelief:
"Against Jervell, in Acts Jewish antagonism is connected causally with the
reorientation of mission. But against the standard theory of reciprocal rejection, it is connected with the gentile mission only when Paul is involved."[70]
The meaning seems to be that the turning away from Jews and to Gentiles is a
personal decision of Paul, but Brawley also makes it clear that, according to
Luke, the reorientation is in accordance with the will of God. Important also
is the observation that, even after announcing his resolve to go to Gentiles

(Acts 13:46–47; 18:6), Paul goes back to preach to Jews: "Although Paul meets Jewish obduracy with severe warnings, he never gives up on the Jews as such."[71] Further, says Brawley, although Luke never delineates Paul's gospel, we may infer its contents from the apostolic decree, his sermons, and his apologetic speeches. These uniformly give us a glimpse of a Christian missionary who stresses continuity with Judaism. Paul himself is described as faithful to the Jewish law and customs and loyal to the Jewish people. His belief in the resurrection is said to conform with Pharisaic belief and constitutes the hope of Israel. Paul's adherence to an ancient tradition is important to Luke's legitimizing techniques.

(2) Pharisees are treated positively and with respect in Luke-Acts.
Pharisees function in part as an aspect of Luke's legitimization of Jesus and the apostles. Brawley maintains that, in the world of the author of Luke-Acts, Pharisees were persons of great respect. In showing that they came to Jesus and discussed points of Torah observance with him, Luke elevates the position of Jesus in the mind of the reader. Brawley admits that Luke does not always treat the Pharisees favorably, and he cites special Lukan material such as the parable in Luke 18:9–14 as an example. But he calls attention to certain differences between Luke and the other synoptic gospels that show that Luke's intent is to compare Jesus with Pharisees and thus to show that his teaching is superior to theirs. They are not hostile to Jesus, and at least on one occasion (Luke 17:20) they come to him as "honest inquirers." The Lukan portrayal is even more positive in Acts, and Brawley calls attention to the roles of Gamaliel (Acts 5:34–39), the Christian Pharisees (Acts 15:5), and the Pharisaic supporters of Paul in the Sanhedrin (Acts 23:6–10). He refers to an article by Jack Sanders, the substance of which appeared later in the book we discussed above.[72] Brawley writes appreciatively of Sanders's article and expresses agreement with many of its points. He disagrees vigorously, however, with Sanders's identification of Pharisees in Luke with Jewish Christians in Acts. He scores Sanders for his failure to consider the context within which Luke wrote: "But beyond these incorrect turns, Sanders misses the point that Luke writes in an environment where the Pharisees hold a rather respectable position for both Luke and his readers. And this accounts for the positive way the Pharisees function in Luke-Acts."[73] Brawley concludes the chapter on the Pharisees thus: "Luke takes over the Pharisees in a historical, cultural, and religious context in which they demand admiration and assigns them a commensurate role. In Acts they legitimate the apostles, Paul, and Christianity. In Luke, they legitimate even Jesus. They can fulfill their function in Acts only because they occupy a position of respect and authority."[74]

(3) The end of Acts does not announce the rejection of the Jews.
Here, of course, the focus of attention is on the two meetings of Paul with Roman Jews (Acts 28:17–28). Brawley acknowledges that, at the end of the

second meeting, Paul announces his intention to go to Gentiles and that this is due to the negative response of some of the Roman Jews. But he calls attention to the fact that Paul's words in Acts 28:28 do not include a specific anathema of Jews. Finally, he refers to Acts 28:30: "He [Paul] lived there two whole years at his own expense and welcomed all who came to him." The key to this verse is the word, "all" (πάντας). Brawley writes: "If 'all' is consistent within its context, it would include Jews, both the curious and the believers. At any rate, *Paul's preaching no longer rouses Jewish opposition in Rome.* Is Paul at peace because Luke has written off the Jews, or because Luke wishes to leave the impression that Paul's mission among gentiles has been adequately explained? Since the second half of Acts concentrates on Paul and his mission in the diaspora, including a mission among gentiles, and since the last quarter of Acts focuses on a defense of Paul, is not the second possibility the only viable one?"[75] The key to understanding the context is that the meetings of Paul with the Roman Jews have been devoted, as have the previous several chapters of Acts, to Paul's defense. In meeting with the Roman Jews, Paul emphasizes his innocence of any act against his people and his explanation that his arrest stands for the hope of Israel. The question that stands behind all this calls for an explanation of Paul's mission to Gentiles, and the quotation of Isa 6:9–10 is intended to provide that explanation. Paul turns to the Gentiles because some Jews do not believe. But this does not mean a turning away from the Jews, as Acts 28:30 makes clear: Paul welcomes both Jews and Gentiles.

In the conclusion to his book, Brawley consciously sets himself on the side of Jervell and over against the views that he thinks have hitherto prevailed. For him Luke-Acts does not describe the triumph of Gentile Christianity over Judaism but rather a binding to it.

Brawley's contention that Luke is less interested in the Gentile mission than in Paul himself functions more as an assumption than a conclusion. Little compelling evidence is offered for it, and a rigid separation between a concern for the Christian mission and a concern for the one who, in Acts, is its chief spokesperson is not convincing. At some points it is difficult to determine the effect of this assumption on Brawley's interpretations. It has long been recognized that the Lukan Paul is very Jewish, even by those scholars who maintain that Acts tells the story of the Gentile mission. The task of determining the meaning of the three announcements about turning to Gentiles (Acts 13:46–47; 18:6; 28:28) is not made less difficult by reading Acts as a biography of Paul. Supposedly, we may regard Luke's task in a different way by conceiving it as Brawley suggests, but the resulting reading of Luke's treatment of Judaism and the Jewish people does not seem to be seriously affected by Brawley's suggestion.

What Brawley says about the Pharisees demonstrates that a significant aspect of his interpretation assumes a particular construction of the historical context of Luke the author. Brawley claims that Luke is writing at a time when Pharisees had reputations as admirable religious leaders and that Luke's community shared this view or at least was acquainted with it. The reader of the gospel who thought of the Pharisees in this way would then be impressed that Jesus was frequently in contact with them, sometimes at their initiative. As Brawley says, "In Luke the Pharisees set Jesus off to advantage. But Luke does not compare them as hero and villain, good against the bad. He contrasts them as superior over reputable."[76] Since Brawley has, for the most part, treated Luke-Acts as a literary work and interpreted it within the limits of the world of the text, the introduction of a supposed historical context of the supposed author is somewhat surprising at this point. He has, in fact, objected to some aspects of the work of S. G. F. Brandon and Charles Talbert on the grounds that they employ external history to account for Luke's text.[77] Brawley's own principle is that "the internal evidence in Acts takes precedence over external history,"[78] but at this point the reverse seems to be the case. An assumed historical reconstruction, in which Pharisees are respected, is cited to explain a phenomenon in Luke's text.

Has Brawley provided us a coherent and convincing interpretation of the Pharisees in Luke-Acts? His insistence that they are not treated unfavorably needs to be tested by more extensive studies of apparently conflicting narratives and parables than Brawley has included here. The parable of the Pharisee and the tax collector (Luke 18:9–14), which contrasts the piety of two almost stereotypical figures, is a case in point. Brawley refers to the parable, which is unique in Luke, only once and by way of concession: "A Pharisee plays the role of an unsuspecting self-righteous person upon whom the tables are turned in 18:9–14. But they are not merely typical opponents."[79] This brief comment ignores the fact that this particular Pharisee appears in a parable of Jesus, where he serves as an example of a person who did not go down to his home justified and who suffers by comparison with the tax collector. Can we infer from this parable that the Pharisee is not cited by Luke as typical? These verses and others in Luke deserve a more extensive analysis than Brawley has given them. He is right, of course, to call attention to a more favorable treatment of Pharisees in some Lukan passages. But this only means that the role of Pharisees in Luke-Acts is complicated, as Sanders readily recognized.

Because of its importance to the argument and to the entire position that he represents, Brawley's reading of Acts 28:28, 30 requires a brief comment. He observes that here "there is no anathema against the Jews as such."[80] Both Acts 13:46 and 18:6 have negative judgments against the Jews: "You reject it [the word] and regard yourselves as unworthy of eternal life" (Acts 13:46); "Your blood be on your own heads" (Acts 18:6). But in Acts 28:28, we have only, "Let it be known to you then that this salvation of God has been sent to the Gentiles; they will listen." It is true that Acts 28:28 has no explicitly negative judgment against the Jews. But the last words, "they will listen," as applied to Gentiles, surely are meant to form a contrast with the quoted description from Isaiah ("their ears are hard of hearing"), which is applied to Paul's audience of Roman Jews.

Brawley then emphasizes the statement in Acts 28:30, that Paul welcomed *all* who came to him. He thinks it obvious that the "all" here is to be taken literally and includes both Jews and Gentiles. If so, Acts does not end on a note of Jewish rejection, but of a continuing openness to Jews. But what grounds are there for insisting on a literal interpretation of Luke's "all" at this point? Brawley himself makes a point of saying that this word is often to be understood as an exaggeration. Just a few pages earlier he writes, "As I have shown, Luke frequently uses πᾶς not in a strictly literal sense, but to refer to a large number."[81] He makes this statement specifically in reference to Acts 25:24, where Festus says to Agrippa that all the Jewish community petitioned him about Paul. Luke, who wrote Acts 25:2, 7, knows that this statement is not to be taken literally, for here it is only some Jews who are mentioned. If Brawley is right in understanding "all" in Acts 25:24 to mean "a large number," as I think he is, how can he then insist on a literal understanding of "all" in Acts 28:30? And if we should understand the latter verse as saying that a large number of people came to Paul, how can we then go on to define the makeup of this large number? Indeed, an interpretation that excludes Jews from this constituency seems more plausible. We read in Acts 28:28 that Gentiles will listen, and so the following verse provides an illustration of this very point: their listening is shown by the very large numbers of them who come to Paul for this very purpose. The inclusion of Jews in the "all" who come to Paul in Acts 28:30 adds something that does not fit with the contention that Jews are unhearing (Acts 28:27) and that Gentiles will listen (Acts 28:28).

As a contrast to the point of view espoused by Sanders and as support for Jervell's position, Brawley's work is significant. We next examine a study of Luke and Acts that exhibits subtle differences from both Sanders and Brawley, as well as Jervell.

Robert C. Tannehill

Robert C. Tannehill is professor of New Testament at the Methodist Theological School in Ohio. His two-volume study of Luke-Acts constitutes a groundbreaking attempt to read these texts by making a selective use of modern literary-critical theories.[82] It is, as the title announces, a narratological reading that stresses the unity of the two works at the level of story. Tannehill's own description states the purpose of the study: "The following study will emphasize the unity of Luke-Acts. This unity is the result of a single author working within a persistent theological perspective, but it is something more. It is a *narrative* unity, the unity appropriate to a well-formed narrative. Change and development are expected in such a narrative, yet unity is maintained because the scenes and characters contribute to a larger story that determines the significance of each part."[83] The monographs by Sanders and Brawley also made use of narrative-critical approaches, but as a commentary-like study, Tannehill's is an exhaustive and inclusive reading of our texts. Although not specifically intended to answer questions about Israel in Luke-Acts, Tannehill's volumes nevertheless have made an important contribution to this quest.

Tannehill understands the story of Israel in Luke's narrative as a tragedy. It begins with a number of expressions of great hope, angelic announcements, and prophetic hymns that speak of "the establishment of a messianic kingdom for Israel and the fulfillment of God's saving purpose universally, embracing both Jews and Gentiles."[84] But the story takes a tragic turn. The projected hope does not materialize, because the Messiah is rejected and killed. Tannehill insists that the hopes for the restoration of a kingdom for Israel, expressed in the nativity stories of Luke 1–2, are meant to be taken quite literally: "To suppose that the author could not be thinking in such political terms because all would know that Israel did not become an independent state with its own king ignores the tragic line of the story: the story is presenting a real possibility and a valid hope which was tragically rejected at the moment of fulfillment."[85] Tannehill's contrast of the beginning of the gospel with the end of Acts emphasizes the tragic aspect of our texts.

> The story that begins by proclaiming that "all flesh will see the salvation of God" ends on a tragic note. All flesh has not seen God's salvation.
>
> More than the fate of the Roman Jews is at stake. God's promise in Scripture, which the narrator presented to us as a key to understanding God's purpose in history, has not been fulfilled. Here is a theological problem that the narrator does not solve, for the narrative ends with an unresolved tension between promise and reality.[86]

But Luke's narrative is also intended to provide assurance to the reader, as Luke 1:4 had stated. This assurance has, however, an ironic character: "As part of its strategy of bringing assurance through story, the Lukan narrative highlights this rejection so that it may show how resistance, conflict, and disappointment are being absorbed into a larger pattern which points toward God's victory—an ironic victory because the forces of rejection and experiences of suffering are themselves becoming the means by which God's purpose is accomplished in the world."[87]

In Tannehill's reading of the Gospel of Luke, the Jewish crowd, in distinction from the leaders, is initially favorable to Jesus, but as the narrative progresses even the crowd is absorbed into the opposition to him. As Jesus approaches Jerusalem, the attitude of the crowd is hardly distinguishable from that of the leaders, and in the trial scenes the Jewish authorities lead the people to make the tragic error of calling for Jesus' crucifixion: "The story of Jesus and the Jewish people comes to a climax in Jerusalem. There the religious authorities lead a major portion of this people into the tragic error of refusing the offered peace of the messianic kingdom. This has serious consequences for Israel's history in the narrator's view. Whether Israel can recover from this tragic error is an important question in the rest of Luke-Acts."[88] But some in the crowd express a sense of remorse, projecting an expectation of repentance that will be narrated in the early chapters of Acts (esp. Acts 2:37–41).

Tannehill sees some variations in the roles of the Jewish leaders in Luke, but for the most part they are simply Jesus' opponents. Pharisees object to Jesus' treatment of the poor and sinners; they use their positions for social advancement; they are greedy, and they customarily exalt themselves. Tannehill acknowledges that Pharisees are not explicitly associated with the death of Jesus, but he notes that their objection in Luke 19:39, the last reference to Pharisees in the Gospel of Luke, connects them with the charges to be brought against Jesus in his trials: "The Pharisees who object in 19:39 stand in the same camp as the Sanhedrin in rejecting Jesus as Messiah."[89] The opposition to Jesus in Jerusalem is more powerful but is not dissimilar to that that Jesus encountered earlier in the gospel: "Not only are scribes mentioned in both contexts, but there is a similar set of attitudes and actions from the two sets of opponents, indicating that the kind of opposition which Jesus met earlier is encountered in a more powerful and dangerous form in Jerusalem."[90] Even the disciples are implicated in Jesus' passion: "They resist Jesus' arrest, are not prepared to follow him in suffering, and are concerned about their own status instead of following Jesus' path of lowly service."[91] But Tannehill fully recognizes Luke's stress on the guilt of the Jewish people and leaders in bringing about the death of Jesus. Pilate, in succumbing to the pressures of the chief priests and people to execute a person he has repeatedly pronounced to be innocent, is no model of justice: "But the focus of attention in Luke 23:13–25 is on the innocence of Jesus, to which Pilate bears repeated witness, and on the determination of the people and their rulers that Jesus die in spite of this."[92]

At the end of his first volume Tannehill includes a narratological and theological explanation for Luke's writing a second volume. In terms of the narrative he says that the story is not complete with Jesus' resurrection. The story "includes the preaching to all nations, and this preaching is important enough to be narrated, not just previewed."[93] Furthermore, the story must continue because of "the implied author's great concern with the Jewish people's reaction to Jesus and the gospel."[94]

In his second volume, devoted to Acts, Tannehill stresses many of the contentions of Jervell and Brawley. In the introduction to this volume he announces his project: "I will argue at various points that the narrator of Acts, like the Lukan Paul, is loyal to Israel and believes the scriptural promises to the Jewish people. The persistence of the mission to the Jews, even when it frequently meets rejection, is a sign of this loyalty. . . . This mission, in a reduced form, is assumed to continue even beyond the end of Acts, according to my interpretation."[95]

This volume takes on more of the form of a traditional commentary than does the first, going through the Acts narrative in its own order and commenting on the various incidents. Throughout Tannehill insists on the theme announced in the introduction, namely that repeated incidents of Jewish rejection do not suggest that Luke has "written off the Jews." Typical is the following comment on Acts 1:1–26: "After the mission's initial success in Jerusalem, the emphasis in Acts will fall on Jewish resistance and rejection. Even this does not mean that the hope for Israel is dead. After all, the messianic reign for Israel was promised by God through the prophets. . . . But the story in Acts, so far as the author takes us, is not the story of the fulfillment of this hope for Israel as a people but the story of a tragic turn away from fulfillment when it was readily available."[96]

Tannehill is quite clear in maintaining that, despite the fact that the Christian missionaries become involved in conflicts with Gentiles on a number of occasions, "the central conflict of the plot, repeatedly emphasized and still present in the last major scene of Acts, is a conflict within Judaism provoked by Jewish Christian preachers (including Paul)."[97] Notably, the narrative in Acts begins optimistically, and Tannehill underscores Jervell's contention that the author of Acts is not describing a Gentile church "with a withering Jewish arm, for the mission in the Jewish homeland is very successful, and the church there is vigorous."[98] But "the story will move from harmony between believers and Jewish society through developing conflict to a major crisis."[99] The speech of Stephen (Acts 7:2–53) seems to be based upon a Deuteronomic pattern, as it speaks of God's punishment for disobedience. But this punishment, which probably for Luke and his readers meant the destruction of Jerusalem and the Temple, "severe as it is, does not mean that unbelieving Jews have been eliminated from God's people once and for all."[100] Stephen's speech, nevertheless, marks a major turn in the narrative: "The early openness to the apostles and their message has ended, and a wall of suspicion separates the disciples from others in Jerusalem, so that 'the Jews' can be used to refer to a hostile group."[101]

The concluding verses of Acts are of special importance to Tannehill's project and for the issues we have been tracing. Tannehill recognizes that the final scene of a narrative carries special weight: "The final scene of a narrative is an opportunity to clarify central aspects of plot and characterization in the preceding story and to make a final, lasting impression on the readers. The fact that the narrator has chosen to end the work with a scene that focuses on Paul's encounter with Jews shows how extraordinarily important the issues of this encounter are to the narrator."[102]

Tannehill seems to be in partial agreement with Sanders in his understanding of Acts 28:24. He notes that Luke has written that some of the Roman Jews were "being persuaded" while others refused to believe. The verb ἐπείθοντο, according to Tannehill, expresses something short of belief. He understands Luke to say that "they were in the process of being persuaded but had made no lasting decision."[103] Under these circumstances the words quoted from Isaiah in Acts 28:26–27 seem inappropriate and unduly harsh. But Tannehill notes that they are appropriate if what Paul is after here is the conversion of the entire population of Roman Jews. Partial acceptance is insufficient, for past incidents have shown that the mission is disrupted by the opposition of the unconverted Jews: "The presence of disagreement among the Jews is enough to show that Paul has not achieved what he sought. He was seeking a communal decision, a recognition by the Jewish community as a whole that Jesus is the fulfillment of the Jewish hope. The presence of significant opposition shows that this is not going to happen."[104] This is not to be understood to signify the end of a Christian mission to Jews. Tannehill cites what he calls "signs of the narrator's concern to keep a mission to Jews alive in spite of this situation."[105] The return of the missionaries to speak in synagogues after the announcements of Acts 13:46–47 and 18:6 provides a precedent that would lead the reader to expect a similar return at Rome. Further, some Roman Jews did express an openness to Paul, and the themes about which Paul preached in Acts 28:31 are the same themes he had proclaimed to Jews on many earlier occasions, namely the Kingdom of God and the Messiahship of Jesus. Tannehill does not stress the meaning of "all" in Acts 28:30 in the same way that Brawley does, but he says that "the reference in v. 30 to Paul welcoming 'all' those coming to him should not be dismissed as an idle remark."[106] "The situation has changed in that Paul can no longer speak in synagogues to the Jews assembled as a community, but he continues to welcome all people who are willing to hear his message, including Jews."[107]

Tannehill's chief concern in both volumes of his study has been to show that the story of Israel in Luke-Acts ends in tragedy. He writes, "Discussion of the Lukan attitude toward Israel must take account of two fundamental points: a persistent concern with the realization of scriptural promises that, the narrator recognizes, apply first of all to the Jewish people, and the stinging experience of rejection of the message that the hope of Israel is now being fulfilled. The resulting tension . . . is not resolved in the narrative."[108]

He notes that there are indications in the narrative that would allow the reader to complete the story of Paul and to conclude that he was convicted and executed in Rome. But he insists that Luke provides no way to resolve the fundamental tension that he himself has developed through the narrative, the tension between the promises of God and their nonfulfillment for Israel. Tannehill, nevertheless, ends on something of a wistful note: "Because God is God, hope remains that God's comprehensive saving purpose will somehow be realized, but there is no indication of how that can happen. In the meantime, Acts can only suggest that the church welcome those Jews who are still willing to listen and continue its mission to the more responsive gentile world."[109]

There is much to admire in Tannehill's magisterial study of Luke-Acts. His close reading has resulted in a sound solution to many thorny problems. He has avoided certain pitfalls in the understanding of the Lukan Pharisees, adopting neither Sanders's identification of those in the gospel with the Jewish Christians of Acts nor Brawley's stress on the positive Lukan treatment of them. He has recognized and made use of Jervell's emphasis on the Jewish character of Lukan Christianity but has not overlooked the importance of the rejection of the Christian preachers by Jews. Tannehill's most important contribution to the discussion of Israel in Luke-Acts is his emphasis on the tension between the Christian message as the fulfillment of God's promises for Israel and the recognition of Jewish nonacceptance of this message. This tension between promise and reality is what constitutes, for Tannehill, the tragedy in Luke-Acts.

The characterization of the story of Israel in Luke-Acts as tragedy has been debated in recent Lukan scholarship. David Moessner, for example, rejects the designation and prefers to think of the tension between promise and fulfillment as ironic.[110] He maintains that certain of the expectations expressed in Luke 1–2 are actually undermined in the subsequent texts. In the temptation story in Luke 4:1–13, Jesus rejects "a way for the anointed Son as outlined in Mary's and Zechariah's expectations or hopes,"[111] and such undermining of the political expectations of Luke 1–2 continues through the narrative. Moessner notes that Luke draws on the servant passages of 2 Isaiah to explain much of the story in both volumes, and he shows that in these Isaianic passages God is glorified through the servant's rejection and humiliation. The same, he maintains, is the case in Luke-Acts: God is glorified even by Jewish rejection. But, according to Moessner, Luke also adopts a Deuteronomistic pattern for the interpretation of history, so that Israel is punished for sins. With respect to the end of Acts, Moessner claims that the use of Isaiah in Acts 28:26–27 is intended to express both disaster and hope. He writes, "Although its solemn finality surely decrees an inevitable disaster upon a monolith of rejection that has formed again, parallel to the gospel, yet it also spells hope if Israel repents."[112] So, Moessner claims, if God is glorified through Israel's rejection and eventual repentance, "tragedy" is at best a misnomer for Luke-Acts.

David Tiede acknowledges the plausibility of using the term "tragedy" for Luke-Acts, but he finds in the prophecy of Simeon in Luke 2:34–35 the concept that controls the entire narrative.[113] Simeon predicts the falling and the rising of many in Israel, and Tiede understands these phenomena sequentially. First, many will fall, and later many will rise. The end of Acts "is, therefore, not the end of the story, but it is a resumption of the themes sounded in Simeon's oracles."[114] Tiede continues, "God is determined that this salvation and reign of Jesus be for light to the Gentiles, and unto the glory of Israel, but for the present the hearts of many in Israel have been disclosed to be hardened against the understanding and healing which God intends for Israel."[115]

Despite their differences, the approaches of Tannehill, Brawley, Moessner, and Tiede share the contention that Acts 28 is not the end of Luke's story. Tannehill is more tentative than the others on this matter, expressing only a hope that somehow the tension developed in Luke-Acts will be resolved. It is important to recognize that he does not attribute this hope to Luke and sees little in the narrative itself that would contribute to a resolution. The hope that

Tannehill expresses is essentially a theological one—"because God is God, hope remains that God's comprehensive saving purpose will somehow be realized . . . "[116]—and it is unclear whether the theology is Tannehill's or Luke's. But Tannehill is clear that the narrative itself ends without resolution.

As a narratological move, the projection of the story beyond the end of the narrative is highly questionable. To be sure, texts may refer to action that takes place before the story in the narrative begins or after it ends. In Acts, however, there is no explicit reference beyond the ending except for the promise of Jesus' return in Acts 1:11, an eschatological promise that has no explicit relation to the matter of the evangelization of Jews. For the end of Acts we are not dealing with references within the text but with interpretations by modern scholars. Sanders's judgment about the end of Acts is sound: "the Book of Acts is here at an end, and so is the cycle."[117] Similarly Gerhard Schneider insists, "The turning to the Gentiles is now final. It does not exclude the conversion of individual Jews. But it becomes clear: the church of the post-Pauline time will be a Gentile-Christian church."[118]

Tannehill may have been able to find a resolution of promise and fulfillment within the text of Luke-Acts by regarding the quotation of Isa 6:9–10 in Acts 28:26–27 as Luke's final word about promise. He is quite right to maintain that the promises that are made in Luke 1–2 are not fulfilled, and Moessner is right to show that the subsequent narrative of Luke-Acts undermines these predictions. But when we come finally to the end of the story and Luke turns one more time to the scriptures, he quotes a promise that is fulfilled on the spot. Paul, like Isaiah, is told to go to the people and tell them that they are blind, deaf, and unheeding. And this is precisely the situation that Luke has described not only in the immediate episode with Roman Jews but in virtually all the narratives of Paul in the Diaspora. *This* promise has been fulfilled.

Finally, it may be observed that the perspective of the reader has a great deal to do with the ways in which narratives are perceived, and this perception has a great deal to do with the social setting of the reader. Whether or not the story of Israel in Luke-Acts is a tragedy depends to a great extent on how it is perceived by readers. Tannehill's view is clearly congenial to late twentieth-century thought, which is sensitive to anti-Jewish tendencies. But, as we have seen, critical scholarship in earlier times was more apt to find some version of triumphalism in Luke-Acts. We shall take a longer look at this phenomenon in the closing chapter of this book.

CHAPTER 8

Luke-Acts at the Beginning of the Third Millennium

Although this chapter constitutes the conclusion to this book, it is not intended to be the conclusion to the discussion of Jews and Judaism in Luke-Acts. Nor could it be. The issues that have been and are being addressed are complex, the methods of study are diverse, and the stakes in the outcome of the discussion are high. Several scholars whose publications have been treated here are still working on the topic, and younger scholars will almost certainly continue to ask serious questions of Luke-Acts. It should not be expected that a history of scholarship such as this will provide definitive answers to questions about the role of Jews and Judaism in Luke-Acts. Rather, one of the chief values of a review such as this is that it can serve as a reminder of the richness of this history and as an occasion to reconsider views that may have been hastily discarded.

This study also provides a good opportunity to reflect on significant shifts that have occurred in critical scholarship on issues relating to Jews and Judaism in Luke-Acts. The differences between the earlier scholars, such as Harnack, and the later ones, such as Tannehill, are dramatic. We began this study with questions about the relationship of social-historical factors and the ways in which various scholars interpret Luke-Acts. Did nineteenth-century culture exercise a negative influence on the ways in which the scholars we examined here interpreted Luke's portrayal of Judaism? Were scholars who wrote in the wake of the Shoah led to see more benign images of Jews in Luke-Acts because they had seen the disastrous results of antisemitism? A major change in the character of NT scholarship generally seems to have taken place in the period following the Holocaust. Before 1933–45, most scholars followed the tradition of anti-Judaism, portraying early Judaism as legalistic, casuistic, demanding, dry, and hopeless. After the twentieth-century tragedy of the Jewish people became widely known, NT scholars began to exhibit a more positive attitude toward second-temple Judaism and described it in very different terms.

Although it seems clear that the Shoah does mark a turning point in the history of NT scholarship, the present study requires a more carefully nuanced verdict in respect to the study of Luke-Acts. It is true that the earlier scholars we have examined here fit the mold that was described in chapter 1. For the most part, these scholars understood early Judaism in negative terms and found that Luke did the same. There were exceptions, especially among English and American scholars, such as the editors of the historic *Beginnings of Christianity*.[1] But for the most part, Lukan scholars agreed in their descriptions of Jews and Judaism and of Luke's treatment of them. This was the case right up to the time of the rise of Hitler, as we saw in the work of Adolf Schlatter. But in many respects the tradition of anti-Judaism described by Karl Hoheisel and others continued in Lukan studies for several decades after World War II. While both Ernst Haenchen and Hans Conzelmann questioned the anti-Jewish tradition of critical scholarship at a number of points, they nevertheless emphasized negative aspects in their treatment of Luke and Acts.

The turning point in Lukan scholarship came over twenty years after the end of World War II with Jacob Jervell, who broke with the Conzelmann-Haenchen consensus and reversed almost all the earlier judgments about Luke-Acts. Jervell characterized Luke as pro-Jewish through and through, as believing that the very legitimacy of the Christian movement rested on its relation to Judaism. According to Jervell, Luke believed that it was absolutely essential for the first generation of Christian believers to adhere meticulously to Torah. Luke also thought that the only non-Jews to join with these Jewish-Christians were Gentiles who had previously been associated with synagogues, namely God-fearers. In Jervell's view, Luke insisted that salvation is impossible outside Israel.

More recent Lukan scholars who have addressed the issues of Judaism in these texts have taken account of the work of Jervell, but there is now no consensus. Judgments about Jews and Judaism in Luke range from those of Jack Sanders, who recovers many of the insights of prewar scholars, to those of Robert Brawley, who follows closely in the footsteps of Jervell.

Rarely is this shift in outlook explicitly attributed to the influence of historical events or social forces. I have found no mention of the Holocaust or contemporary Jewish-Christian relationships in the writings of Jervell. Sanders, however, acknowledges that his own concern about Christian anti-semitism, which he describes as "one of the more pressing social issues of our day,"[2] influenced his own interest in issues about Jews in Luke-Acts. And at the end of his study he includes a warning about the danger of Luke's polemic against the Jews.[3] In a recent monograph on the theology of Luke, Günter Wasserberg quite explicitly distinguishes between scholarship on Luke-Acts before and after Auschwitz, and he comments, "Since Auschwitz, anti-Judaism in Christianity is increasingly recognized as a central problem affecting the foundations of Christian theology."[4] Although he concludes that Luke is not basically anti-Jewish despite the inclusion of some polemical details, Wasserberg says that Luke's approach should not be ours today. He writes,

"No longer must Christian identity be formulated in terms of dissimilarity with Judaism, but in consciousness of the common roots and the special responsibility which Christians have after Auschwitz."[5]

After the Holocaust Christian leaders and scholars gradually became aware of the complex relations between historic Christian teaching about the Jews and attitudes of acceptance, complicity, and approval that supported the political aims of the National Socialist party in Germany and throughout Europe.[6] Undoubtedly this awareness played a role in the history of NT scholarship in general and of scholarship on Luke-Acts in particular. But it would be a mistake to conclude that the Nazi Holocaust is the only influence on recent NT and Lukan scholarship.

The negative portrayal of Jews and Judaism in the earlier scholarship resulted from a number of different factors, including the prevailing anti-Judaism in contemporary Christian theology and practice. But the strength of tradition within scholarly circles must also be considered. Scholars stand on the shoulders of their predecessors and learn from them. They tend to read the primary texts through the lenses supplied by secondary texts written by their predecessors. The earlier scholarship also tended to suffer from a deficient understanding of early Judaism, brought about by a neglect of early Jewish texts and a lack of contact with Jewish scholars.

The more benign interpretations today may likewise result from a similar group of factors, including a greater sensitivity to the dangers of Christian anti-Judaism. But of great importance is the increased knowledge that today's scholars have about early Judaism, knowledge that has come out of research on ancient texts, such as the Qumran scrolls, which were not known before 1947. Study of the scrolls has energized scholarly attempts to produce more accurate descriptions of early Judaism, and thus new studies of the Apocrypha, Pseudepigrapha, and rabbinical texts have burgeoned. Further, the integration of Jewish studies within the academy has been an important factor. Christian and Jewish scholars increasingly work in tandem, and this scholarship has produced a wealth of information that is generally free of anti-Judaism.[7]

Whatever may be the complex of influences on Lukan studies today, the contrasts with earlier scholarship are dramatic. When Harnack or Schlatter pointed to the negative images of Jews and Judaism in Luke-Acts, they did so without recognizing that there might be social problems. Scholars today may not do so, but they encounter serious problems nonetheless. Many modern scholars not only are concerned about the meaning of NT texts, but they also recognize that these texts function as authoritative documents for modern Christians, and they are concerned about the possible influence of their interpretations on Christian-Jewish relations. One way to resolve the problem is to mitigate or deny the alleged anti-Judaism in canonical texts such as Luke-Acts. Jack Sanders has recently called attention to a prevailing tendency in post-Shoah scholarship, which he contrasts with earlier scholarship. He writes that earlier scholars "did not shy away from and twist the meaning of those statements in Luke-Acts that are hostile and defamatory toward Jews. . . ."[8] He condemns more recent scholars for doing just this.

It is notable that two issues have received attention from almost all scholars who have been concerned about the role of Jews and Judaism in Luke-Acts. One issue relates directly to the ways in which scholars have perceived the presence of pro-Jewish and anti-Jewish elements in Luke-Acts, an issue that I call ambivalence.[9] The other relates to the varying ways in which the end of Acts may be read. We turn now to a discussion of these issues.

Ambivalence in Luke-Acts

In general the scholars we have examined have explicitly noted either those materials in Luke-Acts that appear to be anti-Jewish or those that appear to be pro-Jewish. But in ways that are not usually acknowledged, a certain recognition of ambivalence, i.e., an awareness of both pro-Jewish and anti-Jewish materials in Luke-Acts, appears to underlie the work of many of them. Indeed, it may be the case that it is this recognition of ambivalence that stands at the heart of the problems addressed in the history of Lukan scholarship.

Ferdinand Christian Baur understood Luke-Acts in terms of conflict between two forms of early Christianity. He posited a serious conflict between a Petrine, or Jewish, form of Christianity and a Pauline, or Gentile, form, and he saw Acts as intended to provide a basis for conciliation between the two forms. For this reason Luke can speak positively of the Jewish elements and character in the early Christian movement. But Baur also claimed that Luke's effort to bring peace to the two factions of Christians was aided by his attempt to focus hatred toward the non-Christian Jews. The hostility the two Christian parties had toward each other was, in the mind of the author of Luke-Acts, to be redirected toward the Jews. And so, the non-Christian Jews may be shown in very negative ways. For these reasons we have ambivalence in Acts: incidents that speak glowingly of the growth of Jewish Christianity as well as incidents that show how virulently Jews opposed the mission of Paul. Ultimately for Baur, Luke-Acts is anti-Jewish, and Judaism in Luke-Acts is a religion that emphasizes formalism, materialism, particularism, and legalism, and the Jewish people are disobedient, unbelieving, and obdurate. But Baur observes that Paul is made to sound like a Jewish Christian and Peter like a Gentile Christian. The attempt to reconcile opposing parties in early Christianity requires Luke to express ambivalent attitudes.

The situation with the Gospel of Luke, as explained by Baur, is more complicated. Original Luke was a revision of Matthew that omitted the Jewish-Christian tendencies, and as such it was adaptable to Marcionite uses. A second author, who intended to reconcile the Jewish-Christian and Gentile-Christian wings of the church, revised original Luke and reintroduced some pro-Jewish sections from Matthew. As a result, canonical Luke has both anti-

Jewish materials from the first author and pro-Jewish materials from the reviser. Baur's solution to the ambivalence in Luke's gospel is to apportion the different views to different rescensions.

Adolf von Harnack also recognized both pro-Jewish and anti-Jewish leanings in Luke-Acts. He noted that Luke accepted the divine rejection of the Jewish people but that he also included favorable notes about them whenever he was able to do so. For Harnack this was a sign of the author's fairness and lack of bias against the Jews. Luke is, for Harnack, very much like Paul, who had both pro-Jewish and anti-Jewish emphases, but Luke's ambivalence is to be explained in terms of his own religious sentiments. Harnack recognizes Luke's hostility to the Jews as seen in the incidents of opposition to Paul, but he also insists that Luke had a deep reverence for the Hebrew Bible, which Harnack understood to be a pro-Jewish sentiment. As a Gentile Christian, Luke did not have the struggles with Judaism that Paul had. Harnack's own views about the newness of Christianity, growing on the soil of the Old Testament, probably affect his understanding of Luke-Acts. At another point, however, Harnack anticipates the approach taken later by Jacob Jervell, when he denies that Luke thought of the Christians as a new people of God. He writes that Luke has no new "People" taking the place of the Jews, but rather "the Jewish nation still remains the People, to the believing section of which the Gentiles are added."[10]

Adolf Schlatter demonstrated an ambivalence in his own attitude toward Jews of his own time. He called them enemies of Christians but encouraged Christians to honor God's faithfulness to the covenant with them. They are beloved of God. But Schlatter stressed the negative portrayals of Jews and Judaism in Luke-Acts and described Jewish piety as characterized by meticulous observance of Torah and reverence of the Temple. Still, Schlatter insisted on the continuity between Jewish expectation and Christian fulfillment and maintained that neither Luke nor his major source was an opponent of Judaism. Luke's major source in the gospel, the "New Narrator," that is, Lukan *Sondergut,* did not oppose the dominance of law or Jewish particularism. The opponent was "Mammon," the love of possessions and money. But in Schlatter's analysis of Luke-Acts, mammon turned out to be a prime characteristic of Jewish people, and so he carefully pointed out other Jewish practices that have little to do with love of possessions and showed Luke's negativity toward these practices.

Ernst Haenchen clearly recognizes ambivalence as a primary characteristic of Luke-Acts. He notes, for example, that Acts begins with stories in which the Christian preachers meet with a great deal of success among Jewish people. But he claims that this positive tendency must be seen as fitting the aim which Luke had in writing. According to Haenchen, Luke was addressing a particular historical problem, namely, understanding Christianity as a stage in continuity with Judaism and at the same time explaining why most Jews of Luke's day had not responded to the Christian message. For these reasons

Luke had two images of Jews: one as the people of Moses and the prophets; and the other as obdurate enemies of the Christians. The two images are not fully resolved in Luke-Acts. Luke continues to hope that bridges between Christians and Pharisees may be built, and so he portrays Paul as a loyal Pharisee. But in the end, "the Jews are 'written off.'"[11]

In part due to his decision to omit an analysis of Luke 1–2, Hans Conzelmann emphasizes only the negative portrayal of Judaism in Luke-Acts. He says that Luke blamed the Jews for the death of Jesus and believed that they had lost the right to be Israel, the people of God. Conzelmann acknowledges a connection between the church and Israel, but that only means that, for Luke, the church has taken over the role of Israel as the elect of God. Conzelmann is aware of aspects of early Judaism that run counter to the ways in which Luke understood them. His comment on Acts 15:10, for example, shows that he knows that Torah observance was not considered an intolerable burden by Jews in the first century, even if the Lukan Peter says the opposite. He also insists that the characterization of Jews as killers of Jesus is unhistorical. Despite these recognitions on Conzelmann's part, he insists that Luke believed that the age of Israel had ended with the coming of Jesus, and thus he had little of a positive nature to say about Judaism.

The positive images of Jews and Judaism in Luke-Acts are fully recognized by Jacob Jervell. In emphasizing these images to the neglect of the negative ones, Jervell stands at the opposite pole from Conzelmann. He firmly asserts that, in Luke's theology, "*extra Israel nulla salus est,*"[12] and he emphasizes the Jewish acceptance of the Christian message. Further, according to Jervell's interpretation of Luke-Acts, it is the most Torah-observant Jews who repent and accept belief in Jesus. The only Gentile converts are God-fearers, and the inclusion of such Gentiles is a standard feature of Jewish expectation. Jervell is aware of the important role that nonbelieving Jews play in Luke-Acts, but he seems to have no genuine interest in them.

Jack T. Sanders says that he undertook his study because he felt that the ambivalence in Luke-Acts required explanation. In his view, the clue to Lukan ambivalence is to be found in the differences between the narratives and the speeches. The narrative in Acts distinguishes between believing and nonbelieving Jews, but the speeches do not. Sanders notes a further ambivalence in the treatment of the Pharisees in Acts, where Jewish Pharisees provide the sense of continuity that Luke needs, and Christian Pharisees (surrogates for Jewish Christians) are condemned. So, in Sanders's interpretation of Luke-Acts, both Jews and Jewish Christians are condemned, because of their opposition to the inclusion of Gentiles with Jews in the same movement, but Jewish Pharisees are needed to provide continuity.

Like Jervell, Robert L. Brawley sees only positive images of Judaism in Luke-Acts. Pharisees, for example, are treated with respect throughout the narrative and are used by Luke to legitimate Jesus and his followers. Any movement of early Christians toward Gentiles is in fact an accommodation to

Judaism, and Luke ties Gentile Christianity to Judaism. In fact, however, Acts does not tell the story of the Gentile mission but rather the story of Paul, who is not to be regarded as a representative Christian. Brawley maintains that throughout Luke-Acts, Pharisees are treated with respect and are used to legitimate Jesus and his followers.

Robert C. Tannehill characterizes the ambivalence in Luke-Acts as tension between promise and fulfillment. Luke begins with a number of hopeful expressions by pious Jewish people, but this hope does not materialize. In Luke 3:6, we have the prophecy that "all flesh shall see the salvation of God," but by the end of Acts it is clear that this is not to be. Thus, says Tannehill, "the narrative ends with an unresolved tension between promise and reality,"[13] and Luke provides no way for the reader to resolve this tension.

There is, therefore, an impressive if generally unacknowledged agreement underlying much of the scholarship on Luke-Acts. Despite the use of different source-critical theories and different methodologies, most of our scholars have recognized that there are both pro-Jewish and anti-Jewish materials in Luke-Acts. Although Conzelmann paid little attention to the positive aspects and Jervell neglected the negative, others have more clearly seen this problematic aspect of Luke's writings. For Baur, the basic solution to the problem lay in recognizing the purpose of Luke-Acts as a conciliatory document that sought to make peace between a Jewish and a Gentile form of early Christianity. For Haenchen also, the problem arose from Luke's historical context and purpose in writing. He needed to explain the continuity between Judaism and Christianity as well as the rejection by Jews. Sanders saw the ambivalence in terms of the differences between narrative and discourse, and Tannehill saw it as an unresolved conflict between promise and fulfillment. The point to be stressed is that almost all modern scholars who have worked on issues relating to Jews and Judaism in Luke-Acts have perceived a problem and have recognized, implicitly for the most part, that the problem is at least partially due to the fact that Luke had both pro-Jewish and anti-Jewish materials.[14] Even without the implicit recognition of ambivalence, our study would compel us to admit it. For it would be naïve to say that Conzelmann and Jervell are both totally wrong, that anti-Judaism in Luke-Acts is a figment in the eyes of all nineteenth-century scholars, or that those twentieth-century scholars who find Luke to be more benign to Jews are indulging in wishful thinking.

The End of Luke-Acts

It may be tempting to find a satisfactory solution to the problem of ambivalence by resorting to a source analysis of Luke-Acts, or by positing different rescensions separated by a significant period of time, or by reference to different genres with different authorial intentions.[15] But many scholars today do not find any of these alternatives to be satisfactory. Instead, scholars are turning increasingly to the use of literary-critical tools, especially for the interpretation of the gospels and Acts.[16] A literary approach requires that we consider the whole of Luke's narrative, as we have it in the best reconstituted text, in reaching judgments about its meaning. Indeed, to regard Luke-Acts as a narrative means not only that we read it as a story, with considerations about characters and plot, but also pay close attention to the rhetorical devices employed in the text and the direction in which the narrative moves. A narrative is not a logical argument, but a story, whose meaning is determined by the reader in the process of reading. A reader of a narrative is required by the movement of the narrative to form tentative judgments that may be altered many times before the end of the narrative. The end may or may not resolve the problems encountered in the process of reading, but the direction of the narrative can only be learned by reading to the end. Thus, the end of Luke-Acts continues to be of great significance in the discussion of issues relating to Jews and Judaism.

In his study of scholarship on Luke-Acts, Günter Wasserberg begins the analysis of texts with the end of Acts.[17] His title for the chapter is illuminating: "The End at the Beginning—the Concluding Pericope, Acts 28:16–31, as the Hermeneutic Key to the Total Understanding of Luke-Acts." He notes that Luke could have chosen some other theme or incident with which to end his narrative but that he chose to conclude with an episode about Paul and the Roman Jews. Wasserberg claims that the controversy of Paul with the Roman Jews is not just an episode with local character but that it has significance for the whole of Luke-Acts.

Most of the scholars whose work we have examined here agree on the importance of the end of Acts, but there is presently some controversy about its meaning. Although most scholars from Baur to Jervell accepted the end of Acts as marking the end of a Christian mission to Jews, some recent scholars have raised questions about this position. Brawley is representative of a group of scholars who believe that Acts is open-ended. He most emphatically states that the end of Acts does not announce a rejection of the Jews, and he calls attention to Acts 28:30, which says that Paul welcomed *all* who came to him. Tannehill is more tentative. He notes that the end of Acts shows that Paul desires the conversion of all the Jews, not just some, but he admits that Acts shows no way in which this can happen.

It is significant that Jervell and Sanders, who share little else in their interpretations of Luke-Acts, at least agree that the end of Acts means the end of a mission to Jews. Wasserberg likewise reads the end of Acts as a final condemnation of Jewish rejection. Paul's statement in Acts 28:28 may, he acknowledges, be compared with the two previous statements in 13:46–47 and 18:6, after which Paul returned to speak to Jews in synagogues. Also, in Acts 13 and 18, there is a division among Jews. Some respond, and some don't. But Wasserberg says that, in Acts 28, after saying that some Jews were persuaded, Luke has no further interest in them. The episode in Acts 28 has an element that does not appear in Acts 13 or 18, namely, in Acts 28, the Jewish refusal of Paul's message is "conceived to be a divinely willed stubbornness."[18] Paul's reference to Isaiah means that the stubbornness of the Jews here is neither local nor temporary but that unbelieving Jews are eternally condemned. Wasserberg also asks who are they who depart from Paul in 28:25. Luke has written that some Roman Jews were persuaded but others disbelieved, and then he writes that "as they were leaving, Paul made one further statement" (Acts 28:25). Luke uses here an indefinite third-person-plural pronoun, and Wasserberg comments that it may be logical to assume that only the unbelieving Jews departed but that Luke had no interest in such hair-splitting: "His basic theme is to demonstrate and theologically to clarify the Jewish rejection of the Christian message."[19] For Wasserberg, the Roman Jews stand for collective Jewish unbelief in Jesus.

For a variety of reasons, I find Wasserberg's argument convincing. To be sure, there are problems with his position. We may mention three. (1) After the solemn announcements in Acts 13 and 18, Paul did return to speak to Jews in synagogues. (2) Paul's quotation from Isaiah is inappropriate as a condemnation of both believing and unbelieving Jews. (3) Acts 28:30 says that even after his announcement in 28:28, Paul welcomed all who came to him. I include some brief comments on each of these problems.

(1) It is true that, after the previous announcements in Acts 13 and 18 Paul returned to speak to Jews in synagogues. In many respects the episodes in Acts 13 and 28 are similar. In Acts 13 Paul speaks first to Jews and God-fearers in Pisidian Antioch (Acts 13:16–41) with some apparent success (Acts 13:42–43). On the next Sabbath Paul and Barnabas speak to a larger group from the whole city but meet with opposition and hostility from the Jews (Acts 13:44–45), and as a result they make the solemn declaration directed to the Jews: "It was necessary that the word of God should be spoken first to you. Since you reject it and judge yourselves to be unworthy of eternal life, we are turning now to the Gentiles" (Acts 13:46).[20] This announcement is followed by expressions of joy from Gentiles and more harassment from Jews (Acts 13:48–52). But in Acts 14:1 Paul and Barnabas proceed to Iconium, where they immediately speak to Jews and Greeks in the synagogue.

The announcement in Acts 18 follows a more general description of Paul's activity in Corinth. After weekly debates in the synagogue, when he attempted to convert Jews and Greeks but met opposition (Acts 18:4–5), Paul proclaims, "Your blood be on your own heads! I am innocent. From now on I will go to the Gentiles" (Acts 18:6). Here we have no specific incident or series of incidents, but only a kind of summary description. Nothing is said of any success that Paul may have had either among Jews or Gentiles. Further, the events that follow immediately in Acts 18 do not show Paul addressing Jews specifically, although an official of the synagogue, Crispus, is converted in the house of Titius Justus, a God-fearer (Acts 18:7–8). But when Paul moves on to Ephesus, he again speaks with Jews in a synagogue (Acts 18:19).

For these reasons some scholars argue that the narrative leads the reader of Acts to expect that, after the announcement in Acts 28, Paul will return to speak to Jews in synagogues. In their view, the three announcements are intended only for the locations in which they are pronounced (Asia, Greece, and Italy) but have no universal or permanent significance. Further, a Pauline decision to preach among Gentiles does not necessarily exclude a continued mission among Jews.

But there are good reasons to reject these conclusions. We must seriously consider the significance of the fact that the third Pauline announcement about going to Gentiles comes at the very end of the book. Narrative endings carry special weight and often supply just the ingredient that is necessary for a full understanding of the text. In the present case we have a motif that has appeared twice before (Acts 13:46–47; 18:6), with some confusion about its implications. At the end it comes again (Acts 28:28), but now with a sense of finality. On principle, there is no reason to reject the supposition that a text may refer to an event that is beyond the temporal scope of its narrative world. But here the only clear reference is to the reception of the gospel by Gentiles: "they will listen" (Acts 28:28), and nothing further is said about Jewish reception.

(2) Some scholars have correctly pointed out that Paul's quotation from Isaiah is not appropriate to the situation that Luke describes in Acts 28:17–31. Although Luke has described a situation of division among Jews, the quotation from Isaiah, together with the application, does not maintain the same sense of division. Rather it suggests that all Jews are unhearing, unperceptive, and unreceptive of God's messenger. Jervell and others are quite right to observe that the condemnation, strictly interpreted, can apply only to those who did not accept Paul's message, but the quotation speaks of the people as a whole. It is the people who lack understanding and perception, whose hearing is defective and whose eyes have closed. The prophet is told to speak the oracle to this people (Πορεύθητι πρὸς τὸν λαὸν τοῦτον καὶ εἰπόν). Nils Dahl long ago showed that the term ὁ λαός in Luke-Acts almost always designates the Jewish people, and Luke clearly understands the quotation from Isaiah to refer to them.[21] To remove any doubt about who is intended, Paul refers to the people of Isaiah's oracle as, "your ancestors" (Acts 28:25), and thus we have here a prophetic condemnation of Israel in the time of Isaiah and, by implication, the time of Paul. So, if the author of Acts is thinking of a divided people, the quotation of the Isaiah passage against the people as a whole appears to be inappropriate.

But this observation overlooks the rhetorical effect of Luke's text. Tannehill has correctly observed that Luke thinks in corporate rather than individual terms. To be sure, from one perspective the mission to Jews has been successful, and repentant Jews have joined the Jesus movement in large numbers. But what we actually read in Acts 28 is a description of a division among the Roman Jews in Paul's audience, followed by a condemnation of the Jewish people as a whole. The effect of this reading is to show that, although the positive response of some Jews is to be joyfully received, it is not sufficient to remove the condemnation on the people as a whole. Although the text gives every confidence that the conversion of individual Jews should be noted and celebrated, these responses are not enough, since what is intended is the conversion of the people as a whole, and that, since this wholesale conversion has not occurred, the Pauline mission will hereafter be directed toward Gentiles.

Luke has also created a subtle distancing of Paul from the Jewish people in this text. In the first meeting of Paul with the Roman Jews, he spoke of "the customs of *our* ancestors" (Acts 28:17), but in introducing the quotation from Isaiah, he uses the language, *your* ancestors (28:25). In this way Luke creates a gulf between the preacher and the Jewish people.

Wasserberg has correctly pointed out that the announcement in Acts 28 is unlike the others in a major respect, namely, it involves an expression of divine judgment on the Jews.[22] Although Isa 49:6 is quoted in Acts 13:47, it is not a quotation that involves a judgment on the Jewish people but rather serves as a justification for the Gentile mission. The quotation from Isa 6:9–10 in Acts 28:26–27, however, is expressly invoked by Paul against the Roman Jews, whose ancestors were described by the prophet Isaiah. The description shows the people of Israel, both in Isaiah's day and Paul's, to be deficient in understanding and perception.

(3) It is true that Acts 28:30 says that Paul "welcomed all who came to him." Brawley and others have insisted that this verse cannot be interpreted to mean the exclusion of Jews from the mission of Paul. We should note, however, that Acts 28:30 gives no hint of a continuation of a mission of any sort. Paul is not pictured as engaged in a preaching mission but rather of receiving those who come to him. The initiative that is suggested here lies with those who seek out Paul, and there is no hint that Paul initiates the contact. In addition, Acts 28:30 should not be interpreted apart from its context. We have just read that God's salvation has been sent to the Gentiles and that they will listen (Acts 28:28). All that remains is for the reader to have some confirmation, example, or illustration that demonstrates the truth of Acts 28:28. Acts 28:30 does precisely this: it shows that Paul receives those (Gentiles) who come to him. Of course, it is not impossible that Luke is still thinking of Jews (as well as Gentiles) in Acts 28:30. The point would seem to be that Paul turns away no one who is a seeker after the truth he can supply. So, theoretically, a Jew might be welcomed by Paul, but we have already been told in the quotation from Isaiah that Jews are unreceptive of Paul's truth, and so they are not to be found in the group of those who would seek to hear his message.

Thus, in my judgment, it is better to read the end of Acts as proclaiming the end of the mission to the Jews than it is to read it as maintaining a continued openness to the Jewish people. If this is right, the end of Acts provides a resolution to the apparent ambivalence in the narrative. Luke-Acts is a story that begins with images of Jews as piously devoted to God and hopeful for the future of God's people, but it ends with images of Jews as unperceptive and opposed to God's will. The text that exhibits such profound ambivalence in regard to Jews and Judaism moves toward a resolution without ambivalence or ambiguity: an image of Jewish people as rejecting the gospel and thus as a people without hope.

Robert Tannehill has eloquently articulated the ambivalence in Luke-Acts and the negative direction of the narrative.[23] He is most concerned about the disjunction in Luke-Acts between promise and fulfillment. But he also sees in the narrative a number of differences in the ways Luke portrays the Jewish people. The two factors are not unrelated. The promises that Tannehill talks about are to be found mostly in Luke 1–2, in the context of the Lukan birth narratives, which speak glowingly of Jewish piety. The nonfulfillment is finally to be found at the end of Acts, for there it becomes clear that not all flesh shall see the salvation of God, since the larger part of the Jewish people has rejected it. Promise goes with a positive image of the Jewish people; nonfulfillment goes with a negative image of the Jewish people. Tannehill concludes that the story of Israel in Luke-Acts is a tragedy. Divine promises that somehow do not get fulfilled constitute a theological problem that, according to Tannehill, does not achieve resolution in Luke's narrative. And finally he is able to express only a wistful hope that, since God is God the tragedy of the Jewish people may not be final.

There is much to commend Tannehill's approach to Luke-Acts. But there is a different, and in my view a more fruitful, way to ask these questions about Luke's text and its meaning. If we accept the contention of some reader-response critics that meaning is a result of the reading process that occurs at the intersection of text and reading, we would ask about the probable effect on the reader who follows through the narrative from Luke 1 to Acts 28. In *Images of Judaism in Luke-Acts,* I argued that there is an embedded reader in the text, and I made an attempt to discern something about the reader, "the implied reader," by determining the qualifications required simply to understand this text.[24] I concluded that the implied reader of Luke-Acts is similar to those characters in Acts who are called God-fearers.[25] I do not want to reproduce the argument here but would suggest that those who are interested should look at chapter 2 of *Images of Judaism* for a full discussion of the issue. Whatever one may think about this proposal, it is useful simply to ask what is likely to happen to a reader who takes the ambivalence of Luke-Acts and the direction of the narrative seriously. In my judgment, such a reader would find in the text much that would confirm a positive view of the Jewish people. Unfortunately, this reader would finally be persuaded to agree with the negative judgment that Paul expressed through the quotation of Isaiah 6 in Acts 28:26–27.

A history of scholarship such as this does not lead to a simple and straightforward conclusion. It does, however, seem clear that the major shift we have observed in the understanding of Luke's treatment of Jews and Judaism was, to a significant degree, influenced by a recognition of the connections between NT scholarship, Christian anti-Judaism, and the antisemitism that prevailed in the late nineteenth and early twentieth centuries. The tragedy that met the Jewish people in the Shoah, clearly a watershed event in human history and especially the history of Judaism, also served as a signal to scholars that ideas sometimes have disastrous social consequences. Many of the earlier scholars we have treated here saw no problems with highlighting and approving the negative treatment of Jews and Judaism in Luke-Acts. But scholars today are not able to proceed so easily. Although some scholars continue to walk in the pre-Shoah traditions, others are unable to dissociate their work from contemporary history. Some of these latter attempt to deny the presence of anti-Judaism in these NT texts; others recognize it and attempt to mitigate its effect; and still others call attention to it and condemn it. If Luke-Acts is again a "storm-center in contemporary scholarship," as Wasserberg claims,[26] it is largely because issues about the treatment of Jews and Judaism in these texts have not yet been resolved.

ABBREVIATIONS

CBQ	*Catholic Biblical Quarterly*
CurrTheoMiss	*Currents in Theology and Mission*
EKK	Evangelisch-katholischer Kommentar zum Neuen Testament
ETL	*Ephemerides theologicae lovanienses*
Haer.	Epiphanius, *Haereses*
HTR	*Harvard Theological Review*
ICC	International Critical Commentary
Int	*Interpretation*
ITQ	*Irish Theological Quarterly*
JBL	*Journal of Biblical Literature*
JJS	*Journal of Jewish Studies*
JR	*Journal of Religion*
JTS	*Journal of Theological Studies*
NTS	*New Testament Studies*
RB	*Revue biblique*
ResQ	*Restoration Quarterly*
RSV	Revised Standard Version of the Bible
RGG	*Religion in Geschichte und Gegenwart*
SBL	Society of Biblical Literature
SBLMS	SBL Monograph Series
SBL*SP*	SBL *Seminar Papers*
SCM	Student Christian Movement
SJT	*Scottish Journal of Theology*
SNTSMS	Society for New Testament Studies Monograph Series
SPCK	Society for the Promotion of Christian Knowledge
ST	*Studia theologica*
Str-B	[H. Strack and] P. Billerbeck, *Kommentar zum neuen Testament*
TDNT	G. Kittel and G. Friedrich, eds., *Theological Dictionary of the New Testament*
ThLZ	*Theologische Literaturzeitung*
TS	*Theological Studies*
WW	*Word and World*
ZNTW	*Zeitschrift für die neutestamentliche Wissenschaft*
ZTK	*Zeitschrift für Theologie und Kirche*

NOTES

CHAPTER 1: ANTI-JUDAISM AND NEW TESTAMENT SCHOLARSHIP

1. See Karl Hoheisel, *Das Antike Judentum in Christlicher Sicht: Ein Beitrag zur neueren Forschungsgeschichte,* Studies in Oriental Religions 2 (Wiesbaden: Otto Harrassowitz, 1978).

2. Emil Schürer, *A History of the Jewish People in the Time of Jesus Christ,* trans. Sophia Taylor and Peter Christie (Edinburgh: T. & T. Clark, 1897), Div. 2, 2:93.

3. Emil Schürer, *The History of the Jewish People in the Age of Jesus Christ (175 B.C.–A.D. 135),* rev. and ed. Geza Vermes, Fergus Millar, and Matthew Black (Edinburgh: T. & T. Clark, 1979), 2:466.

4. Hoheisel, *Antike Judentum,* p. 215.

5. Ibid.

6. George Foot Moore, "Christian Writers on Judaism," *HTR* 14 (1921): 197–254.

7. E. P. Sanders, *Paul and Palestinian Judaism: A Comparison of Patterns of Religion* (Philadelphia: Fortress Press, 1977), esp. pp. 33–59.

8. Geza Vermes, "Jewish Studies and New Testament Interpretation," *JJS* 31 (1980): 1–17.

9. Susannah Heschel, "The Image of Judaism in Nineteenth-Century Christian New Testament Scholarship in Germany," in *Jewish-Christian Encounters over the Centuries: Symbiosis, Prejudice, Holocaust, Dialogue,* ed. Marvin Perry and Frederick M. Schweitzer (New York: Peter Lang, 1994), pp. 215–40. See also Heschel, *Abraham Geiger and the Jewish Jesus* (Chicago: University of Chicago Press, 1998).

10. Heschel, "Image of Judaism," p. 233.

11. Moore, "Christian Writers," p. 221.

12. Ibid.

13. Ibid., pp. 221–22.

14. Ibid., p. 197.

15. Ibid., p. 225.

16. Ibid., p. 226. Hoheisel agrees that Gförer opened a new epoch in scholarship. He writes that Gförer's studies have made him a "forerunner of that modern teaching that highly esteems rabbinic literature for knowledge about Judaism in the early Tanaaitic period" (Hoheisel, *Antike Judentum,* p. 11).

17. Heschel, "Image of Judaism," p. 218.

18. Ibid., p. 219.

19. Moore, "Christian Writers," p. 232.

20. Ibid., p. 233.

21. Sanders, *Paul,* p. 37.

22. Ibid., p. 38.

23. Hoheisel, *Antike Judentum,* p. 12.

24. Moore, "Christian Writers," p. 252.

25. Hoheisel, *Antike Judentum,* p. 19.

26. Vermes, "Jewish Studies," p. 7.

27. Ferdinand Weber, *Jüdische Theologie auf Grund des Talmud und verwandter Schriften,* 2d ed. (Leipzig: Dörffling & Franke, 1897), p. xii.

28. Heschel, "Image of Judaism," p. 228.

29. Martin Hengel and Roland Deines, "E. P. Sanders' 'Common Judaism,' Jesus, and the Pharisees," *JTS* 46 (1995): 68–69.

30. Sanders, *Paul,* p. 42.

31. Ibid., p. 43.

32. Ibid., pp. 234–35.

33. Ibid., p. 235.

34. Hoheisel, *Antike Judentum,* p. 43.

35. See ibid. Vermes points out that Billerbeck depended heavily on Weber: "Very often the choice of the illustrative material in the famous *Commentary to the New Testament from Talmud and Midrash* is governed by Weber's understanding of Judaism" (Vermes, "Jewish Studies," p. 7).

36. Moore, "Christian Writers," p. 242.

37. Ibid., p. 243.

38. Ibid., pp. 244–45.

39. Hoheisel, *Antike Judentum,* p. 26.

40. See Sanders, *Paul,* p. 39.

41. Heschel, "Image of Judaism," p. 230.

42. See Hoheisel, *Antike Judentum,* p. 31.

43. D. Wilhelm Bousset, *Die Religion des Judentums im neutestamentlichen Zeitalter,* 2d ed. (Berlin: Reuther und Reichard, 1906), p. 136.

44. Ibid., p. 156.

45. See ibid., p. 151.

46. Sanders, *Paul,* pp. 39–40.

47. See Bousset, *Religion des Judentums,* p. 158.

48. Ibid., p. 158.

49. See ibid., p. 153.

50. Hoheisel, *Antike Judentum,* pp. 19–20.

51. Ibid., p. 20.

52. Heschel, "Image of Judaism," pp. 229–30.

53. Schürer, *History of the Jewish People* (1897 ed.), Div. 2, 2:91.

54. Ibid., Div. 2, 2:95.

55. Ibid.

56. Ibid., Div. 2, 2:125.

57. Sanders, *Paul,* p. 44.

58. Ibid., p. 45.

59. Ibid., p. 47.

60. Hoheisel, *Antike Judentum,* pp. 58–59.

61. See Rudolf Bultmann, *Primitive Christianity in Its Contemporary Setting,* trans. R. H. Fuller (New York: Meridian Books, 1957), p. 59.

62. Ibid., p. 62.

63. Ibid., p. 65.

64. Ibid.

65. Ibid., p. 67.

66. Ibid., p. 69.

67. Ibid.

CHAPTER 2: FERDINAND CHRISTIAN BAUR

1. See Jacob Jervell, "The Divided People of God: The Restoration of Israel and Salvation for the Gentiles," in *Luke and the People of God* (Minneapolis: Augsburg Publishing House, 1972), pp. 41–74.

2. Ibid., p. 42.

3. Horton Harris, *The Tübingen School: A Historical and Theological Investigation of the School of F. C. Baur,* 2d ed. (Grand Rapids: Baker Book House, 1990), p. 1.

4. See David Friedrich Strauss, *Das Leben Jesu, kritisch bearbeitet,* 2 vols. (Tübingen: C. F. Osiander, 1835); trans. from the 4th ed. by George Eliot as *The Life of Jesus Critically Examined,* ed. Peter Hodgson, Lives of Jesus (Philadelphia: Fortress Press, 1972).

5. Quoted by Harris, *Tübingen,* p. 27.

6. Ferdinand C. Baur, *The Church History of the First Three Centuries,* trans. Allan Menzies (London: Williams and Norgate, 1878), 1:17. The first German edition was published in 1853.

7. Ibid., 1:18.

8. Ibid., 1:30.

9. Alan Richardson, *History Sacred and Profane: Bampton Lectures for 1962* (London: SCM Press, 1964), p. 121.

10. See Peter C. Hodgson, *The Formation of Historical Theology: A Study of Ferdinand Christian Baur* (New York: Harper & Row, 1966); idem, *Ferdinand Christian Baur on the Writing of Church History* (New York: Oxford University Press, 1968). See also Klaus Penzel, "Will the Real Ferdinand Christian Baur Stand Up?" *JR* 48 (1968): 310–23. In this article Penzel provides a critique of two recent authors on Baur, namely Hodgson and Wolfgang Geiger.

11. Hodgson, *Formation,* pp. 3–4.

12. See Hodgson, *Ferdinand Christian Baur,* p. 4.

13. Ibid., p. 5 n. 5.

14. Baur did not publish a commentary on Acts. His most extensive treatment is in *Paul, the Apostle of Jesus Christ, His Life and Work, His Epistles and His Doctrine: A Contribution to a Critical History of Primitive Christianity,* trans. Allan Menzies, 2 vols. (London: Williams & Norgate, 1876). The English is a translation of the second German edition edited by Eduard Zeller, 1866–67. Other comments are to be found in several journal articles, as cited below.

15. See A. J. Mattill, Jr., "The Purpose of Acts: Schneckenburger Reconsidered," in *Apostolic History and the Gospel: Biblical and Historical Essays Presented to F. F. Bruce on His 60th Birthday,* ed. W. Ward Gasque and Ralph P. Martin (Grand Rapids: Wm. B. Eerdmans, 1970), pp. 108–22. See also Matthias Schneckenburger, *Über den Zweck der Apostelgeschichte* (Bern: Fischer, 1841).

16. Quoted by Mattill, "The Purpose of Acts," p. 112.

17. Ibid., p. 109.

18. A case can be made for the contention that Peter in Acts sounds like Paul. But how does one make the case that Paul is made to sound like Peter? To say that Paul in

Acts does not sound like Paul in his own letters is one thing, but to say that Paul in Acts sounds like Peter is quite another. How does Baur know what the historical Peter should sound like, since he is not able to cite anything he has written? To be quite accurate, we should say that Luke has made Paul speak and act in ways that Baur conceived to be appropriate for a first generation Jewish Christian.

19. Baur, *Historisch-Kritische Untersuchungen zum Neuen Testament* (Stuttgart: Friedrich Frommann, 1963), p. 462. This is a reprint of selected writings by Baur. The quotation above is from "Über Zweck und Veranlassung des Römerbriefs und die damit zusammenhängenden Verhältnisse der römischen Gemeinde," *Tübinger Zeitschrift für Theologie* 9 (1836): 59–178.

20. Baur, *Paul, the Apostle,* 1:6.

21. Baur, *Church History,* 1:55.

22. See Baur, "Die Christuspartei in der korinthischen Gemeinde, der Gegensatz des petrinischen und paulinischen Christenthums in der ältesten Kirche, der Apostel Petrus in Rom," *Tübinger Zeitschrift für Theologie* 5 (1831): 61–206.

23. Baur, *Church History,* 1:75.

24. Ibid., 1:132.

25. Ibid., 1:135.

26. Baur, *Paul, the Apostle,* 1:89.

27. Ibid., 1:119.

28. Ibid., 1:125.

29. Baur defends the proposition by observing that the statement is confirmed by Epiphanius, *Haer.* 30, which says that the Ebionites were poor because they voluntarily laid their possessions at the feet of the apostles. The Ebionites would not have taken this from Acts, says Baur, because of their opposition to Paul, so the statement has independent verification from an unfriendly source. See Baur, *Paul, the Apostle,* 1:29–33.

30. Baur, *Paul, the Apostle,* 1:38.

31. Ibid.

32. Ibid., 1:57.

33. Ibid., 1:46–47.

34. Ibid., 1:49.

35. Ibid., 1:49–50.

36. Ibid., 1:195.

37. Ibid.

38. Ibid., 1:324.

39. Ibid.

40. Baur, *Historisch-Kritische Untersuchungen,* p. 462.

41. See Baur, *Church History,* 1:77–82.

42. See Baur, *Kritische Untersuchungen über die kanonischen Evangelien, ihr Verhältniss zu einander, ihren Charakter und Ursprung* (Tübingen: Ludw. Fr. Fues, 1847), pp. 391–531. In 1939, Mary E. Andrews complained that Baur's work on Luke was not well known. See her, "*Tendenz* versus Interpretation: F. C. Baur's Criticisms of Luke," *JBL* 58 (1939): 263–76. Sadly, her complaint is still valid.

43. See Albrecht Ritschl, *Das Evangelium Marcions und das kanonische Evangelium des Lucas* (Tübingen: Osiander, 1846).

44. The post-Marcionite location of canonical Luke is an important factor that contributes to Baur's late dating of the NT documents.

45. Baur, *Kritische Untersuchungen,* p. 428.

46. Note the textual variants in Luke 10:1,17, which allow one to make a strong case for the number seventy-two as original.

47. Actually Jesus' words in Luke 10:16 are different from those in Matt 10:40, and the audience for Luke 10:16 is undefined. The words are spoken by Jesus before the seventy return in Luke 10:17 and are attached to his condemnation of Chorazin and Bethsaida, cities that are addressed in the second person.

48. Baur, *Kritische Untersuchungen,* p. 441.

49. Ibid., p. 502.

50. Ibid., p. 503. The meaning of Baur's term *Phantasie* is not altogether clear. There may be an allusion to the poetic imagination, which would probably evoke images from Jewish apocalyptic literature. But its use here, modified only by the term *jüdische,* seems more likely to carry an evaluation of Jewish messianic expectation as illusion. It is probably the more negative, and hence anti-Jewish, sense that is conveyed to most readers of Baur.

51. See ibid., p. 507.

52. Ibid., p. 508.

53. Baur, *Church History,* 1:78–79.

54. See Eduard Zeller, *Die Apostelgeschichte nach ihrem Inhalt und Ursprung kritisch untersucht* (Stuttgart: C. Mäcken, 1854); trans. Joseph Dare as *The Contents and Origin of the Acts of the Apostles, Critically Investigated,* 2 vols. (London: Williams and Norgate, 1875–76).

55. Zeller, *Contents and Origin,* 2:78; emphasis in original.

56. Ibid., 2:123.

57. Ibid., 2:154.

58. Ibid., 2:155.

59. See Franz Overbeck's introduction to W. M. L. DeWette, *Kurze Erklärung der Apostelgeschichte* (Leipzig: S. Hirzel, 1870). Overbeck's introduction also appears as the introduction to the English translation of Zeller's commentary on Acts. See Zeller, *Contents and Origin,* 1:3–81.

60. Overbeck in Zeller, *Contents and Origin,* 1:20–21; emphasis in original.

61. Ibid., 1:24.

62. See Albrecht Ritschl, *Die Enstehung der altkatholischen Kirche: Eine kirchen- und dogmengeschichtliche Monographie,* 2d ed. (Bonn: Adolph Marcus, 1857). Horton Harris refers to Ritschl as "the apostate of the Tübingen School" (*Tübingen,* p. 101).

CHAPTER 3: ADOLF VON HARNACK

1. Susannah Heschel, *Abraham Geiger and the Jewish Jesus* (Chicago: University of Chicago Press, 1998), esp. pp. 122–26.

2. Ibid., p. 123.

3. Ibid., pp. 123–24.

4. Quoted by Martin Rumscheidt, ed., *Adolf von Harnack: Liberal Theology at Its Height* (London: Collins, 1988), p. 12.

5. Rumscheidt, *Adolf von Harnack,* p. 10.

6. See ibid., p. 22.

7. Ibid., p. 14.

8. See Heinrich J. Holtzmann, *Die synoptischen Evangelien: Ihr Ursprung und geschichtlicher Charakter* (Leipzig: W. Engelmann, 1863).

9. Werner Georg Kümmel, *The New Testament: The History of the Investigation of Its Problems,* trans. S. McLean Gilmour and Howard C. Kee (Nashville: Abingdon Press, 1972), p. 151.

10. William R. Farmer, *The Synoptic Problem: A Critical Analysis* (New York: Macmillan, 1964), p. 46.

11. See Abraham Geiger, *Urschrift und Übersetzungen der Bibel in ihrer Abhängigkeit von der inneren Entwickelung des Judentums* (Breslau: Julius Hainauer, 1857); idem, *Sadducäer und Pharisäer* (Breslau: H. Skutsch, 1863); idem, *Das Judentum und seine Geschichte von der Zerstörung des zweiten Tempels bis zum Ende des zwölften Jahrhunderts* (Breslau: Schlettersche Buchhandlung, 1865).

12. See Geiger, *Judentum und seine Geschichte.*

13. Heschel, "The Image of Judaism in Nineteenth-Century Christian New Testament Scholarship in Germany," in *Jewish-Christian Encounters over the Centuries: Symbiosis, Prejudice, Holocaust, Dialogue,* ed. Marvin Perry and Frederick M. Schweitzer (New York: Peter Lang, 1994), p. 226.

14. Adolf Harnack, *What Is Christianity?* trans. Thomas Bailey Saunders (New York: Harper and Row, 1957), p. 47. The original, taken from sixteen lectures delivered by Harnack in 1899–1900, was published as *Das Wesen des Christentums* (Leipzig: J. C. Hinrichs, 1900).

15. *Fläche* is a generally neutral term for area or surface. A better translation of the phrase in question might be, "For them everything was on one level. . . ."

16. Harnack, *What Is Christianity?* p. 48.

17. Alfred Loisy took Harnack to task for drawing similarly sharp distinctions between early Judaism and early Christianity. He noted that the two faiths, together with Islam, share much in common and should be defined in connection not only with their differences but also in terms of what they share. Loisy wrote: "It is, therefore, in the highest degree arbitrary to decide that Christianity in its essence must be all that the gospel has not borrowed of Judaism, as if all that the gospel has retained of the Jewish tradition must be necessarily of secondary value. Herr Harnack finds it quite natural to place the essence of Christianity in the faith in God the Father, because he supposes, somewhat hastily by the way, that this element of the gospel is foreign to the Old Testament." See Loisy, *The Gospel and the Church,* trans. Christopher Home (New York: Charles Scribner's Sons, 1912), p. 10.

18. Harnack, *What Is Christianity?* pp. 70–71.

19. Ibid., p. 71.

20. See Harnack, *The Expansion of Christianity in the First Three Centuries,* trans. James Moffatt (London: Williams and Norgate, 1904), 1:1–18.

21. Ibid., 1:15.

22. Harnack, *History of Dogma,* trans. Neil Buchanan (Boston: Little, Brown and Company, 1905), 1:41.

23. Ibid., 1:42.

24. Ibid.

25. Ibid.

26. Ibid., 1:43.

27. Ibid., 1:47.

28. See Harnack, *Marcion: Das Evangelium vom Fremden Gott: Eine Monographie zur Geschichte der Grundlegung der katholischen Kirche* (Leipzig: J. C. Hinrichs,

1921), trans. John E. Steely and Lyle D. Bierma as *Marcion: The Gospel of the Alien God* (Durham, N.C.: Labyrinth Press, 1990). Unless otherwise noted, quotations here are from the English translation.

29. Harnack, *Marcion,* p. 21; emphasis in original.

30. Ibid., p. 133; emphasis in original.

31. Ibid., p. 134; emphasis in original.

32. Harnack, *Expansion,* 1:81–82; emphasis mine.

33. See Harnack, *Lukas der Arzt, der Verfasser des dritten Evangeliums und der Apostelgeschichte* (Leipzig: Hinrichs, 1906), trans. J. R. Wilkinson as *Luke the Physician: The Author of the Third Gospel and the Acts of the Apostles* (London: Williams and Norgate, 1908); idem, *Die Apostelgeschichte* (Leipzig: Hinrichs, 1908), trans. Wilkinson as *The Acts of the Apostles* (London: Williams and Norgate, 1909); idem, *Neue Untersuchungen zur Apostelgeschichte und zur Abfassungszeit der synoptischen Evangelium* (Leipzig: Hinrichs, 1911), trans. Wilkinson as *The Date of the Acts and of the Synoptic Gospels* (London: Williams and Norgate, 1911). Unless otherwise noted, quotations below are from the English editions.

34. See Harnack, *Sprüche und Reden Jesu* (Leipzig: Hinrichs, 1907), trans. Wilkinson as *The Sayings of Jesus: The Second Source of St. Matthew and St. Luke* (London: Williams and Norgate, 1908).

35. Harnack, *Luke the Physician,* p. 2.

36. Ibid., p. 12.

37. Ibid., p. 13.

38. William K. Hobart, *The Medical Language of St. Luke* (Dublin: Hodges, Figgis and Co., 1882).

39. See Harnack, *Luke the Physician,* pp. 175–98.

40. Ibid., pp. 52–53.

41. Ibid., pp. 126–27.

42. Ibid., p. 127.

43. Ibid., p. 142.

44. See Harnack, *The Date of the Acts,* pp. 30–89.

45. Ibid., p. 43.

46. Ibid., p. 49.

47. Ibid., p. 51.

48. Ibid., pp. 60–61; emphasis in original.

49. Ibid., p. 88.

50. Harnack, *The Acts of the Apostles,* p. 194.

51. Ibid., pp. xxiv–xxv.

52. Harnack, *Luke the Physician,* p. 135; emphasis in original.

53. Ibid., p. 127.

54. Harnack, *The Acts of the Apostles,* p. xxv n.

55. Ibid., p. xxiv.

56. Ibid.

57. Harnack, *Luke the Physician,* p. 128.

58. Harnack, *The Date of the Acts,* p. 112.

59. Harnack, *Luke the Physician,* p. 127.

60. Elsewhere Harnack observed that Luke placed 16:17 where he did in order to correct the apparent antinomianism of 16:16. See Harnack, *The Sayings of Jesus,* p. 198.

CHAPTER 4: ADOLF SCHLATTER

1. English translation, Albert Schweitzer, *The Quest of the Historical Jesus: A Critical Study of Its Progress from Reimarus to Wrede,* trans. W. Montgomery (London: A. & C. Black, 1910). Unless otherwise noted, quotations here are from this edition.

2. F. C. Burkitt, preface, in Schweitzer, *Quest,* p. v.

3. See William Wrede, *Das Messiasgeheimnis in den Evangelien: Zugleich ein Beitrag zum Verständnis des Markusevangeliums* (Göttingen: Vandenhoeck & Ruprecht, 1901). See also Schweitzer, *Das Messianitäts und Leidengeheimnis: Eine Skizze des Lebens Jesu* (Tübingen: J. C. B. Mohr [Paul Siebeck], 1901).

4. Schweitzer, *Quest,* p. 339.

5. Ibid., p. 345.

6. Ibid., p. 371.

7. Ibid.

8. Ibid., p. 398.

9. See Karl Ludwig Schmidt, *Der Rahmen der Geschichte Jesu: Literarkritische Untersuchungen zur ältesten Jesusüberlieferung* (Berlin: Trowitzsch & Sohn, 1919).

10. See Martin Dibelius, *Die Formgeschichte des Evangeliums* (Tübingen: J. C. B. Mohr [Paul Siebeck], 1919), trans. Dibelius and Bertram Lee Woolf as *From Tradition to Gospel* (New York: Charles Scribner's Sons, 1935). Quotations below are from the English edition.

11. Dibelius, *From Tradition to Gospel,* p. 1.

12. Ibid., p. 61.

13. See Dibelius, "Stilkritisches zur Apostelgeschichte," in *Aufsätze zur Apostelgeschichte,* ed. Heinrich Greeven (Göttingen: Vandenhoeck & Ruprecht, 1951), pp. 9–28; trans. Mary Ling as *Studies in the Acts of the Apostles* (London: William Clowes and Sons, 1956), pp. 1–25. The essay first appeared in *Eucharisterion für H. Gunkel* (Göttingen: Vandenhoeck & Ruprecht, 1923), 2:27–49. Quotations below are from the English edition.

14. See Rudolf Bultmann, *Die Geschichte der synoptischen Tradition* (Göttingen: Vandenhoeck & Ruprecht, 1921), trans. John Marsh as *The History of the Synoptic Tradition* (New York: Harper and Row, 1963). Quotations below are from the English edition.

15. Bultmann, *Synoptic Tradition,* p. 41.

16. Ibid., p. 50.

17. See Adolf Deissmann, *Light from the Ancient East: The New Testament Illustrated by Recently Discovered Texts of the Graeco-Roman World,* trans. Lionel R. M. Strachan (New York: George H. Doran Co., 1927). First German edition, 1908.

18. See Richard Reitzenstein, *Die hellenistischen Mysterienreligion: Ihren Grundgedanken und Wirkungen* (Leipzig: B. G. Teubner, 1910), trans. John E. Steely as *Hellenistic Mystery-Religions: Their Basic Ideas and Significance* (Pittsburgh: Pickwick Press, 1978).

19. See Wilhelm Bousset, *Kyrios Christos: Geschichte des Christusglaubens von den Anfängen des Christentums bis Irenaeus* (Göttingen: Vandenhoeck & Ruprecht, 1913), trans. John E. Steely as *Kyrios Christos: A History of the Belief in Christ from the Beginnings of Christianity to Irenaeus* (Nashville: Abingdon Press, 1970).

20. See Bousset, *Die Religion des Judentums in neutestamentlichen Zeitalter* (Berlin: Reuther & Reichard, 1903).

21. See H. L. Strack and Paul Billerbeck, *Kommentar zum Neuen Testament aus Talmud und Midrasch,* 6 vols. (Munich: Beck, 1922–61).

22. Stephen Neill, *The Interpretation of the New Testament 1861–1961* (London: Oxford University Press, 1964), p. 292. But for a vigorous critique of Strack-Billerbeck, see E. P. Sanders, *Paul and Palestinian Judaism: A Comparison of Patterns of Religion* (Philadelphia: Fortress Press, 1977), esp. pp. 33–59.

23. See George Foot Moore, *Judaism in the First Centuries of the Christian Era: The Age of the Tannaim,* 3 vols. (Cambridge: Harvard University Press, 1927). See also Moore's review of eighteenth- and nineteenth-century scholarship on early Judaism, "Christian Writers on Judaism," *HTR* 14 (1921) 197–254.

24. Moore, "Christian Writers," p. 245.

25. See C. G. Montefiore, *Rabbinic Literature and Gospel Teachings* (London: Macmillan, 1930).

26. See Montefiore, *The Synoptic Gospels,* 3 vols. (London: Macmillan, 1909).

27. See W. M. Ramsay, *The Bearing of Recent Discovery on the Trustworthiness of the New Testament,* 4th ed. (London: Hodder and Stoughton, 1920); idem, *Luke the Physician and Other Studies in the History of Religion* (London: Hodder and Stoughton, 1908).

28. See Theodor Zahn, *Das Evangelium des Lucas* (Leipzig: Deichert, 1913); idem, *Die Apostelgeschichte des Lucas,* 2 vols. (Leipzig: Deichert, 1919).

29. See Eduard Meyer, *Ursprung und Anfänge des Christentums,* 3 vols. (Stuttgart: J. G. Cotta, 1921–23).

30. See F. J. Foakes-Jackson and Kirsopp Lake, eds., *The Beginnings of Christianity,* part 1, *The Acts of the Apostles,* 5 vols. (London: Macmillan, 1920–33). All five volumes are now available in a paperback reprint: Grand Rapids, Mich.: Baker Book House, 1979. References below are to this edition.

31. W. Ward Gasque, *A History of the Interpretation of the Acts of the Apostles* (Peabody, Mass.: Hendrickson, 1989), p. 170.

32. Beverly Roberts Gaventa, "The Peril of Modernizing Henry Joel Cadbury," in *Cadbury, Knox, and Talbert: American Contributions to the Study of Acts,* ed. Mikeal C. Parsons and Joseph B. Tyson (Atlanta: Scholars Press, 1992), p. 8.

33. Ernst Haenchen, *The Acts of the Apostles: A Commentary,* trans. Bernard Noble et al. (Oxford: Basil Blackwell, 1971), p. 37.

34. Haenchen conceded that "the rich abundance of linguistic, historical and archaeological details renders the work, now as then, indispensable to the scholar, and ensures its value even on the Continent" (ibid.). It is also notable that Haenchen dedicated the English translation of the commentary to H. J. Cadbury and referred to him as "the doyen of Anglo-Saxon research on Acts" (ibid., p. 43).

35. See Foakes-Jackson and Lake, eds., *Beginnings,* 1:35–81.

36. Ibid., 1:36; emphasis in original.

37. Ibid., 1:46.

38. Ibid., 1:66.

39. Ibid., 1:79.

40. Ibid.; emphasis in original.

41. See ibid., 1:82–136.

42. Ibid., 1:136.

43. See Gasque, *History of the Interpretation,* p. 181 and 181 n.

44. Foakes-Jackson and Lake, eds., *Beginnings,* 4:279.

45. Ibid., 4:350.

46. Ibid., 4:174.

47. Ibid., 4:348.

48. Ibid.

49. Werner Neuer, *Adolf Schlatter: A Biography of Germany's Premier Biblical Theologian,* trans. Robert W. Yarbrough (Grand Rapids: Baker Books, 1995), p. 56. Originally published as *Adolf Schlatter* (Wuppertal: R. Brockhaus, 1988). Quotations below are from the English edition. I am heavily dependent on Neuer for biographical information about Schlatter.

50. Ibid., p. 95.

51. Martin Hengel, *Vorwort,* in *Paulus und das antike Judentum,* ed. Martin Hengel and Ulrich Heckel (Tübingen: J. C. B. Mohr [Paul Siebeck], 1991), p. vii.

52. Mark Noll, foreword, in Neuer, *Adolf Schlatter,* p. 7.

53. Peter Stuhlmacher, foreword, in Schlatter, *Romans: The Righteousness of God,* trans. Siegfried S. Schatzmann (Peabody, Mass.: Hendrickson, 1995), p. xxi. Originally published as *Gottes Gerechtigkeit: Ein Kommentar zum Römerbrief* (Stuttgart: Calwer Verlag, 1935).

54. Ibid., p. xxiv.

55. Adolf Schlatter, *The Church in the New Testament Period,* trans. Paul P. Levertoff (London: SPCK, 1955), p. 2. Originally published as *Die Geschichte der ersten Christenheit* (Gütersloh: C. Bertelmann, 1926). Quotations below are from the English edition.

56. Schlatter, *The Church,* p. 59.

57. See Schlatter, *Die Theologie des Judentums nach dem Bericht des Josefus* (Gütersloh: Gerd Mohn, 1932).

58. See Schlatter, *Die Geschichte des Christus* (Stuttgart: Calwer, 1923), trans. Andreas J. Köstenberger as *The History of the Christ: The Foundation of New Testament Theology* (Grand Rapids: Baker Books, 1997). See also Schlatter, *Romans.* Quotations below are from the English editions.

59. Schlatter, *History of the Christ,* p. 205.

60. Ibid., p. 206.

61. Ibid., p. 206 n.

62. Ibid., p. 217.

63. Schlatter, *Romans,* p. 200.

64. Ibid., p. 223.

65. Ibid., p. 225.

66. Schlatter, *The Church,* pp. 5–6.

67. Neuer, *Adolf Schlatter,* p. 151.

68. See Schlatter, *Die neue deutsche Art in der Kirche* (Bethel: Anstalt Bethel, 1933).

69. Lenore Siegele-Wenschkewitz, "Adolf Schlatters Sicht des Judentums im politischen Kontext: Die Schrift *Wird der Jude über uns siegen?* von 1935," in *Christlicher Antijudaismus und Antisemitismus: Theologische und kirchliche Programme Deutscher Christen,* ed. Siegele-Wenschkewitz (Frankfurt: Haag & Herchen, 1994), p. 107.

70. See Schlatter, *Wir Christen und die Juden* (Essen: Freizeiten, 1930).

71. See Schlatter, *Wird der Jude über uns siegen?* (Essen: Freizeiten, 1935).

72. See Schlatter, *Rückblick auf seine Lebensarbeit* (Gütersloh: C. Bertelsmann, 1952), pp. 262–63. The bulk of the book is autobiographical, but Theodor Schlatter

added a concluding chapter to a previously unpublished manuscript of his father's. The chapter deals with the last fifteen years of Adolf Schlatter's life.

73. See Walter Grundmann, *Jesus der Galiläer und das Judentum* (Leipzig: Georg Wigand, 1940). For a study of Grundmann, see Susannah Heschel, "Theologen für Hitler: Walter Grundmann und das 'Institut zur Erforschung und Beseitigung des jüdischen Einflusses auf das deutsche kirchliche Leben," in *Christlicher Antijudaismus,* pp. 125–70.

74. See Neuer, *Adolf Schlatter,* p. 151.

75. See Siegele-Wenschkewitz, "Adolf Schlatters Sicht," pp. 95–110.

76. See Neuer, *Adolf Schlatter: Ein Leben für Theologie und Kirche* (Stuttgart: Calwer, 1996).

77. See ibid., p. 760.

78. Siegele-Wenschkewitz, "Adolf Schlatters Sicht," pp. 99–100.

79. See Reijo E. Heinonen, *Anpassung und Idenität: Theologie und Kirchenpolitik der Bremer Deutschen Christen 1933–1945* (Göttingen: Vandenhoeck & Ruprecht, 1978), p. 155. The quotation of Grundmann is taken from an article in *Kommende Kirche* 33 (1937). Heinonen says that *Kommende Kirche* reported on nobody else's theology in greater detail than Schlatter's.

80. Heinonen, *Anpassung,* pp. 154–66.

81. Schlatter, *Der neue deutsche Art,* p. 16; quoted in Heinonen, *Anpassung,* p. 157.

82. Heinonen, *Anpassung,* p. 157.

83. See Schlatter, *Erläuterungen zum Neuen Testament,* 3 vols. (Stuttgart: Verlag der Vereinsbuchhandlung, 1908).

84. See Schlatter, *Die Apostelgeschichte ausgelegt für Bibelleser* (Stuttgart: Verlag der Vereinsbuchhandlung, 1902); idem, *Die Apostelgeschichte* (Stuttgart: Calwer, 1962).

85. See Schlatter, *Erläuterungen,* 1:851.

86. Ibid., 1:856.

87. Ibid., 1:1010.

88. Ibid., 1:877.

89. Ibid., 1:879.

90. Ibid.

91. Ibid., 1:881.

92. Ibid., 1:884.

93. Ibid., 1:950.

94. Schlatter, *The Church,* p. 136.

95. See Schlatter, *Erläuterungen,* 1:1053.

96. See Schlatter, *Das Evangelium des Lukas: Aus seinen Quellen erklärt* (Stuttgart: Calwer, 1931).

97. Ulrich Luck, *Kerygma und Tradition in der Hermeneutik Adolf Schlatters* (Köln und Oplanden: Westdeutscher Verlag, 1955), p. 12.

98. See ibid., pp. 7–13.

99. See Schlatter, *Lukas,* pp. 5–6.

100. See ibid., pp. 48–49.

101. "The New Edition of Mark" has 114 pages, "The Gospel of Matthew in Luke," 90 pages, and "The New Narrator," 325 pages.

102. Schlatter, *Lukas,* p. 463.

103. Ibid., p. 464.
104. Ibid., p. 147.
105. Ibid., p. 149.
106. See ibid., pp. 194–97.
107. Ibid., p. 210.
108. Ibid., p. 212.
109. Ibid., p. 232.
110. See ibid., p. 284.
111. Ibid., p. 304.
112. See ibid., p. 330.
113. Ibid., p. 389.
114. Ibid., p. 399.

CHAPTER 5: ERNST HAENCHEN AND HANS CONZELMANN

1. Ulrich Busse, "Ernst Haenchen und sein Johanneskommentar," *ETL* 57 (1981): 128–29. On the role of Hirsch in support of National Socialism, see Robert P. Ericksen, *Theologians under Hitler: Gerhard Kittel, Paul Althaus, and Emanuel Hirsch* (New Haven: Yale University Press, 1985).

2. See Ernst Haenchen, *Der Weg Jesu: Eine Erklärung des Markus-Evangeliums und der kanonischen Parallelen,* 2d ed. (Berlin: Walter de Gruyter & Co., 1968).

3. See Haenchen, *Das Johannesevangelium: Ein Kommentar,* ed. Ulrich Busse (Tübingen: J. C. B. Mohr [Paul Siebeck], 1980).

4. See Haenchen, *Die Apostelgeschichte* (Göttingen: Vandenhoeck & Ruprecht, 1956). This volume constitutes the 10th edition of the Meyer commentaries (Kritisch-exegetischer Kommentar über das Neue Testament). The English translation is from the 14th German edition of 1965. See Haenchen, *The Acts of the Apostles: A Commentary,* trans. Bernard Noble et al. (Oxford: Basil Blackwell, 1971). Quotations below are from the English edition.

5. I am indebted to Busse, "Ernst Haenchen," for the preceding biographical information.

6. See Haenchen, "Volk und Staat in der Lehre der Kirche," in *Volk, Staat, Kirche: Ein Lehrgang der Theolog Fakultät Giessen* (Giessen: Alfred Töpelmann, 1933), pp. 53–72.

7. Ibid., p. 71. I have deliberately left the term *Volkstum* untranslated, because of its significance at the time that Haenchen was writing. In the present context, it probably stands for one's national identity.

8. Ibid., p. 63.
9. Ibid., p. 64.
10. See ibid., pp. 68–69.
11. See Haenchen, "Matthäus 23," *ZTK* 48 (1951): 38–63; republished in *Gott und Mensch: Gesammelte Aufsätze* (Tübingen: J. C. B. Mohr [Paul Siebeck], 1965), pp. 29–54. References here are to the 1965 edition.

12. Ibid., p. 42.
13. Ibid., p. 51.
14. See Haenchen, *Der Weg Jesu.*
15. Ibid., p. 112.
16. Ibid., p. 114.

17. Ibid., p. 129.

18. Ibid., p. 121.

19. See Haenchen, *Acts.*

20. See ibid., pp. 14–50.

21. Ibid., p. 37.

22. Ibid., p. 41.

23. Ibid., p. 100; emphasis in original.

24. Ibid.

25. Ibid., p. 116.

26. Ibid., p. 221.

27. Ibid., p. 223.

28. Ibid., pp. 289–90.

29. See Haenchen, "Judentum und Christentum in der Apostelgeschichte," *ZNTW* 54 (1963): 155–87.

30. Ibid., p. 165.

31. Haenchen, *Acts,* p. 417.

32. Ibid.

33. Ibid., pp. 417–18.

34. Ibid., p. 535.

35. Ibid., pp. 539–40.

36. Ibid., p. 461.

37. Ibid., p. 459. Haenchen cites Str-B 1:608ff., and Foakes-Jackson and Lake, eds., *Beginnings,* 4:173ff., as support for the contention that this negative attitude toward the law is not Jewish. He says further, "The Jewish saw in the law a privilege and a help: the idea of 'the yoke (of the law)' denoted the religious duties and contained no complaint that the law was hard or intolerable" (Haenchen, p. 446n).

38. Haenchen, *Acts,* p. 469; emphasis in original.

39. Ibid., p. 470.

40. Ibid., p. 643.

41. Ibid., p. 659.

42. Ibid., pp. 693–94.

43. Ibid., p. 730.

44. Ibid., p. 128.

45. Dietz Lange, "In Memoriam Hans Conzelmann," in *Gentiles—Jews—Christians: Polemics and Apologetics in the Greco-Roman Era,* by Hans Conzelmann, trans. M. Eugene Boring (Minneapolis: Fortress Press, 1992), p. xiv. Originally published as *Heiden—Juden—Christen: Auseinandersetzungen in der Literatur der hellenistisch-römischen Zeit* (Tübingen: J. C. B. Mohr [Paul Siebeck], 1981). Quotations below are from the English edition.

46. See Conzelmann, *Die Mitte der Zeit: Studien zur Theologie des Lukas,* Beiträge zur historischen Theologie 17 (Tübingen: J. C. B. Mohr [Paul Siebeck], 1954), trans. Geoffrey Buswell as *The Theology of St. Luke* (New York: Harper & Bros., 1960). References below are to the English edition unless otherwise noted.

47. Conzelmann, Χάρος, in *TDNT,* ed. Gerhard Kittel, trans. G. W. Bromiley (Grand Rapids: Eerdmans, 1973–76), 9:388.

48. Ibid.

49. Conzelmann, *An Outline of the Theology of the New Testament,* trans. John Bowden (London: SCM Press, 1969). Originally published as *Grundriss der Theologie*

des Neuen Testaments, 2d ed. (Munich: Christian Kaiser, 1968). Quotations below are taken from the English edition.

50. Ibid., p. 13.

51. Ibid., p. 14.

52. Ibid.

53. Ibid., p. 21.

54. Ibid.

55. Ibid.

56. Ibid.

57. See Hans Conzelmann and Andreas Lindemann, *Interpreting the New Testament: An Introduction to the Principles and Methods of N.T. Exegesis,* trans. Siegfried S. Schatzmann (Peabody, Mass.: Hendrickson, 1988). Originally published as *Arbeitsbuch zum Neuen Testament* (Tübingen: J. C. B. Mohr [Paul Siebeck], 1985). Quotations below are taken from the English edition.

58. Ibid., p. 130.

59. Ibid., p. 131.

60. Ibid.

61. Conzelmann, "Jesus Christ," in *Die Religion in Geschichte und Gegenwart: Handwörterbuch für Theologie und Religionswissenschaft,* ed. Kurt Galling et al., 3d edition (Tübingen: J. C. B. Mohr [Paul Siebeck], 1959), 3:619–53; trans. Raymond Lord as *Jesus: The Classic Article from RGG Expanded and Updated,* ed. John Reumann (Philadelphia: Fortress Press, 1973). Quotations below are taken from the English edition.

62. Conzelmann, *Jesus,* p. 18.

63. Ibid., pp. 52–53.

64. Ibid., p. 53.

65. Ibid., p. 54; emphasis in original.

66. Ibid., pp. 84–85.

67. Ibid., p. 86.

68. Conzelmann, "History and Theology in the Passion Narratives of the Synoptic Gospels," *Int* 24 (1970): 179; trans. Charles B. Cousar from "Historie und Theologie in den synoptischen Passionsberichten," in *Zur Bedeutung des Todes Jesu,* ed. Fritz Viering (Gütersloh: Gerd Mohn, 1967), pp. 35–53. Quotations below are taken from the English edition.

69. Ibid.

70. Ibid., p. 197.

71. Ibid.

72. Conzelmann, "The First Christian Century as Christian History," in *The Bible in Modern Scholarship: Papers Read at the 100th Meeting of the Society of Biblical Literature, December 28–30, 1964,* ed. J. Philip Hyatt (Nashville: Abingdon Press, 1965), p. 222.

73. Ibid., p. 220.

74. See Conzelmann, *Gentiles—Jews—Christians.*

75. See ibid., pp. 1–5.

76. See ibid., pp. 253–54.

77. Ibid., p. 257.

78. Ibid., p. 342.

79. Ibid.

80. Ibid., p. 133.

81. Ibid., p. 342; emphasis in original.

82. See n. 46 above.

83. Conzelmann, *Theology,* pp. 13–14.

84. Ibid., p. 9.

85. Ibid., p. 12.

86. Ibid., p. 9.

87. Ibid.

88. For examples of narratological and literary approaches to Luke-Acts, see chap. 7 below.

89. Conzelmann, *Theology,* p. 20.

90. Ibid., p. 23 .

91. Ibid., p. 172.

92. See H. H. Oliver, "The Lucan Birth Stories and the Purpose of Luke-Acts," *NTS* 10 (1964): 202–26.

93. See Paul S. Minear, "Luke's Use of the Birth Stories," in *Studies in Luke-Acts,* ed. by Leander E. Keck and J. Louis Martyn (Nashville: Abingdon Press, 1966), pp. 111–30.

94. Ibid., p. 113. In drawing up this list Minear depended on Alfred Plummer, *A Critical and Exegetical Commentary on the Gospel according to St. Luke,* ICC, 5th ed. (Edinburgh: T. & T. Clark, 1922), pp. lix–lx.

95. Minear, "Luke's Use," pp. 114–18. At this point Minear draws on Robert Morgenthaler, *Lukanische Geschichtsschreibung als Zeugnis: Gestalt und Gehalt der Kunst des Lukas* (Zurich: Zwingli-Verlag, 1948) and *Statistik des neutestamentlichen Wortschatzes* (Zurich: Gotthelf-Verlag, 1958).

96. Minear, "Luke's Use," p. 120.

97. Ibid., p. 121.

98. Ibid.

99. See B. H. Streeter, "Fresh Light on the Synoptic Problem," *Hibbert Journal* 20 (1921): 103–112; *The Four Gospels: A Study of Origins* (London: Macmillan, 1924), pp. 201–22; Vincent Taylor, *Behind the Third Gospel: A Study of the Proto-Luke Hypothesis* (Oxford: Clarendon Press, 1926).

100. Taylor, *Third Gospel,* pp. 164–66.

101. Conzelmann, *Theology,* p. 118.

102. Ibid., p. 9.

103. Ibid., p. 87.

104. Ibid., p. 90.

105. Ibid.

106. Ibid., p. 145.

107. Ibid., p. 147.

108. Ibid., p. 160.

109. Ibid., p. 165.

110. Ibid., p. 167.

111. See n. 4 above.

112. See Conzelmann, "Geschichte, Geschichtsbild und Geschichtsdarstellung bei Lukas," *ThLZ* 85 (1960): 241–50.

113. See Conzelmann, *Die Apostelgeschichte,* Handbuch zum Neuen Testament 7 (Tübingen: J. C. B. Mohr [Paul Siebeck], 1963), trans. James Limburg, A. Thomas

Kraabel, and Donald H. Juel as *The Acts of the Apostles: A Commentary on the Acts of the Apostles,* Hermeneia Series (Philadelphia: Fortress Press, 1987). Quotations below are from the English edition.

114. Ibid., p. 103.
115. Ibid., p. 106.
116. Ibid., p. xlviii.
117. Ibid., p. 106.
118. Ibid., p. 115.
119. Ibid., p. 117.
120. See ibid., p. 188. Conzelmann had not, however, given attention to this parable in his *Theology of St. Luke.*
121. Ibid.
122. Ibid., p. 227.
123. See Haenchen, *Acts,* p. 128.
124. See, e.g., Conzelmann, *Theology,* p. 167.
125. See Conzelmann, *Gentiles—Jews—Christians,* pp. 253–54.

CHAPTER 6: JACOB JERVELL

1. See Jacob Jervell, *Die Apostelgeschichte,* Meyers Kritisch-Exegetischer Kommentar über das Neue Testament, 17th ed. (Göttingen: Vandenhoeck & Ruprecht, 1998). See also Haenchen, *The Acts of the Apostles: A Commentary,* trans. Bernard Noble et al. (Oxford: Basil Blackwell, 1971). The English is a translation of the 14th edition of the German commentary, published in 1965.

2. See Jervell, *Imago Dei: Gen 1.26f. im Spätjudentum, in der Gnosis und in den paulinischen Briefen* (Göttingen: Vandenhoeck & Ruprecht, 1960).

3. Trans. by Harris E. Kaasa as *The Continuing Search for the Historical Jesus* (Minneapolis: Augsburg Publishing House, 1965). Quotations below are from the English edition.

4. See Ernst Käsemann, "The Problem of the Historical Jesus," in *Essays on New Testament Themes,* trans. W. J. Montague (London: SCM Press, 1964), pp. 15–47. The essay was originally delivered as a lecture in 1953 and first published in *ZTK* 51 (1954): 125–53.

5. Jervell, *Continuing Search,* p. 36.

6. Ibid.

7. Ibid., p. 42.

8. See Joachim Jeremias, *Abba: Studien zur neutestamentlichen Theologie und Zeitgeschichte* (Göttingen: Vandenhoeck & Ruprecht, 1966).

9. Jervell, *Continuing Search,* p. 40.

10. Ibid., p. 50.

11. Ibid., p. 76.

12. See Jervell, *Luke and the People of God: A New Look at Luke-Acts* (Minneapolis: Augsburg Publishing House, 1972).

13. See ibid., pp. 41–74.

14. Ibid., p. 41.

15. Ibid., p. 55.

16. Ibid., p. 46.

17. See Jervell, "The Church of Jews and Godfearers," in *Luke-Acts and the Jew-*

ish People: Eight Critical Perspectives, ed. Joseph B. Tyson (Minneapolis: Augsburg Publishing House, 1988), pp. 11–20.

18. Ibid., p. 18.

19. Jervell, *Luke and the People,* p. 45.

20. Ibid., p. 125.

21. Ibid., p. 141.

22. Ibid., p. 137.

23. Ibid., p. 138.

24. Ibid., p. 140.

25. First published in *Svensk Exegetisk Aarsbok* 37–38 (1972–73): 145–55; trans. in Jervell, *The Unknown Paul: Essays in Luke-Acts and Early Christian History* (Minneapolis: Augsburg Publishing House, 1984), pp. 138–45. Quotations below are from the English edition.

26. Jervell, *Unknown Paul,* p. 144.

27. Ibid., p. 145.

28. Jervell, *Luke and the People,* p. 144.

29. See Jervell, "Das Aposteldekret in der lukanischen Theologie," in *Texts and Contexts: Biblical Texts in Their Textual and Situational Contexts,* ed. Todd Fornberg and David Hellholm (Oslo: Scandinavian University Press, 1995), pp. 227–43.

30. Ibid., p. 229.

31. Ibid., p. 238.

32. Jervell, *Unknown Paul,* p. 21.

33. Ibid., p. 23.

34. Ibid., p. 38.

35. Ibid., pp. 26–27; emphasis in original.

36. See Jervell, *Luke and the People,* pp. 153–83.

37. Ibid., p. 165.

38. Ibid., p. 199.

39. Ibid., p. 177.

40. See Philipp Vielhauer, "On the 'Paulinism' of Acts," in *Studies in Luke-Acts,* ed. Leander E. Keck and J. Louis Martyn (Nashville: Abingdon Press, 1966), pp. 33–50.

41. Jervell, *Unknown Paul,* p. 90.

42. Ibid., pp. 68–76.

43. Ibid., p. 70.

44. Ibid., p. 59.

45. Ibid., p. 71.

46. Ibid., p. 67.

47. But see below, p. 13. Jervell notes that Acts 28:26–27 holds out no prospect for a future conversion of Israel, as does Rom 11:11–24. See Jervell, *Apostelgeschichte,* pp. 627–28.

48. Jervell, *Unknown Paul,* p. 75.

49. Ibid., p. 72.

50. Jervell, *The Theology of the Acts of the Apostles* (Cambridge: Cambridge University Press, 1996), p. 3.

51. Ibid., p. 4.

52. See Jervell, "Paulus in der Apostelgeschichte und die Geschichte des Urchristentums," *NTS* 32 (1986): 378–92.

53. Jervell, *Apostelgeschichte,* p. 89.

54. Ibid., p. 346.

55. Ibid., p. 626.

56. Ibid., p. 627.

57. Ibid., p. 628.

58. Jervell, "Retrospect and Prospect in Luke-Acts Interpretation," in SBL*SP,* ed. Eugene H. Lovering, Jr. (Atlanta: Scholars Press, 1991), p. 384.

59. See John T. Carroll, "Review of *The Unknown Paul,*" *Princeton Seminary Bulletin* 7 (1986): 298–301.

60. Ibid., p. 300.

61. E. Earle Ellis, "Review of *Luke and the People of God,*" *Int* 28 (1974): 98.

62. See Schuyler Brown, "Review of *The Unknown Paul,*" *Int* 40 (1986): 428–30.

63. See ibid., p. 430.

64. See C. K. Barrett, "What Minorities?" in *Mighty Minorities? Minorities in Early Christianity—Positions and Strategies,* ed. David Hellholm, Halvor Moxnes, and Turid Karlsen Seim (Oslo: Scandinavian University Press, 1995), pp. 1–10. Barrett also noted that it was not meaningful to talk about majorities and minorities without more precise numbers, which are unavailable to the modern scholar.

65. Ibid., p. 6.

66. Ibid., p. 7.

67. Jervell, "Retrospect and Prospect," p. 383.

68. Jervell, "The Future of the Past: Luke's Vision of Salvation History and Its Bearing on His Writing of History," in *History, Literature, and Society in the Book of Acts,* ed. Ben Witherington III (Cambridge: Cambridge University Press, 1996), p. 123.

69. Jervell, *Theology of Acts,* p. 131.

70. Jervell, *Luke and the People,* pp. 42–43.

71. Ibid., p. 43.

72. Ibid., p. 68; emphasis mine.

73. Jervell, "God's Faithfulness to the Faithless People: Trends in Interpretation of Luke-Acts," *WW* 12 (1992): 35.

74. C. K. Barrett, *The Acts of the Apostles,* ICC (Edinburgh: T. & T. Clark, 1994), 1:210.

75. Jervell, *Apostelgeschichte,* p. 332.

76. Ibid., p. 370.

77. Jervell, "Retrospect and Prospect," p. 391.

78. On Acts 21:20 see Michael J. Cook, "The Mission to the Jews in Acts: Unraveling Luke's 'Myth of the "Myriads,"'" in *Luke-Acts and the Jewish People,* pp. 102–23.

79. For a discussion of the major options for interpreting the meaning of Hebrews and Hellenists in Acts 6:1, see Everett Ferguson, "The Hellenists in the Book of Acts," *ResQ* 12 (1969): 159–80.

80. See my article, "The Jewish Public in Luke-Acts," *NTS* 30 (1984): 574–83.

81. See Jervell, "The Church of Jews and Godfearers." Jervell's contention that the two named converts at Athens (Acts 17:34) were God-fearers rests on an earlier reference to Paul's preaching at the synagogue there (Acts 17:17). He thus infers the character of the converts from this reference. See ibid., p. 19.

82. See Jervell, "Retrospect and Prospect," pp. 390–91.

83. But see J. M. Reynolds and M. Tannenbaum, *Jews and God-Fearers at Aphro-*

disias: Greek Inscriptions with Commentary (Cambridge: Cambridge Philological Society, 1987); Paul R. Trebilco, *Jewish Communities in Asia Minor* (Cambridge: Cambridge University Press, 1991).

84. Jervell, *Unknown Paul*, p. 145.

85. Jervell, *Theology of Acts*, p. 37.

86. Jervell, *Apostelgeschichte*, p. 631.

CHAPTER 7: LATE-TWENTIETH-CENTURY AMERICAN SCHOLARSHIP

1. Recent commentaries on Luke and Acts have often included comments on the treatment of Judaism and Jews in these texts but have not focused sustained attention on this issue. Among recent commentaries, see Joel B. Green, *The Gospel of Luke*, The New International Commentary on the New Testament (Grand Rapids: William B. Eerdmans, 1997); Howard C. Kee, *To Every Nation under Heaven: The Acts of the Apostles*, The New Testament in Context (Harrisburg, Pa.: Trinity Press International, 1997); Charles H. Talbert, *Reading Acts: A Literary and Theological Commentary on the Acts of the Apostles* (New York: Crossroad Publishing Company, 1997); Ben Witherington III, *The Acts of the Apostles: A Socio-Rhetorical Commentary* (Grand Rapids: William B. Eerdmans, 1998). See also Bruce W. Winter, *The Book of Acts in Its First Century Setting*, 5 vols. (Grand Rapids: William B. Eerdmans, 1993–96); I. Howard Marshall and David Peterson, eds., *Witness to the Gospel: The Theology of Acts* (Grand Rapids: William B. Eerdmans, 1998).

2. See Gerhard Lohfink, *Die Sammlung Israels: Eine Untersuchung zur lukanischen Ekklesiologie* (Munich: Kösel, 1975).

3. Ibid., p. 55.

4. Ibid., p. 57.

5. See Matthias Klinghardt, *Gesetz und Volk Gottes: Das lukanische Verständnis des Gesetzes nach Herkunft, Funktion und seinem Ort in der Geschichte des Urchristentums* (Tübingen: J. C. B. Mohr [Paul Siebeck], 1988).

6. Ibid., p. 206.

7. See Luke Timothy Johnson, *The Acts of the Apostles*, Sacra Pagina 5 (Collegeville, Minn.: Liturgical Press, 1992); see also Johnson, *The Gospel of Luke*, Sacra Pagina 3 (Collegeville, Minn.: Liturgical Press, 1991).

8. Johnson, *Acts*, p. 8.

9. Ibid., p. 9; emphasis in original.

10. Ibid., p. 475.

11. See James D. G. Dunn, *The Acts of the Apostles*, Narrative Commentaries (Valley Forge, Pa.: Trinity Press International, 1996); see also Dunn, *The Partings of the Ways between Christianity and Judaism and Their Significance for the Character of Christianity* (London: SCM Press, 1991).

12. Dunn, *Acts*, p. xx.

13. Ibid., p. 353.

14. Ibid.

15. See Robert Maddox, *The Purpose of Luke-Acts*, ed. John Riches (Edinburgh: T. & T. Clark, 1982).

16. Ibid., p. 184.

17. Ibid., p. 42.

18. Ibid., p. 46.

19. See François Bovon, *Das Evangelium nach Lukas,* 3 vols., EKK (Zurich: Benziger Verlag, 1989).

20. Ibid., 1:25.

21. See S. G. Wilson, *Luke and the Law,* SNTSMS 50 (Cambridge: Cambridge University Press, 1983).

22. Ibid., p. 117.

23. See M.-E. Boismard, *Les Actes des Deux Apôtres,* Etudes Bibliques 12–14, n.s. (Paris: J. Gabalda, 1990). The entire project will extend to six volumes, of which Boismard wrote the first three. Justin Taylor has published volumes five (1994) and six (1996) and is currently working on volume four. Taylor makes use of Boismard's source theory but is most interested in the historical context and aspects of the book of Acts.

24. See W. C. van Unnik, "Luke-Acts, a Storm Center in Contemporary Scholarship," in *Studies in Luke-Acts: Essays Presented in Honor of Paul Schubert,* ed. Leander E. Keck and J. Louis Martyn (Nashville: Abingdon Press, 1966), pp. 15–32.

25. See Jack T. Sanders, *The Jews in Luke-Acts* (Philadelphia: Fortress Press, 1987).

26. Ibid., p. xv.

27. Ibid.

28. Ibid., p. 7.

29. Ibid., p. 13.

30. Ibid., p. 227.

31. Ibid., p. 26.

32. Ibid., p. 28.

33. Ibid., p. 33.

34. Ibid., p. 47.

35. Ibid., p. 58.

36. Ibid., p. 53.

37. Ibid., p. 234.

38. Ibid., p. 63; emphasis in original.

39. Ibid., p. 65.

40. Ibid., p. 77; emphasis in original.

41. Ibid., p. 80; emphasis in original.

42. Ibid., p. 81; emphasis in original.

43. Ibid., pp. 298–99.

44. Ibid., pp. 88–89.

45. For a different view about Gamaliel, see Johnson, *Acts,* pp. 101–3. Johnson objects to the interpretation that the speech of Gamaliel is benign and hence conveys a positive image of the Pharisees. In Johnson's interpretation, Gamaliel argues that the same thing will happen to the Christian preachers as happened to Theudas and Judas.

46. Sanders, *Jews in Luke-Acts,* p. 101.

47. Ibid., p. 123.

48. Ibid., p. 129.

49. Ibid., p. 130.

50. Ibid., p. 110.

51. Ibid., p. 113.

52. Ibid., p. 316.
53. See, e. g., Dunn, *Partings,* pp. 150–51.
54. Sanders, *Jews in Luke-Acts,* p. 161.
55. Ibid., p. 33.
56. Ibid., p. 172.
57. Ibid., pp. 179–80.
58. Ibid., p. 289.
59. See Ernst Haenchen, "The Book of Acts as Source Material for the History of Early Christianity," in *Studies in Luke-Acts,* p. 278. See also Haenchen, *The Acts of the Apostles: A Commentary,* trans. Bernard Noble et al. (Oxford: Basil Blackwell, 1971), p. 128.
60. See Sanders, *Jews in Luke-Acts,* p. 39.
61. Ibid., p. 317.
62. Ibid.
63. Robert L. Brawley, *Luke-Acts and the Jews: Conflict, Apology, and Conciliation,* SBLMS 33 (Atlanta: Scholars Press, 1987), p. 3.
64. See Brawley, "Paul in Acts: Lucan Apology and Conciliation," in *Luke-Acts: New Perspectives from the Society of Biblical Literature Seminar,* ed. Charles H. Talbert (New York: Crossroad, 1984), pp. 129–47; Sanders, "The Parable of the Pounds and Lucan Anti-Semitism," *TS* 42 (1981): 660–68; idem, "The Pharisees in Luke-Acts," in *The Living Text: Essays in Honor of Ernest W. Saunders,* ed. Dennis Groh and Robert Jewett (Lanham, Md.: University Press of America, 1985), pp. 141–88; idem, "The Salvation of the Jews in Luke-Acts," in *Luke-Acts: New Perspectives,* pp. 104–28.
65. See Brawley, *Luke-Acts and the Jews,* p. 151.
66. Ibid., p. 159.
67. See Talbert, *Literary Patterns, Theological Themes and the Genre of Luke-Acts,* SBLMS 20 (Missoula, Mont.: Scholars Press, 1974).
68. Brawley, *Luke-Acts and the Jews,* p. 55.
69. Ibid., p. 39.
70. Ibid., p. 71.
71. Ibid., p. 72.
72. See Sanders, "Pharisees in Luke-Acts."
73. Brawley, *Luke-Acts and the Jews,* p. 92.
74. Ibid., p. 105. For a critique of Sanders, Brawley, and John Darr on the characterization of the Pharisees, see Steve Mason, "Chief Priests, Sadducees, Pharisees and Sanhedrin in Acts," in *The Book of Acts in Its Palestinian Setting,* ed. Richard Bauckham, The Book of Acts in Its First Century Setting 4 (Grand Rapids: Eerdmans, 1995), pp. 115–77; see also John A. Darr, *On Character Building: The Reader and the Rhetoric of Characterization in Luke-Acts,* Literary Currents in Biblical Interpretation (Louisville: Westminster/John Knox, 1992).
75. Brawley, *Luke-Acts and the Jews,* pp. 143–44; emphasis in original.
76. Ibid., p. 158.
77. See S. G. F. Brandon, *The Fall of Jerusalem and the Christian Church* (London: SPCK, 1975); Talbert, *Luke and the Gnostics* (New York: Abingdon, 1966).
78. Brawley, *Luke-Acts and the Jews,* p. 78.
79. Ibid., p. 88.
80. Ibid., p. 74. But for a contrary view, see Günter Wasserberg, *Aus Israels*

Mitte—Heil für die Welt: Eine narrativ-exegetische Studie zur Theologie des Lukas (Berlin: Walter de Gruyter, 1998), pp. 87–88.

81. Brawley, *Luke-Acts and the Jews,* p. 139.

82. See Robert C. Tannehill, *The Narrative Unity of Luke-Acts: A Literary Interpretation,* 2 vols., Foundations and Facets (Philadelphia and Minneapolis: Fortress Press, 1986, 1990).

83. Ibid., 1:xiii; emphasis in original.

84. Ibid., 1:8.

85. Ibid., 1:26.

86. Ibid., 1:40–41.

87. Ibid., 1:12.

88. Ibid., 1:160.

89. Ibid., 1:188.

90. Ibid., 1:191.

91. Ibid., 1:273.

92. Ibid., 1:198.

93. Ibid., 1:294.

94. Ibid., 1:295.

95. Ibid., 2:3.

96. Ibid., 2:16.

97. Ibid., 2:34.

98. Ibid., 2:82.

99. Ibid., 2:47.

100. Ibid., 2:95.

101. Ibid., 2:157.

102. Ibid., 2:344.

103. Ibid., 2:347.

104. Ibid. For a similar view see Joseph B. Tyson, "The Problem of Jewish Rejection in Acts," in *Luke-Acts and the Jewish People: Eight Critical Perspectives,* ed. Tyson (Minneapolis: Augsburg Publishing House, 1988), pp. 124–37.

105. Tannehill, *Narrative Unity,* 2:350.

106. Ibid., 2:351.

107. Ibid., 2:352.

108. Ibid.

109. Ibid., 2:357.

110. See David P. Moessner, "The Ironic Fulfillment of Israel's Glory," in *Luke-Acts and the Jewish People,* pp. 35–50.

111. Ibid., p. 43.

112. Ibid., p. 49.

113. See David L. Tiede, "'Glory to Thy People Israel': Luke-Acts and the Jews," in *Luke-Acts and the Jewish People,* pp. 21–34.

114. Ibid., p. 29.

115. Ibid.

116. . Tannehill, *Narrative Unity,* 2:357.

117. Sanders, *Jews in Luke-Acts,* p. 299.

118. Gerhard Schneider, *Die Apostelgeschichte,* Herders Theologischer Kommentar zum Neuen Testament (Freiburg, Basel, Wien: Herder, 1980, 1982) 2:419–20.

CHAPTER 8: LUKE-ACTS AT THE BEGINNING OF THE THIRD MILLENNIUM

1. See F. J. Foakes-Jackson and Kirsopp Lake, eds., *The Beginnings of Christianity,* part 1, *The Acts of the Apostles,* 5 vols. (London: Macmillan, 1920–33).

2. Jack T. Sanders, *The Jews in Luke-Acts* (Philadelphia: Fortress Press, 1987), p. xv.

3. Ibid., p. 317.

4. Günter Wasserberg, *Aus Israels Mitte—Heil für die Welt: Eine narrativexegetische Studie zur Theologie des Lukas* (Berlin: Walter de Gruyter, 1998), p. 17.

5. Ibid., p. 366.

6. See, e. g., Robert P. Ericksen, *Theologians under Hitler: Gerhard Kittel, Paul Althaus, and Emanuel Hirsch* (New Haven: Yale University Press, 1985); Craig A. Evans and Donald A. Hagner, eds., *Anti-Semitism and Early Christianity: Issues of Polemic and Faith* (Minneapolis: Fortress Press, 1993); Edward H. Flannery, *The Anguish of the Jews: Twenty-Three Centuries of Anti-Semitism* (New York: Macmillan, 1976); Lillian C. Freudmann, *Antisemitism in the New Testament* (Lanham, Md.: University Press of America, 1994); John C. Gager, *The Origins of Anti-Semitism: Attitudes toward Judaism in Pagan and Christian Antiquity* (New York: Oxford University Press, 1983); Daniel Jonah Goldhagen, *Hitler's Willing Executioners: Ordinary Germans and the Holocaust* (New York: Alfred A. Knopf, 1996); Jules Isaac, *The Teaching of Contempt: Christian Roots of Anti-Semitism,* ed. Claire Huchet-Bishop, trans. Helen Weaver (New York: Holt, Rinehart and Winston, 1964); William Nicholls, *Christian Antisemitism: A History of Hate* (Northvale, N.J.: Jason Aronson, 1993); Peter Richardson, ed., with David Granskou, *Anti-Judaism in Early Christianity,* vol. 1 (Waterloo: Wilfrid Laurier University Press, 1986); Rosemary Radford Ruether, *Faith and Fratricide: The Theological Roots of Anti-Semitism* (New York: Seabury, 1974); Samuel Sandmel, *Anti-Semitism in the New Testament?* (Philadelphia: Fortress Press, 1978); Clark M. Williamson, *Has God Rejected His People?: Anti-Judaism in the Christian Church* (Nashville: Abingdon, 1982); Stephen G. Wilson, ed., *Anti-Judaism in Early Christianity,* vol. 2 (Waterloo: Wilfrid Laurier University Press, 1986).

7. See, e.g., Shaye J. D. Cohen, *From the Maccabees to the Mishnah,* Library of Early Christianity 7 (Philadelphia: Westminster Press, 1987); W. D. Davies and Louis Finkelstein, eds., *The Cambridge History of Judaism,* 2 vols. (Cambridge: Cambridge University Press, 1984–89); Martin Hengel, *Judaism and Hellenism: Studies in Their Encounter in Palestine during the Early Hellenistic Period,* trans. John Bowden, 2 vols. (Philadelphia: Fortress Press, 1974); Robert A. Kraft and George W. E. Nickelsburg, eds., *Early Judaism and Its Modern Interpreters* (Philadelphia: Fortress Press; Atlanta: Scholars Press, 1986); Jacob Neusner, *The Rabbinic Traditions about the Pharisees before 70* (Leiden: E. J. Brill, 1971); Neusner, *From Testament to Torah: An Introduction to Judaism in Its Formative Age* (Englewood Cliffs: Prentice Hall, 1988); Neusner and Ernest S. Frerichs, eds., *"To See Ourselves as Others See Us": Christians, Jews, "Others" in Late Antiquity,* Scholars Press Studies in the Humanities (Chico: Scholars Press, 1985); Neusner, William S. Green, and Ernest Frerichs, eds., *Judaisms and Their Messiahs at the Turn of the Christian Era* (Cambridge: Cambridge University Press, 1987); George W. E. Nickelsburg, *Jewish Literature between the Bible and the Mishnah: A Historical and Literary Introduction* (Philadelphia: Fortress Press, 1981);

Anthony J. Saldarini, *Pharisees, Scribes and Sadducees in Palestinian Society: A Sociological Approach* (Wilmington, Del.: Michael Glazier, 1988); E. P. Sanders, *Jesus and Judaism* (Philadelphia: Fortress Press, 1985); M. E. Stone, *Scriptures, Sects and Visions: A Profile of Judaism from Ezra to the Jewish Revolts* (Philadelphia: Fortress Press, 1980); Geza Vermes, *Jesus and the World of Judaism* (Philadelphia: Fortress Press, 1983).

8. Jack T. Sanders, "Can Anything Bad Come out of Nazareth, or Did Luke Think That History Moved in a Line or in a Circle?" in *Literary Studies in Luke-Acts: Essays in Honor of Joseph B. Tyson,* ed. Richard P. Thompson and Thomas E. Phillips (Macon, Ga.: Mercer University Press, 1998), p. 309.

9. I use the term "ambivalence" simply to express the apparent presence of both pro-Jewish and anti-Jewish materials in Luke-Acts, not to suggest in advance that any specific scholar has explicitly perceived the issue as one of ambivalence.

10. Adolf von Harnack, *The Date of the Acts and of the Synoptic Gospels,* trans. J. R. Wilkinson (London: Williams and Norgate, 1911). p. 112.

11. Ernst Haenchen, *The Acts of the Apostles: A Commentary,* trans. Bernard Noble et al. (Oxford: Basil Blackwell, 1971), p. 128.

12. Jacob Jervell, "The Future of the Past: Luke's Vision of Salvation History and Its Bearing on His Writing of History," in *History, Literature, and Society in the Book of Acts,* ed. by Ben Witherington III (Cambridge: Cambridge University Press, 1996), p. 123.

13. Robert C. Tannehill, *The Narrative Unity of Luke-Acts: A Literary Interpretation,* Foundations and Facets (Philadelphia: Fortress Press, 1986), 1:41.

14. This examination bears out the paradoxical truth of Lloyd Gaston's well-known statement, "Luke-Acts is one of the most pro-Jewish and one of the most anti-Jewish writings in the New Testament." Gaston, "Anti-Judaism and the Passion Narrative in Luke and Acts," in *Anti-Judaism in Early Christianity,* ed. Peter Richardson, with David Granskou (Waterloo: Wilfrid Laurier University Press, 1986), 1:153.

15. See Mikeal C. Parsons and Richard I. Pervo, *Rethinking the Unity of Luke and Acts* (Minneapolis: Fortress Press, 1993), for a discussion of some of the problems that accompany the conception of the unity of Luke and Acts.

16. See, for example, the works cited in chap. 7 of this volume.

17. See Wasserberg, *Aus Israels Mitte,* pp. 71–115.

18. Ibid., p. 88.

19. Ibid., p. 95.

20. In Greek, the last phrase is simply, "We are turning to the Gentiles."

21. See Nils Dahl, "A People for His Name," *NTS* 4 (1958): 319–27. Dahl lists only two exceptions, Acts 15:14; 18:10.

22. See Wasserberg, *Aus Israels Mitte,* pp. 87–88.

23. Others have, of course, perceived the ambivalence or the negative direction of the narrative, but not both. Jack Sanders, like Tannehill, has emphasized both ambivalence and the negative direction, but he sees the ambivalence in terms of the different functions of narrative and discourse within the text. Tannehill sees the ambivalence as embedded within the text as a whole.

24. See Joseph B. Tyson, *Images of Judaism in Luke-Acts* (Columbia: University of South Carolina Press, 1992), pp. 19–41.

25. Wasserberg has argued against this proposal on two grounds. First, he says that reader-response criticism requires the search for all possible groups of readers, and so

he thinks that God-fearers are not the only group envisaged by Luke. Second, he understands that the term "God-fearer" in Acts designates any pious person and so can include both Jews and Gentiles. See Wasserberg, *Aus Israels Mitte*, pp. 31–67. The point at issue between us seems to be the distinction between an implied reader and an intended reader. There is every reason to think that the author of Luke-Acts intended to address a wide and perhaps diverse community, but the reader implied by the text can be conceived as a single individual with certain definable characteristics. Wasserberg may well be right, however, in his definition of a God-fearer, when he says that "Anyone who fears the God of Israel is for Luke a God-fearer" (Wasserberg, p. 48). This may mean that I should have called the implied reader in Luke-Acts a character similar to the *Gentile* God-fearers in the text, but it does not alter the substance of my description of this reader.

    26. See Wasserberg, *Aus Israels Mitte*, p. 13.

SELECTED BIBLIOGRAPHY

The bibliography is keyed to the various topics and scholars treated here. It is not intended to be exhaustive in terms of scholarship on Luke-Acts, but it includes the major works that have been consulted in the course of this study and cited in the text. A few entries appear more than once because of their relevance to more than one topic.

ANTI-JUDAISM AND NEW TESTAMENT SCHOLARSHIP

Bousset, D. Wilhelm. *Die Religion des Judentums im neutestamentlichen Zeitalter,* 2d ed. Berlin: Reuther und Reichard, 1906.

Bultmann, Rudolf. *Primitive Christianity in Its Contemporary Setting.* Translated by R. H. Fuller. New York: Meridian Books, 1957.

Hengel, Martin, and Roland Deines, "E. P. Sanders' 'Common Judaism,' Jesus, and the Pharisees," *JTS* 46 (1995): 1–70.

Heschel, Susannah. "The Image of Judaism in Nineteenth-Century Christian New Testament Scholarship in Germany." In *Jewish-Christian Encounters over the Centuries: Symbiosis, Prejudice, Holocaust, Dialogue,* edited by Marvin Perry and Frederick M. Schweitzer, 215–40. New York: Peter Lang, 1994.

———. *Abraham Geiger and the Jewish Jesus.* Chicago: University of Chicago Press, 1998.

Hoheisel, Karl. *Das Antike Judentum in Christlicher Sicht: Ein Beitrag zur neueren Forschungsgeschichte,* Studies in Oriental Religions 2. Wiesbaden: Otto Harrassowitz, 1978.

Moore, George Foot. "Christian Writers on Judaism." *HTR* 14 (1921): 197–254.

Sanders, E. P. *Paul and Palestinian Judaism: A Comparison of Patterns of Religion.* Philadelphia: Fortress Press, 1977.

Schürer, Emil. *A History of the Jewish People in the Time of Jesus Christ.* Translated by Sophia Taylor and Peter Christie. Edinburgh: T. & T. Clark, 1897.

———. *The History of the Jewish People in the Age of Jesus Christ (175 B.C.–A.D. 135).* Revised and edited by Geza Vermes, Fergus Millar, and Matthew Black. Edinburgh: T. & T. Clark, 1979.

Strack, Hermann L., and Paul Billerbeck. *Kommentar zum Neuen Testament aus Talmud und Midrasch.* 6 vols. Munich: Beck, 1922–61.

Vermes, Geza. "Jewish Studies and New Testament Interpretation." *JJS* 31 (1980): 1–17.

Weber, Ferdinand. *Jüdische Theologie auf Grund des Talmud und verwandter Schriften,* 2d ed. Leipzig: Dörffling & Franke, 1897.

FERDINAND CHRISTIAN BAUR

Andrews, Mary E. "*Tendenz* versus Interpretation: F. C. Baur's Criticisms of Luke." *JBL* 58 (1939): 263–76.

Baur, Ferdinand C. "Die Christuspartei in der korinthischen Gemeinde, der Gegensatz des petrinischen und paulinischen Christenthums in der ältesten Kirche, der Apostel Petrus in Rom." *Tübinger Zeitschrift für Theologie* 5 (1831): 61–206.

———. "Über Zweck und Veranlassung des Römerbriefs und die damit zusammenhängenden Verhältnisse der römischen Gemeinde." *Tübinger Zeitschrift für Theologie* 9 (1836): 59–178.

———. *Kritische Untersuchungen über die kanonischen Evangelien, ihr Verhältniss zu einander, ihren Charakter und Ursprung.* Tübingen: Ludw. Fr. Fues, 1847.

———. *Paul, the Apostle of Jesus Christ, His Life and Work, His Epistles and His Doctrine: A Contribution to a Critical History of Primitive Christianity.* Translated by Allan Menzies. 2 vols. London: Williams & Norgate, 1876.

———. *The Church History of the First Three Centuries.* Translated by Allan Menzies. 2 vols. London: Williams and Norgate, 1878.

———. *Historisch-Kritische Untersuchungen zum Neuen Testament.* Stuttgart: Friedrich Frommann, 1963.

DeWette, W. M. L. *Kurze Erklärung der Apostelgeschichte.* Leipzig: S. Hirzel, 1870.

Harris, Horton. *The Tübingen School: A Historical and Theological Investigation of the School of F. C. Baur.* 2d ed. Grand Rapids: Baker Book House, 1990.

Hodgson, Peter C. *The Formation of Historical Theology: A Study of Ferdinand Christian Baur.* New York: Harper & Row, 1966.

———. *Ferdinand Christian Baur on the Writing of Church History.* New York: Oxford University Press, 1968.

Mattill, A. J., Jr. "The Purpose of Acts: Schneckenburger Reconsidered." In *Apostolic History and the Gospel: Biblical and Historical Essays Presented to F. F. Bruce on His 60th Birthday,* edited by W. Ward Gasque and Ralph P. Martin, 108–22. Grand Rapids: Wm. B. Eerdmans, 1970.

Penzel, Klaus. "Will the Real Ferdinand Christian Baur Stand Up?" *JR* 48 (1968): 310–23.

Richardson, Alan. *History Sacred and Profane: Bampton Lectures for 1962.* London: SCM Press, 1964.

Ritschl, Albrecht. *Das Evangelium Marcions und das kanonische Evangelium des Lucas.* Tübingen: Osiander, 1846.

———. *Die Enstehung der altkatholischen Kirche: Eine kirchen- und dogmengeschichtliche Monographie.* 2d ed. Bonn: Adolph Marcus, 1857.

Schneckenburger, Matthias. *Über den Zweck der Apostelgeschichte.* Bern: Fischer, 1841.

Strauss, David Friedrich. *Das Leben Jesu, kritisch bearbeitet.* 2 vols. Tübingen: C. F. Osiander, 1835. Translated from the 4th ed. by George Eliot as *The Life of Jesus Critically Examined,* edited by Peter Hodgson. Lives of Jesus. Philadelphia: Fortress Press, 1972.

Zeller, Eduard. *Die Apostelgeschichte nach ihrem Inhalt und Ursprung kritisch untersucht.* Stuttgart: C. Mäcken, 1854. Translated by Joseph Dare as *The Contents and Origin of the Acts of the Apostles, Critically Investigated.* 2 vols. London: Williams and Norgate, 1875–76.

ADOLF VON HARNACK

Blass, Friedrich. *Professor Harnack und die Schriften des Lukas.* Gütersloh: C. Bertelmann, 1907.

Farmer, William R. *The Synoptic Problem: A Critical Analysis.* New York: Macmillan, 1964.

Geiger, Abraham. *Das Judentum und seine Geschichte von der Zerstörung des zweiten Tempels bis zum Ende des zwölften Jahrhunderts.* Breslau: Schlettersche Buchhandlung, 1865.

———. *Sadducäer und Pharisäer.* Breslau: H. Skutsch, 1863.

———. *Urschrift und Übersetzungen der Bibel in ihrer Abhängigkeit von der inneren Entwickelung des Judentums.* Breslau: Julius Hainauer, 1857.

Glick, G. Wayne. *The Reality of Christianity: A Study of Adolf von Harnack as Historian and Theologian.* New York: Harper & Row, 1967.

Harnack, Adolf. *Die Apostelgeschichte.* Leipzig: Hinrichs, 1908. Translated by J. R. Wilkinson as *The Acts of the Apostles.* New Testament Studies 3. London: Williams & Norgate, 1909.

———. *The Expansion of Christianity in the First Three Centuries.* Translated by James Moffatt. 2 vols. London: Williams & Norgate, 1904.

———. *Geschichte der altchristlichen Literatur bis Eusebius.* Leipzig: Hinrichs, 1896.

———. *History of Dogma.* Translated by Neil Buchanan. 7 vols. Boston: Little, Brown, 1905–10.

———. *Lukas der Arzt, der Verfasser des dritten Evangeliums und der Apostelgeschichte.* Leipzig: Hinrichs, 1906. Translated by J. R. Wilkinson as *Luke the Physician: The Author of the Third Gospel and the Acts of the Apostles.* New Testament Studies 1. London: Williams & Norgate, 1908.

———. *Marcion: Das Evangelium vom Fremden Gott: Eine Monographie zur Geschichte der Grundlegung der katholischen Kirche.* Leipzig: Hinrichs, 1921. Translated by John E. Steely and Lyle D. Bierma as *Marcion: The Gospel of the Alien God.* Durham, N.C.: Labyrinth Press, 1990.

———. *Neue Untersuchungen zur Apostelgeschichte und zur Abfassungszeit der synoptischen Evangelium.* Leipzig: Hinrichs, 1911. Translated by J. R. Wilkinson as *The Date of the Acts and of the Synoptic Gospels.* New Testament Studies 4. London: Williams & Norgate, 1911.

———. *Sprüche und Reden Jesu.* Leipzig: Hinrichs, 1907. Translated by J. R. Wilkinson as *The Sayings of Jesus: The Second Source of St. Matthew and St. Luke.* New Testament Studies 2. London: Williams & Norgate, 1908.

———. *Das Wesen des Christentums.* Leipzig: Hinrichs, 1900. Translated by Thomas Bailey Saunders as *What Is Christianity?* New York: Harper & Row, 1957.

Harnack, Agnes von Zahn-. *Adolf von Harnack.* 2d ed. Berlin: Walter de Gruyter & Co., 1951.

Heschel, Susannah. *Abraham Geiger and the Jewish Jesus.* Chicago: University of Chicago Press, 1998.

———. "The Image of Judaism in Nineteenth-Century Christian New Testament Scholarship in Germany." In *Jewish-Christian Encounters over the Centuries: Symbiosis, Prejudice, Holocaust, Dialogue,* edited by Marvin Perry and Frederick M. Schweitzer, 215–40. New York: Peter Lang, 1994.

Hobart, William K. *The Medical Language of St. Luke.* Dublin: Hodges, Figgis and Co. 1882.

Holtzmann, Heinrich J. *Die synoptischen Evangelien: Ihr Ursprung und geschichtlicher Charakter.* Leipzig: W. Engelmann, 1863.

Keim, Theodor. *The History of Jesus of Nazara: Freely Investigated in Its Connection with the National Life of Israel, and Related in Detail.* 6 vols. London: Williams & Norgate, 1876.

Kümmel, Werner Georg. *The New Testament: The History of the Investigation of Its Problems.* Translated by S. McLean Gilmour and Howard C. Kee. Nashville: Abingdon Press, 1972.

Loisy, Alfred. *The Gospel and the Church.* Translated by Christopher Home. New York: Charles Scribner's Sons, 1912.

Murrmann-Kahl, Michael, "Nestor der Wissenschaften: Adolf von Harnack (1851–1930)." *Evangelische Kommentare* 28 (1995): 728–31.

Renan, Ernst. *The Life of Jesus.* New York: Modern Library, 1927.

Ritschl, Albrecht. *Die Enstehung der altkatholischen Kirche: Eine kirchen- und dogmengeschichtliche Monographie.* 2d ed. Bonn: Adolph Marcus, 1857.

Rumscheidt, Martin, ed. *Adolf von Harnack: Liberal Theology at Its Height.* The Making of Modern Theology. London: Collins, 1988.

Saunders, Thomas Bailey. *Professor Harnack and His Oxford Critics.* London: Williams & Norgate, 1902.

Smend, Friedrich. *Adolf von Harnack: Verzeichnis seiner Schriften bis 1930.* München: Saur, 1990.

ADOLF SCHLATTER

Bousset, Wilhelm. *Die Religion des Judentums in neutestamentlichen Zeitalter.* Berlin: Reuther und Reichard, 1903.

———. *Kyrios Christos: Geschichte des Christusglaubens von den Anfängen bis Irenaeus.* Göttingen: Vandenhoeck & Ruprecht, 1913. Translated by John E. Steely as *Kyrios Christos: A History of the Belief in Christ from the Beginnings of Christianity to Irenaeus.* Nashville: Abingdon Press, 1970.

Bultmann, Rudolf. *Die Geschichte der synoptischen Tradition.* Göttingen: Vandenhoeck & Ruprecht, 1921. Translated by John Marsh as *The History of the Synoptic Tradition.* New York: Harper & Row, 1963.

Cadbury, Henry J. *The Style and Literary Method of Luke.* Cambridge: Harvard University Press, 1920.

———. *The Making of Luke-Acts.* New York: Macmillan, 1927.

———. *The Peril of Modernizing Jesus.* New York: Macmillan, 1937.

———. *Jesus: What Manner of Man?* New York: Macmillan, 1947.

———. *The Book of Acts in History.* London: Adam and Charles Black, 1955.

———. *The Eclipse of the Historical Jesus.* Wallingford, Pa.: Pendle Hill Publications, 1964.

Deissmann, Adolf. *Light from the Ancient East: The New Testament Illustrated by Recently Discovered Texts of the Graeco-Roman World.* Translated by Lionel R. M. Strachan. New York: George H. Doran Co., 1927.

Dibelius, Martin. *Die Formgeschichte des Evangeliums.* Tübingen: J. C. B. Mohr (Paul

Siebeck), 1919. Translated by Dibelius and Bertram Lee Woolf as *From Tradition to Gospel.* New York: Charles Scribner's Sons, 1935.

———. *Aufsätze zur Apostelgeschichte.* Edited by Heinrich Greeven. Göttingen: Vandenhoeck & Ruprecht, 1951. Translated by Mary Ling as *Studies in the Acts of the Apostles.* London: William Clowes and Sons, 1956.

Dinatman, Stephen F. *Creative Grace: Faith and History in the Theology of Adolf Schlatter.* New York: Peter Lang, 1993.

Egg, Gottfried. *Adolf Schlatters kritische Position: Geseigt an seiner Matthäusinterpretation.* Stuttgart: Calwer Verlag, 1968.

Foakes-Jackson, F. J. *The Rise of Gentile Christianity.* New York: George H. Doran Co., 1927.

———. *The Acts of the Apostles.* Moffatt New Testament Commentary. London: Hodder and Stoughton, 1931.

———, ed. *The Parting of the Roads: Studies in the Development of Judaism and Early Christianity.* London: Edward Arnold, 1912.

Foakes-Jackson, F. J., and Kirsopp Lake, eds. *The Beginnings of Christianity.* Part 1, *The Acts of the Apostles.* 5 vols. London: Macmillan, 1920–33.

Gasque, W. Ward. *A History of the Interpretation of the Acts of the Apostles.* Peabody, Mass.: Hendrickson, 1989.

Grundmann, Walter. *Jesus der Galiläer und das Judentum.* Leipzig: Georg Wigand, 1940.

Haenchen, Ernst. *The Acts of the Apostles: A Commentary.* Translated by Bernard Noble et al. Oxford: Basil Blackwell, 1971.

Heinonen, Reijo E. *Anpassung und Identität: Theologie und Kirchenpolitik der Bremer Deutschen Christen 1933–1945.* Göttingen: Vandenhoeck & Ruprecht, 1978.

Hengel, Martin, and Ulrich Heckel, eds. *Paulus und das antike Judentum.* Tübingen: J. C. B. Mohr (Paul Siebeck), 1991.

Luck, Ulrich. *Kerygma und Tradition in der Hermeneutik Adolf Schlatters.* Köln und Oplanden: Westdeutscher Verlag, 1955.

Meyer, Eduard. *Ursprung und Anfänge des Christentums.* 3 vols. Stuttgart: J. G. Cotta, 1921–23.

Montefiore, Claude G. *The Synoptic Gospels.* 3 vols. London: Macmillan, 1909.

———. *Rabbinic Literature and Gospel Teachings.* London: Macmillan, 1930.

Moore, George Foot. "Christian Writers on Judaism." *HTR* 14 (1921): 197–254.

———. *Judaism in the First Centuries of the Christian Era: The Age of the Tannaim.* 3 vols. Cambridge: Harvard University Press, 1927.

Morgan, Robert. *The Nature of New Testament Theology: The Contribution of William Wrede and Adolf Schlatter.* London: SCM Press, 1973.

Neill, Stephen. *The Interpretation of the New Testament, 1861–1961.* London: Oxford University Press, 1964.

Neuer, Werner. *Adolf Schlatter.* Wuppertal: R. Brockhaus, 1988. Translated by Robert W. Yarbrough as *Adolf Schlatter: A Biography of Germany's Leading Biblical Theologian.* Grand Rapids: Baker Books, 1995.

———. *Adolf Schlatter: Ein Leben für Theologie und Kirche.* Stuttgart: Calwer Verlag, 1996.

Parsons, Mikeal C., and Joseph B. Tyson, eds. *Cadbury, Knox, and Talbert: American Contributions to the Study of Acts.* Atlanta: Scholars Press, 1992.

Ramsay, William M. *Luke the Physician and Other Studies in the History of Religion.* London: Hodder & Stoughton, 1908.

———. *The Bearing of Recent Discovery on the Trustworthiness of the New Testament.* 4th ed. London: Hodder & Stoughton, 1920.

Reitzenstein, Richard. *Die hellenistischen Mysterienreligion: Ihren Grundgedanken und Wirkungen.* Leipzig: B. G. Teubner, 1910. Translated by John E. Steely as *Hellenistic Mystery-Religions: Their Basic Ideas and Significance.* Pittsburgh: Pickwick Press, 1978.

Sanders, E. P. *Paul and Palestinian Judaism: A Comparison of Patterns of Religion.* Philadelphia: Fortress Press, 1977.

Schlatter, Adolf. *Die Apostelgeschichte ausgelegt für Bibelleser.* Stuttgart: Verlag der Vereinsbuchhandlung, 1902.

———. *Erläuterungen zum Neuen Testament.* 3 vols. Stuttgart: Verlag der Vereinsbuchhandlung, 1908.

———. *Die Geschichte des Christus.* Stuttgart: Calwer Verlag, 1923. Translated by Andreas J. Köstenberger as *The History of the Christ: The Foundation of New Testament Theology.* Grand Rapids: Baker Books, 1997.

———. *Erlebtes.* 3d ed. Berlin: Furche Verlag, 1924.

———. *Die Geschichte der ersten Christenheit.* Gütersloh: C. Bertelsmann, 1926. Translated by Paul P. Levertoff as *The Church in the New Testament Period.* London: SPCK, 1955.

———. *Wir Christen und die Juden.* Essen: Freizeiten, 1930.

———. *Das Evangelium des Lukas: Aus seinen Quellen erklärt.* Stuttgart: Calwer Verlag, 1931.

———. *Die Theologie des Judentums nach dem Bericht des Josefus.* Gütersloh: Gerd Mohn, 1932.

———. *Die neue deutsche Art in der Kirche.* Bethel: Anstalt Bethel, 1933.

———. *Gottes Gerechtigkeit: Ein Kommentar zum Römerbrief.* Stuttgart: Calwer Verlag, 1935. Translated by Siegfried S. Schatzmann as *Romans: The Righteousness of God.* Peabody, Mass.: Hendrickson, 1995.

———. *Wird der Jude über uns siegen?* Essen: Freizeiten, 1935.

———. *Rückblick auf seine Lebensarbeit.* Gütersloh: C. Bertelsmann, 1952.

Schmidt, Karl Ludwig. *Der Rahmen der Geschichte Jesu: Literarkritische Untersuchungen zur ältesten Jesusüberlieferung.* Berlin: Trowitzsch & Sohn, 1919.

Schweitzer, Albert. *Das Messianitäts und Leidengeheimnis: Eine Skizze des Lebens Jesu.* Tübingen: J. C. B. Mohr (Paul Siebeck), 1901.

———. *Von Reimarus zu Wrede: Eine Geschichte der Leben-Jesu–Forschung.* Tübingen: J. C. B. Mohr (Paul Siebeck), 1906. Translated by W. Montgomery as *The Quest of the Historical Jesus: A Critical Study of Its Progress from Reimarus to Wrede.* London: A. & C. Black, 1910.

Siegele-Wenschkewitz, Lenore, ed. *Christlicher Antijudaismus und Antisemitismus: Theologische und kirchliche Programme Deutscher Christen.* Frankfurt: Haag & Herchen, 1994.

Wrede, William. *Das Messiasgeheimnis in den Evangelien: Zugleich ein Beitrag zum Verständnis des Markusevangeliums.* Göttingen: Vandenhoeck & Ruprecht, 1901.

Zahn, Theodor. *Das Evangelium des Lucas.* Leipzig: Deichert, 1913.

———. *Die Apostelgeschichte des Lucas.* 2 vols. Leipzig: Deichert, 1919.

ERNST HAENCHEN AND HANS CONZELMANN

Busse, Ulrich. "Ernst Haenchen und sein Johanneskommentar." *ETL* 57 (1981): 125–43.

Conzelmann, Hans. *Die Mitte der Zeit: Studien zur Theologie des Lukas.* Beiträge zur historischen Theologie 17. Tübingen: J. C. B. Mohr (Paul Siebeck), 1954. Translated by Geoffrey Buswell as *The Theology of St. Luke.* New York: Harper & Brothers, 1960.

———. "Jesus Christus." In *Die Religion in Geschichte und Gegenwart: Handwörterbuch für Theologie und Religionswissenschaft,* edited by Kurt Galling et al., 3:619–53. 3d ed. Tübingen: J. C. B. Mohr (Paul Siebeck), 1959. Translated by Raymond Lord as *Jesus: The Classic Article from RGG Expanded and Updated,* edited by John Reumann. Philadelphia: Fortress Press, 1973.

———. "Geschichte, Geschichtsbild und Geschichtsdarstellung bei Lukas." *ThLZ* 85 (1960): 241–50.

———. *Die Apostelgeschichte.* Handbuch zum Neuen Testament 7. Tübingen: J. C. B. Mohr (Paul Siebeck), 1963. Translated by James Limburg, A. Thomas Kraabel, and Donald H. Juel as *The Acts of the Apostles: A Commentary on the Acts of the Apostles.* Hermeneia Series. Philadelphia: Fortress Press, 1987.

———. "The First Christian Century as Christian History." In *The Bible in Modern Scholarship: Papers Read at the 100th Meeting of the Society of Biblical Literature, December 28–30, 1964,* edited by J. Philip Hyatt, 217–26. Nashville: Abingdon Press, 1965.

———. "Luke's Place in the Development of Early Christianity." In *Studies in Luke-Acts: Essays Presented in Honor of Paul Schubert,* edited by Leander E. Keck and J. Louis Martyn, 298–316. Nashville: Abingdon Press, 1966.

———. "Historie und Theologie in den synoptischen Passionsberichten." In *Zur Bedeutung des Todes Jesu,* edited by Fritz Viering, 35–53. Gütersloh: Gerd Mohn, 1967. Translated by Charles B. Cousar as "History and Theology in the Passion Narratives of the Synoptic Gospels." *Int* 24 (1970): 178–97.

———. *Grundriss der Theologie des Neuen Testaments.* 2d ed. Munich: Christian Kaiser, 1968. Translated by John Bowden as *An Outline of the Theology of the New Testament.* London: SCM Press, 1969.

———. *Geschichte des Urchristentums.* Göttingen: Vandenhoeck & Ruprecht, 1969. Translated by John E. Steely as *History of Primitive Christianity.* Nashville: Abingdon Press, 1973.

———. *Heiden—Juden—Christen: Auseinandersetzungen in der Literatur der hellenistisch-römischen Zeit.* Tübingen: J. C. B. Mohr (Paul Siebeck), 1981. Translated by M. Eugene Boring as *Gentiles—Jews—Christians: Polemics and Apologetics in the Greco-Roman World.* Minneapolis: Fortress Press, 1992.

Conzelmann, Hans, and Andreas Lindemann. *Arbeitsbuch zum Neuen Testament.* 8th ed. Tübingen: J. C. B. Mohr (Paul Siebeck), 1985. Translated by Siegfried S. Schatzmann as *Interpreting the New Testament: An Introduction to the Principles and Methods of N.T. Exegesis.* Peabody, Mass.: Hendrickson, 1988.

Ericksen. Robert P. *Theologians under Hitler: Gerhard Kittel, Paul Althaus, and Emanuel Hirsch.* New Haven: Yale University Press, 1985.

Haenchen, Ernst. "Volk und Staat in der Lehre der Kirche." In *Volk, Staat, Kirche: Ein Lehrgang der Theolog Fakultät Giessen,* 53–72. Giessen: Alfred Töpelmann, 1933.

——. "Matthäus 23." *ZTK* 48 (1951): 38–63. Also in Haenchen, *Gott und Mensch: Gesammelte Aufsätze,* 29–54. Tübingen: J. C. B. Mohr (Paul Siebeck), 1965.

——. "Review of Conzelmann, *Die Mitte der Zeit.*" *Zeitschrift für Kirchengeschichte* 66 (1955): 157–60.

——. "Tradition und Komposition in der Apostelgeschichte." *ZTK* 52 (1955): 205–25.

——. *Die Apostelgeschichte.* Kritisch-exegetischer Kommentar über das Neue Testament 10. Göttingen: Vandenhoeck & Ruprecht, 1956. Translated by Bernard Noble et al. as *The Acts of the Apostles: A Commentary.* Oxford: Basil Blackwell, 1971.

——. "Judentum und Christentum in der Apostelgeschichte." *ZNTW* 54 (1963): 155–87.

——. *Der Weg Jesu: Eine Erklärung des Markus-Evangelium und der kanonischen Parallelen.* 2d ed. Berlin: Walter de Gruyter & Co, 1968.

——. *Das Johannesevangelium: Ein Kommentar.* Edited by Ulrich Busse. Tübingen: J. C. B Mohr, 1980.

Minear, Paul S. "Luke's Use of the Birth Stories." In *Studies in Luke-Acts: Essays Presented in Honor of Paul Schubert,* edited by Leander E. Keck and J. Louis Martyn, 111–30. Nashville: Abingdon Press, 1966.

Oliver, H. H. "The Lucan Birth Stories and the Purpose of Luke-Acts." *NTS* 10 (1964): 202–26.

Smend, Rudolf. "Ansprache am Sarge Ernst Haenchens." *ZTK* 72 (1975): 303–9.

Streeter, B. H. "Fresh Light on the Synoptic Problem." *Hibbert Journal* 29 (1921): 103–12.

——. *The Four Gospels: A Study of Origins.* London: Macmillan, 1924.

Taylor, Vincent. *Behind the Third Gospel: A Study of the Proto-Luke Hypothesis.* Oxford: Clarendon Press, 1926.

JACOB JERVELL

Bailey, James L. "Review of Jacob Jervell, *Luke and the People of God.*" *Lutheran Quarterly* 25 (1973): 419–20.

Barrett, C. K. *The Acts of the Apostles.* 2 vols. International Critical Commentary. Edinburgh: T. & T. Clark, 1994, 98.

Boismard, M.-E. "Review of Jacob Jervell, *Imago Dei.*" *RB* 68 (1961): 144–45.

Brown, Schuyler. "Review of Jacob Jervell, *The Unknown Paul.*" *Int* 40 (1986): 428–30.

Carroll, John T. "Review of Jacob Jervell, *The Unknown Paul.*" *Princeton Seminary Bulletin* 7 (1986): 298–301.

Ellis, E. Earle. "Review of Jacob Jervell, *Luke and the People of God.*" *Int* 28 (1974): 94–98.

Geer, Thomas C., Jr. "Review of Jacob Jervell, *The Unknown Paul.*" *ResQ* 29 (1987): 63–64.

Hellholm, David, Halvor Moxnes, and Turid Karlsen Seim, eds. *Mighty Minorities? Minorities in Early Christianity—Positions and Strategies: Essays in Honour of Jacob Jervell on His 70th Birthday 21 May 1995.* Oslo: Scandinavian University Press, 1995.

Hooker, Morna D. "Review of Jacob Jervell, *Imago Dei.*" *JTS* 12 (1961): 83–85.

Jeremias, Joachim. *Abba: Studien zur neutestamentlichen Theologie und Zeit-geschichte.* Göttingen: Vandenhoeck & Ruprecht, 1966.

Jervell, Jacob. *Imago Dei: Gen 1,26f. im Spätjudentum, in der Gnosis und in den paulinischen Briefen.* Forschungen zur Religion und Literatur des Alten und Neuen Testaments, n.s. 58. Göttingen: Vandenhoeck & Ruprecht, 1960.

———. *The Continuing Search for the Historical Jesus.* Minneapolis: Augsburg Publishing House, 1965.

———. *Luke and the People of God: A New Look at Luke-Acts.* Minneapolis: Augsburg Publishing House, 1972.

———. "Das Volk des Geistes." In *God's Christ and His People: Studies in Honour of Nils Alstrup Dahl,* edited by Jacob Jervell and Wayne A. Meeks, 87–106. Oslo: Universitetsforlaget, 1977.

———. "The Acts of the Apostles and the History of Early Christianity." *ST* 17 (1983): 17–32.

———. *The Unknown Paul: Essays in Luke-Acts and Early Christian History.* Minneapolis: Augsburg Publishing House, 1984.

———. "Paulus in der Apostelgeschichte und die Geschichte des Urchristentums." *NTS* 32 (1986): 378–92.

———. "The Church of Jews and Godfearers." In *Luke-Acts and the Jewish People: Eight Critical Perspectives,* edited by Joseph B. Tyson, 11–20. Minneapolis: Augsburg Publishing House, 1988.

———. "The Letter to Jerusalem." In *The Romans Debate,* edited by Karl P. Donfried, 53–64. Rev. and expanded edition. Peabody, Mass.: Hendrickson, 1991.

———. "Retrospect and Prospect in Luke-Acts Interpretation." In *SBLSP,* edited by Eugene H. Lovering, Jr., 383–404. Atlanta: Scholars Press, 1991.

———. "God's Faithfulness to the Faithless People: Trends in Interpretation of Luke-Acts." *WW* 12 (1992): 29–36.

———. "The Lucan Interpretation of Jesus as Biblical Theology." In *New Directions in Biblical Theology: Papers of the Aarhus Conference, 16–19 September 1992,* edited by Sigfred Pedersen, 77–92. Leiden: E. J. Brill, 1994.

———. "Das Aposteldekret in der lukanischen Theologie." In *Texts and Contexts: Biblical Texts in Their Textual and Situational Contexts,* edited by Todd Fornberg and David Hellholm, 227–43. Oslo: Scandinavian University Press, 1995.

———. *The Theology of the Acts of the Apostles.* New Testament Theology. Cambridge: Cambridge University Press, 1996.

———. "The Future of the Past: Luke's Vision of Salvation History and Its Bearing on His Writing of History." In *History, Literature, and Society in the Book of Acts,* edited by Ben Witherington III, 104–26. Cambridge: Cambridge University Press, 1996.

———. *Die Apostelgeschichte.* Meyers Kritisch-exegetischer Kommentar über das Neue Testament. 17th ed. Göttingen: Vandenhoeck & Ruprecht, 1998.

Käsemann, Ernst. *Essays on New Testament Themes.* Translated by W. J. Montague. London: SCM Press, 1964.

Kodell, Jerome. "Review of Jacob Jervell, *Luke and the People of God.*" *CBQ* 35 (1973): 392–93.

Need, Stephen W. "Review of Jacob Jervell, *The Unknown Paul.*" *ITQ* 53 (1987): 77–78.

O'Neill, J. C. "Review of Jacob Jervell, *The Unknown Paul.*" *SJT* 40 (1987): 457–59.

Pfitzner, V. C. "Review of Jacob Jervell, *The Unknown Paul.*" *Lutheran Theological Journal* 19 (1985): 100–101.

Reynolds, J. M., and M. Tannenbaum. *Jews and God-Fearers at Aphrodisias: Greek Inscriptions with Commentary.* Cambridge: Cambridge Philological Society, 1987.

Trebilco, Paul R. *Jewish Communities in Asia Minor.* SNTSMS 69. Cambridge: Cambridge University Press, 1991.

Turro, James C. "Review of Jacob Jervell, *Luke and the People of God.*" *TS* 35 (1974): 182–84.

Tyson, Joseph B. "The Jewish Public in Luke-Acts." *NTS* 30 (1984): 574–83.

Vielhauer, Philipp. "On the 'Paulinism' of Acts." In *Studies in Luke-Acts: Essays Presented in Honor of Paul Schubert,* edited by Leander E. Keck and J. Louis Martyn, 33–50. Nashville: Abingdon Press, 1966.

LATE TWENTIETH-CENTURY AMERICAN SCHOLARSHIP

Bock, Darrell L. *Luke 1. 1:1–9:50.* Baker Exegetical Commentary on the New Testament. Grand Rapids: Baker Books, 1994.

———. *Luke 2. 9:51–24:53.* Baker Exegetical Commentary on the New Testament. Grand Rapids: Baker Books, 1996.

Boismard, M.-E. *Les Actes des Deux Apôtres.* 3 vols. Etudes Bibliques 12–14, n.s. Paris: J. Gabalda, 1990.

Bovon, François. *Luke the Theologian: Thirty-Three Years of Research (1950–1983).* Translated by Ken McKinney. Allison Park, Pa.: Pickwick Publications, 1987.

———. *Das Evangelium nach Lukas.* 3 vols. EKK. Zurich: Benziger Verlag, 1989.

Brandon, S. G. F. *The Fall of Jerusalem and the Christian Church.* London: SPCK, 1975.

Brawley, Robert L. *Luke-Acts and the Jews: Conflict, Apology, and Conciliation.* SBLMS 33. Atlanta: Scholars Press, 1987.

Danker, Frederick W. *Luke.* Proclamation Commentaries. 2d ed. Philadelphia: Fortress Press, 1987.

Darr, John A. *On Character Building: The Reader and the Rhetoric of Characterization in Luke-Acts.* Literary Currents in Biblical Interpretation. Louisville: Westminster/John Knox, 1992.

Dunn, James D. G. *The Partings of the Ways between Christianity and Judaism and Their Significance for the Character of Christianity.* London: SCM Press, 1991.

———. *The Acts of the Apostles.* Narrative Commentaries. Valley Forge, Pa.: Trinity Press International, 1996.

Fitzmyer, Joseph A. *The Gospel according to Luke (I–IX): Introduction, Translation, and Notes.* Anchor Bible 28. Garden City: Doubleday, 1981.

———. *The Gospel according to Luke (X–XXIV): Introduction, Translation, and Notes.* Anchor Bible 28A. Garden City: Doubleday, 1985.

Green, Joel B. *The Gospel of Luke.* The New International Commentary on the New Testament. Grand Rapids: William B. Eerdmans, 1997.

Hengel, Martin. *Acts and the History of Earliest Christianity.* Translated by John Bowden. Philadelphia: Fortress Press, 1979.

Hill, Craig C. *Hellenists and Hebrews: Reappraising Division within the Earliest Church.* Minneapolis: Fortress Press, 1992.

Johnson, Luke T. "The New Testament's Anti-Jewish Slander and the Conventions of Ancient Polemic." *JBL* 108 (1989): 419–41.

———. *The Gospel of Luke.* Sacra Pagina 3. Collegeville, Minn.: Liturgical Press, 1991.

———. *The Acts of the Apostles.* Sacra Pagina 5. Collegeville, Minn.: Liturgical Press, 1992.

Keck, Leander E., and J. Louis Martyn, eds. *Studies in Luke-Acts: Essays Presented in Honor of Paul Schubert.* Nashville: Abingdon Press, 1966.

Kee, Howard C. *To Every Nation under Heaven: The Acts of the Apostles.* The New Testament in Context. Harrisburg, Pa.: Trinity Press International, 1997.

Klinghardt, Matthias. *Gesetz und Volk Gottes: Das lukanische Verständnis des Gesetzes nach Herkunft, Funktion und seinem Ort in der Geschichte des Urchristentums.* Wissenschaftliche Untersuchungen zum Neuen Testament 32. Tübingen: J. C. B. Mohr (Paul Siebeck), 1988.

Lohfink, Gerhard. *Die Sammlung Israels: Eine Untersuchung zur lukanischen Ekklesiologie.* Studien zum Alten und Neuen Testament 39. Munich: Kösel, 1975.

Maddox, Robert. *The Purpose of Luke-Acts.* Edited by John Riches. Edinburgh: T. & T. Clark, 1982.

Marshall, I. Howard. *The Gospel of Luke: A Commentary on the Greek Text.* Grand Rapids: William B. Eerdmans, 1978.

Marshall, I. Howard, and David Peterson, eds. *Witness to the Gospel: The Theology of Acts.* Grand Rapids: William B. Eerdmans, 1998.

Moscato, Mary A. "Current Theories Regarding the Audience of Luke-Acts." *CurrTheoMiss* 3 (1976): 355–61.

Pesch, Rudolf. *Die Apostelgeschichte.* EKK. 2 vols. Zurich: Benziger Verlag, 1986.

Radl, Walter. *Das Lukas-Evangelium.* Erträge der Forschung 261. Darmstadt: Wissenschaftliche Buchgesellschaft, 1988.

Sanders, Jack T. *The Jews in Luke-Acts.* Philadelphia: Fortress Press, 1987.

Schneider, Gerhard. *Die Apostelgeschichte. I. Teil.* Herders Theologischer Kommentar zum Neuen Testament. Freiburg, Basel, Vienna: Herder, 1980.

———. *Die Apostelgeschichte. II. Teil.* Herders Theologischer Kommentar zum Neuen Testament. Freiburg, Basel, Vienna: Herder, 1982.

Spencer, F. Scott. *Acts.* Readings: A New Biblical Commentary. Sheffield: Sheffield Academic Press, 1997.

Talbert, Charles H. *Luke and the Gnostics.* New York: Abingdon, 1966.

———. *Literary Patterns, Theological Themes and the Genre of Luke-Acts.* SBLMS 20. Missoula, Mont.: Scholars Press, 1974.

———. *Reading Luke: A Literary and Theological Commentary on the Third Gospel.* New York: Crossroad, 1982.

———. *Acts.* Knox Preaching Guides. Atlanta: John Knox Press, 1984.

———. *Reading Acts: A Literary and Theological Commentary on the Acts of the Apostles.* New York: Crossroad Publishing Company, 1997.

———, ed. *Luke-Acts: New Perspectives from the Society of Biblical Literature Seminar.* New York: Crossroad, 1984.

Tannehill, Robert C. *The Narrative Unity of Luke-Acts: A Literary Interpretation.* Vol. 1, *The Gospel according to Luke.* Foundations and Facets. Philadelphia: Fortress Press, 1986.

———. *The Narrative Unity of Luke-Acts: A Literary Interpretation.* Vol. 2, *The Acts of the Apostles.* Foundations and Facets. Minneapolis: Fortress Press, 1990.

———. *Luke*. Abingdon New Testament Commentaries. Nashville: Abingdon Press, 1996.

Taylor, Justin. *Les Actes des Deux Apôtres*. 2 vols. Etudes Bibliques 23, 30 n.s. Paris: J. Gabalda, 1994–96.

Thompson, Richard P. "Christian Community and Characterization in the Book of Acts: A Literary Study of the Lukan Concept of the Church." 2 vols. Ph.D. diss., Southern Methodist University, 1996.

Tyson, Joseph B. *Images of Judaism in Luke-Acts*. Columbia: University of South Carolina, 1992.

———, ed. *The Jewish People in Luke-Acts: Eight Critical Perspectives*. Minneapolis: Augsburg Publishing House, 1988.

Wiefel, Wolfgang. *Das Evangelium nach Lukas*. Theologischer Handkommentar zum Neuen Testament 3. Berlin: Evangelische Verlagsanstalt, 1988.

Wilson, S. G. *Luke and the Law*. SNTSMS 50. Cambridge: Cambridge University Press, 1983.

Winter, Bruce W., ed. *The Book of Acts in Its First Century Setting*. 5 vols. Grand Rapids: William B. Eerdmans, 1993–96.

Witherington, Ben, III. *The Acts of the Apostles: A Socio-Rhetorical Commentary*. Grand Rapids: William B. Eerdmans, 1998.

LUKE-ACTS AT THE BEGINNING OF THE THIRD MILLENNIUM

Cohen, Shaye J. D. *From the Maccabees to the Mishnah*. Library of Early Christianity 7. Philadelphia: Westminster Press, 1987.

Dahl, Nils. "A People for His Name." *NTS* 4 (1958): 319–27.

Davies, W. D., and Louis Finkelstein, eds. *The Cambridge History of Judaism*. 2 vols. Cambridge: Cambridge University Press, 1984–89.

Ericksen, Robert P. *Theologians under Hitler: Gerhard Kittel, Paul Althaus, and Emanuel Hirsch*. New Haven: Yale University Press, 1985.

Evans, Craig A., and Donald A. Hagner, eds. *Anti-Semitism and Early Christianity: Issues of Polemic and Faith*. Minneapolis: Fortress Press, 1993.

Flannery, Edward H. *The Anguish of the Jews: Twenty-Three Centuries of Anti-Semitism*. New York: Macmillan, 1976.

Freudmann, Lillian C. *Antisemitism in the New Testament*. Lanham, Md.: University Press of America, 1994.

Gager, John C. *The Origins of Anti-Semitism: Attitudes toward Judaism in Pagan and Christian Antiquity*. New York: Oxford University Press, 1983.

Goldhagen, Daniel Jonah. *Hitler's Willing Executioners: Ordinary Germans and the Holocaust*. New York: Alfred A. Knopf, 1996.

Hengel, Martin. *Judaism and Hellenism: Studies in Their Encounter in Palestine during the Early Hellenistic Period*. Translated by John Bowden. 2 vols. Philadelphia: Fortress Press, 1974.

Isaac, Jules. *The Teaching of Contempt: Christian Roots of Anti-Semitism*. Edited by Claire Huchet-Bishop. Translated by Helen Weaver. New York: Holt, Rinehart and Winston, 1964.

Kraft, Robert A., and George W. E. Nickelsburg, eds. *Early Judaism and Its Modern Interpreters*. Philadelphia: Fortress Press; Atlanta: Scholars Press, 1986.

Neusner, Jacob. *The Rabbinic Traditions about the Pharisees before 70.* Leiden: E. J. Brill, 1971.

———. *From Testament to Torah: An Introduction to Judaism in Its Formative Age.* Englewood Cliffs: Prentice Hall, 1988.

Neusner, Jacob, and Ernest S. Frerichs, eds. *"To See Ourselves as Others See Us": Christians, Jews, "Others" in Late Antiquity.* Scholars Press Studies in the Humanities. Chico: Scholars Press, 1985.

Neusner, Jacob, William S. Green, and Ernest Frerichs, eds. *Judaisms and Their Messiahs at the Turn of the Christian Era.* Cambridge: Cambridge University Press, 1987.

Nicholls, William. *Christian Antisemitism: A History of Hate.* Northvale, N.J.: Jason Aronson, 1993.

Nickelsburg, George W. E. *Jewish Literature between the Bible and the Mishnah: A Historical and Literary Introduction.* Philadelphia: Fortress Press, 1981.

Parsons, Mikeal C., and Richard I. Pervo. *Rethinking the Unity of Luke and Acts.* Minneapolis: Fortress Press, 1993.

Rese, Martin. "'Die Juden' im lukanischen Doppelwerk: Ein Bericht über eine längst nötige 'neuere' Diskussion." In *Der Treue Gottes Trauen: Beiträge zum Werk des Lukas,* edited by Claus Bussmann and Walter Radl, 61–79. Freiburg: Herder, 1991.

Richardson, Peter, ed., with David Granskou. *Anti-Judaism in Early Christianity.* Vol. 1. Waterloo: Wilfrid Laurier University Press, 1986.

Ruether, Rosemary Radford. *Faith and Fratricide: The Theological Roots of Anti-Semitism.* New York: Seabury, 1974.

Saldarini, Anthony J. *Pharisees, Scribes and Sadducees in Palestinian Society: A Sociological Approach.* Wilmington, Del.: Michael Glazier, 1988.

Sanders, E. P. *Jesus and Judaism.* Philadelphia: Fortress Press, 1985.

Sanders, Jack T. "Can Anything Bad Come out of Nazareth, or Did Luke Think That History Moved in a Line or in a Circle?" In *Literary Studies in Luke-Acts: Essays in Honor of Joseph B. Tyson,* edited by Richard P. Thompson and Thomas E. Phillips, 297–312. Macon, Ga.: Mercer University Press, 1998.

Sandmel, Samuel. *Anti-Semitism in the New Testament?* Philadelphia: Fortress Press, 1978.

Stone, Michael E. *Scriptures, Sects and Visions: A Profile of Judaism from Ezra to the Jewish Revolts.* Philadelphia: Fortress Press, 1980.

Thompson, Richard P., and Thomas E. Phillips, eds. *Literary Studies in Luke-Acts: Essays in Honor of Joseph B. Tyson.* Macon, Ga.: Mercer University Press, 1998.

Tyson, Joseph B. *Images of Judaism in Luke-Acts.* Columbia: University of South Carolina Press, 1992.

———. "Jews and Judaism in Luke-Acts: Reading as a Godfearer." *NTS* 41 (1995): 19–38.

Vermes, Geza. *Jesus and the World of Judaism.* Philadelphia: Fortress Press, 1983.

Wasserberg, Günter. *Aus Israels Mitte—Heil für die Welt: Eine narrativ-exegetische Studie zur Theologie des Lukas.* Berlin: Walter de Gruyter, 1998.

Williamson, Clark M. *Has God Rejected His People? Anti-Judaism in the Christian Church.* Nashville: Abingdon, 1982.

Wilson, Stephen G., ed. *Anti-Judaism in Early Christianity.* Vol. 2. Waterloo: Wilfrid Laurier University Press, 1986.

INDEX OF BIBLICAL
AND RABBINIC LITERATURE

INDEX OF
MODERN SCHOLARS